# THE
# COMPLETE
# GEORGE CROSS

# THE COMPLETE GEORGE CROSS

*A Full Chronological Listing of All GC Holders*

by

## Kevin Brazier

*Foreword by*

## Tony Gledhill GC

Pen & Sword
**MILITARY**

First published in Great Britain in 2012 by
Pen & Sword Military
an imprint of
Pen & Sword Books Ltd
47 Church Street
Barnsley
South Yorkshire
S70 2AS

ISBN 978 1 84884 287 8

A CIP catalogue record for this book is available from the British Library.

Typeset in Centaur by
Phoenix Typesetting, Auldgirth, Dumfriesshire, DG2 0XE

Printed and bound in England by
the MPG Books Group Ltd.

Pen & Sword Books Ltd incorporates the Imprints of Pen & Sword Aviation,
Pen & Sword Family History, Pen & Sword Maritime, Pen & Sword Military,
Pen & Sword Discovery, Wharncliffe Local History, Wharncliffe True Crime,
Wharncliffe Transport, Pen & Sword Select, Pen & Sword Military Classics,
Leo Cooper, The Praetorian Press, Remember When, Seaforth Publishing and
Frontline Publishing

For a complete list of Pen & Sword titles please contact
PEN & SWORD BOOKS LIMITED
47 Church Street, Barnsley, South Yorkshire, S70 2AS, England
E-mail: enquiries@pen-and-sword.co.uk
Website: www.pen-and-sword.co.uk

# CONTENTS

For my Mum,
who was always there for me.

# ACKNOWLEDGEMENTS

My initial thanks must go to Rupert Harding for commissioning this book even before my first book on the Victoria Cross was published. I must thank my friends who have helped and supported me throughout this project, especially David Brown, Joe Dever, Paul Murray and Gary Williams, also Lance Renetzke for his knowledge of Indian Army rankings, Andrew Cross for his knowledge of naval rankings and Jill Sugden for her many hours of research.

Tom Johnson BEM has given me a great deal of assistance; his help has, as always, been invaluable. I must also thank Didy Grahame OBE, MVO of the VC&GC Association for her help and for putting me in touch with all the living GC holders; Terry Hissey for his help and for proofreading the finished work; Marion Hebblethwaite who has helped throughout my research; and the *London Gazette*.

I am most grateful also to the Photographic Department of the Imperial War Museum, and to the staff at the many cemeteries I have visited, who have been very helpful in finding the exact location of a great many GC holders, and the staff at many of the museums I have been in contact with. In this context special thanks are due to Carolyn Anand of the RNLI Heritage Trust, Robert Steele of the Royal Highland Fusiliers Museum, Barbara Tomlinson of the National Maritime Museum, Eric Carpenter of the Australian War Memorial, Lynda Powell of the Green Howards Museum, Helen Jones of the Keep Military Museum, Edward Besly of the National Museum Wales, Anne Bradley of the National Coal Mining Museum of England, Anna Lebbell of the Royal Marines Museum, George Streatfeild of the Soldiers of Gloucestershire Museum, Jesper Ericsson of the Gordon Highlanders Museum, Ian Chatfield of the Queen's Royal Surrey Regiment Museum, Mary White of the National Railway Museum, Lynne Lennard of the Royal Gunpowder Mills, Stuart Allan of the National Museum of Scotland, Beverley Williams of the Royal Engineers Museum, Derek Marrison of the Army Medical Service Museum, Jane Rugg of the London Fire Brigade Museum, Andrew Cormack of the RAF Museum, Gary Gibbs of the Guards Museum, Clare Griffiths of the Borough Museum and Art Gallery (Newcastle-under-Lyne), Fergus Read of the Imperial War Museum, Gina Young of the Stranraer Museum, Peter Donnelly of the King's Own Royal Regiment Museum, and Danu Reid of the National Army Museum.

I must thank my editor, Sarah Cook, for her many, many hours of hard work, and for putting up with my constant last-minute changes. My very special thanks go to Tony Gledhill GC, not only for writing the Foreword to this book, but for the photos he has kindly provided from his personal collection. Last, but by no means least, my thanks go to Teresa, my long-suffering wife.

# HMS *HOOD*

When the HMS *Hood* went down in the deep
That was the news that made mothers weep
For their lads who had fought for their country so proud
Now they sleep with the sea for a shroud

They are sleeping in Heavenly sleep
They are resting in Heavenly rest.

Then came the *King George*, the *Prince of Wales* too
They took in hand what the *Hood* tried to do
The *Norfolk*, the *Suffolk*, the *Dorsetshire* as well
Along with the *Rodney* blew the *Bismarck* to hell.

Now the sea's clean and all is well
We are proud of our Navy as well.

That was the day with our guns in full play
The *Bismarck* was sunk on that day in May
Now we finished the job we had to do
Oh we are so proud of our red, white and blue.

Now the ship's sunk and we are glad
But for our boys we are so sad.

Now mothers and wives and sweethearts be proud
Though your lads are asleep with the sea for a shroud
They were fighting for freedom, let's never forget
That our lads were British, as British we are yet.

Now they are sleeping in Heavenly sleep
Now they are resting in Heavenly rest.

*Charles Henry Walker GC*

Reproduced with kind permission of his family.

# FOREWORD

## BY TONY GLEDHILL GC

When I was asked to write the foreword to *The Complete George Cross* I began by reading what must be one of the most remarkable collections of stories ever compiled in one book, and in looking through the list of names and reviewing the deeds of those heroic men and women whose actions led to the award of the George Cross, I felt both humbled and honoured to be counted amongst their ranks. A number of these people I know, and some I can call my friends, and all of them richly deserved the highest civilian award that a grateful nation can bestow upon its citizens.

Each of these men and women faced a moment in their lives when they had to make a decision, always fateful, sometimes fatal. Each chose to go further than they needed to do. For some the decision was made on the spur of the moment, for others it was the result of long consideration.

In some instances they were going about their usual duties, as I was, when they were faced with a situation they had neither expected nor wanted. In other cases they had volunteered to go in secret behind enemy lines, or fight fires, or to operate openly upon unexploded ordnance. In each situation they could have said 'no'; they could have turned away and no one would have blamed them. But in every instance they chose to put themselves in harm's way, either to save others or because they believed it was the right thing to do. None, I am sure, would want to face that kind of situation, nor have to make that kind of decision, a second time.

As well as providing a comprehensive record of the awards of the George Cross, *The Complete George Cross* includes many fascinating details and additional facts. These include the burial locations of George Cross holders, and the location of the medals, where known.

*The Complete George Cross* provides a detailed and precise summary of the actions that were recognised by the award of the George Cross. Read them all and you will feel as humbled and honoured as I did.

# GLOSSARY

| | |
|---|---|
| Aft | Rear of a ship or boat |
| Babu | Indian title equal to Sir |
| Begum | Indian title equal to Mrs |
| Bight of Wire | The centre part of rolled-up wire |
| Bull-ring | Rings for lashing cargo to the deck |
| Bump | Pressure inside a mine that shoots coal from the walls with great force |
| Claymore | Anti-personnel mine |
| Crib | A seaside cottage |
| Dacoit | Burmese or South Asian robber |
| Fathom | Naval means of measuring depth at sea. One fathom = 6 feet |
| Feeder | Aqueduct |
| Firedamp | Methane, which is explosive when mixed with air |
| Flamper | Clay ironstone found in seams |
| Gantline | A line passed through a block, used to hoist sails or rigging |
| Gob fire | An area that has been left void after coal has been extracted, causing spontaneous combustion |
| Godown | Store or warehouse |
| Greaser | Engineer or Mechanic |
| Hoppit | A large bucket for hoisting men |
| Jacob's Ladder | A rope ladder with wooden rungs that hangs over a ship's side |
| Kaid | A major in the Trans-Jordan Frontier Force |
| Lamp black | A dark black pigment consisting of amorphous carbon |
| Lascar | A sailor from India or the Far East serving on a European ship |
| Lathi | Bamboo stick |
| Lighter | A barge or flat-bottomed boat |
| Maquis | French resistance |
| Mulazim | A lieutenant in the Trans-Jordan Frontier Force |
| Parapet | Breastwork of earth in front of trenches |
| Salvo | A battery of guns firing together |
| Sampan | Chinese open flat-bottomed boat |
| Scuppers | Openings for draining water from the deck of a ship |
| Shawish | A sergeant in the Sudan Police Force |
| Skiff | A small one-man boat |
| Spartan | An unarmed fully tracked armoured vehicle |

| Traverse | A pair of right-angled bends incorporated into a trench to avoid enfilading fire |
| Windlass | A large and elaborate type of winch |
| Yuzbashi | A captain in the Sudan Defence Force |

## Coal Mining Job Titles

| Agent | Arranges for the sale of the coal |
| Banksman | Draws the tubs from the cages at the surface |
| Brakesman | Engineman who attends to the winding engines |
| Driver | A boy employed in driving the horses on the underground railway |
| Duty | A man who sets timber for the safety of the work force |
| Hewer | A man who cuts coal from the coal face |
| Onsetter | A man who pushes the full mine wagons on to the cage and takes the empties out, at the shaft bottom |
| Overman | In charge of the working of the colliery where there is no under viewer |
| Under Manager | Manager of the underground workings |
| Viewer | Overall manager both under- and overground |
| Wasteman | A man employed in building pillars for the support of the roof and keeping the airways in good order |

## Acronyms and Abbreviation

| AM | Albert Medal |
| AMF | Australian Military Forces |
| ARP | Air Raid Precaution |
| ATO | Ammunition Technical Officer |
| BEF | British Expeditionary Force |
| BEM | British Empire Medal |
| CO | Commanding Officer |
| DCM | Distinguished Conduct Medal |
| DFC | Distinguished Flying Cross |
| DSC | Distinguished Service Cross |
| DSO | Distinguished Service Order |
| DSR | Department of Scientific Research |
| EGM | Empire Gallantry Medal |
| EM | Edward Medal |
| EOKA | Ethniki Organosis Kyprion Agoniston |
| GC | George Cross |
| GM | George Medal |

| | |
|---|---|
| HMHS | His/Her Majesty's Hospital Ship |
| HQ | Headquarters |
| IED | Improvised Explosive Device |
| INA | Indian National Army |
| IRA | Irish Republican Army |
| LAC | Leading Aircraftman |
| MBE | Member of the Order of the British Empire |
| MC | Military Cross |
| ML | Motor Launch |
| MM | Military Medal |
| MV | Merchant Vessel |
| NCO | Non Commissioned Officer |
| NFS | National Fire Service |
| POW | Prisoner of War |
| RAF | Royal Air Force |
| RAMC | Royal Army Medical Corps |
| RFC | Royal Flying Corps |
| RLC | Royal Logistics Corps |
| RNLI | Royal National Life-boat Institution |
| RUC | Royal Ulster Constabulary |
| SAS | Special Air Service |
| SOE | Special Operations Executive |
| VC | Victoria Cross |
| WAAF | Women's Auxiliary Air Force |

## Indian Army Ranks

| **Indian Army** | **British Army equivalent or role (in *Italics*)** |
|---|---|
| Risaldar | Lieutenant |
| Jemadar | Second Lieutenant |
| Subadar Major | *Company second-in-command* |
| Subadar or | |
| Jemadar/Zemindar | *Platoon commander* |
| Havildar Major | Company Sergeant Major |
| Havildar (infantry) | |
| or Duffadar (cavalry) | Sergeant |
| Naik (infantry) or | |
| Lance Duffadar (cavalry) | Corporal |
| Lance Naik (infantry) or | |
| Acting Lance Duffadar (cavalry) | Lance Corporal |
| Sepoy (infantry) | *Rifleman* |
| Sowar (cavalry) | Trooper |

Note: Variations in spelling may occur depending on which source is being consulted.

# PREFACE

Having finished my first book, *The Complete Victoria Cross*, I started to realise that the story was not 'complete' as the George Cross needed to be covered in the same way. Surprisingly, information on George Cross holders seems to be harder to find, despite the fact that it came into being eighty-four years after the Victoria Cross.

When I started work on this book, I had no idea how many George Crosses had been awarded since its introduction in 1940, nor for what unbelievable deeds of bravery. In layman's terms, the George Cross is the civilian equivalent of the Victoria Cross, but even this is not strictly true. Of the 161 direct awards (those that did not exchange from another award) over 100 have gone to military personnel. It would perhaps be more realistic to say that the George Cross is awarded for bravery 'when not in the face of the enemy'. But this too is not clear, as it depends on exactly how 'the enemy' is defined. Dealing with an enemy bomb is not classed as being in the face of the enemy, nor is bravery under 'friendly fire'. Likewise, bravery when dealing with enemy prisoners or for deeds involving clandestine operations are also not classed in this way. It seems the enemy must be in sight, but with the changing face of modern warfare perhaps we need to rethink what 'in the face of the enemy' really means.

It is worth noting that foreign names and locations have various spelling and that both local and anglicised versions have been used. Every effort has been made to check facts, dates and names, but errors are bound to creep in; the responsibility for these is entirely mine, and mine alone. Should you find any errors, or indeed have any new information, I would be very grateful if you would contact me with the details at kib1856@yahoo.co.uk

I was lucky enough to be invited to the preview of the Lord Ashcroft Gallery at the Imperial War Museum in 2010 and had the good fortune to meet many holders of the George Cross and Victoria Cross. I will never forget the first time I held a George Cross in my hand: what a privilege.

It's an odd thing writing about people who are not only still living but whom I have met; I don't want to get it wrong, especially as these are some of the bravest people in the country so there's always the worry they will come and clip me around the ear if I do! Once again, if I have learnt nothing else during the writing of his book, it is that these men and women have in common their humility, selflessness, courage and determination.

# CHAPTER ONE

# A Short History of the George Cross

I n 1940 King George VI felt the need formally to recognise individual acts of outstanding bravery by the civilian population during the Blitz. He decided to create an award for men and women of the Commonwealth whose courage could not be marked by any other honour.

Many decorations and medals for gallantry had been instituted by the king's predecessors, but these awards were largely restricted to members of the armed forces. It was to meet this evident need that the king instigated the new award. The George Cross came into being when the king signed the royal warrant on 24 September 1940. Announcing the new award, the king said: 'In order that they should be worthily and promptly recognised, I have decided to create, at once, a new mark of honour for men and women in all walks of civilian life. I propose to give my name to this distinction, which will consist of the George Cross, which will rank next to the Victoria Cross.'

The medal, designed by Percy Metcalfe, consists of a plain silver cross, 2 inches (50mm) wide, with the royal cipher 'GVI' in the angle of each limb. In the centre is a circular medallion showing St George and the Dragon, surrounded by the inscription 'For Gallantry'. The reverse is plain and bears the name of the recipient and the date of the award. The suspension bar is decorated with laurel leaves and the cross is suspended from what is described as a dark blue (but is in fact a garter blue) ribbon originally 1¼ inches (32mm) wide; this was increased to 1½ inches (38mm) in 1941. The George Cross is worn before all other decorations except the Victoria Cross. Each cross is made of silver and is struck by the Royal Mint.

Ladies not in uniform wear the George Cross suspended from a wide bow of dark blue ribbon below the left shoulder. Recipients are permitted to use the letters GC after their name. Although its award is recommended by the prime minister, the decoration is bestowed by the sovereign.

Awards of the George Cross have always been announced in the pages of the London Gazette, a process known as being 'Gazetted'. The first investiture took place on 24 May 1941 at Buckingham Palace, when the king presented the decoration to Mr Thomas Alderson, remarking 'you are the first recipient of the George Cross. It gives me very great pleasure to hand it to you.'

Prior to the inception of the George Cross, several other gallantry awards existed for civilians. The Empire Gallantry Medal (EGM), officially called the Medal of the Order of the British Empire for Gallantry, was instituted on 29 December 1922. It was awarded in two classes, Military and Civilian. When the George Cross was introduced, the 108 living recipients of the Empire Gallantry Medal were obliged to exchange their medals for the George Cross. The next of kin of four further Empire Gallantry Medal recipients were also eligible to exchange because their awards had been made after 3 September 1939.

The Albert Medal (AM), instituted on 7 March 1866, was for life-saving on land and sea, and was awarded in two classes, 1st class (Gold) and 2nd class (Bronze). In 1949 the Gold award was 'replaced' by the George Cross, and there-after the Albert Medal was only awarded posthumously in Bronze. In 1971 awards of the Albert Medal ceased and living recipients were invited to exchange their decoration for the George Cross; sixteen decided not to.

The Edward Medal (EM) (Mines), instituted on 13 July 1907, was awarded for life-saving in mines and quarries. The Edward Medal (Industry) was insti-tuted on 1 December 1909 for life-saving in factory accidents and disasters. Both were awarded in two classes, 1st class (Silver) and 2nd class (Bronze). After 1949 the medal was only awarded posthumously. In 1971 awards of the Edward Medal ceased and all living recipients were invited to exchange their decoration for the George Cross; only eight decided not to. Whether exchanging their medals or not, all became holders of the George Cross and were entitled to all of its privileges.

To date (December 2011) 161 direct awards have been made, with a further 245 by exchange or indirect awards, making a total of 406. The George Cross has, on the express instruction of the sovereign, been awarded twice to a collec-tive body, to the island of Malta on 15 April 1942 and to the Royal Ulster Constabulary in 1999. No one has yet been awarded a Bar but, unlike the Victoria Cross, several woman have been awarded the George Cross. The recipients also include fourteen Australians, ten Canadians and one Tasmanian. John Bamford, at 15 years and 7 months, was the youngest direct recipient, but the youngest indi-rect award went to David Western at 10 years and 10 months. The oldest direct recipient was William Foster at 61 years.

Twenty-six people have been awarded it while still in their teens, and thirteen people in their fifties. The largest number of George Crosses awarded indirectly for a single incident was ten, during the aftermath of the Quetta earthquake on 31 May 1935. Thirty-two awards were made during the First World War, 142 between the world wars, 157 in the Second World War and seventy-one in the post-war period.

The George Cross is no longer awarded to Canadians, who now receive the

Canadian Cross of Valour. Likewise, Australians are now awarded the Australian Cross of Valour.

In recent years the George Cross has only been awarded to military personnel serving in Afghanistan and Iraq, and at least one of these has been for an incident that many say should have resulted in the award of the Victoria Cross.

# CHAPTER TWO

# The Terms of the 1940 George Cross Warrant, and its Amendments

WHEREAS We have taken into Our Royal consideration the many acts of heroism performed both by male and female persons, especially during the present war:

And whereas We are desirous of honouring those who perform such deeds:

We do by these presents for Us, Our Heirs and Successors institute and create a new Decoration which We desire should be highly prized and eagerly sought after.

Firstly: It is ordained that the Decoration shall be designated and styled 'The George Cross.'

Secondly: It is ordained that the Decoration shall consist of a plain cross with four equal limbs, the Cross having in the centre a circular medallion bearing a design showing St George and the Dragon, that the inscription 'For Gallantry' shall appear round this medallion, and in the angle of each limb of the cross the Royal cipher 'G.VI' forming a circle concentric with the medallion, that the reverse of the Cross shall be plain and bear the name of the recipient and the date of the award, that the Cross shall be suspended by a ring from a bar adorned with laurel leaves, and that the whole shall be in silver.

Thirdly: It is ordained that the persons eligible for the Decoration of the Cross shall be

(1) Our faithful subjects and persons under Our protection in civil life, male and female, of Our United Kingdom of Great Britain and Northern Ireland, India, Burma, Our Colonies, and of Territories under Our Suzerainty, Protection or Jurisdiction,

(2) Persons of any rank in the Naval, Military or Air Force of Our United Kingdom of Great Britain and Northern Ireland, of India, Burma, of Our Colonies, and of Territories under Our Suzerainty, Protection or Jurisdiction, including the Home Guard and in India members of the Frontier Corps and

Military Police and members of Indian States' Forces and in Burma members of the Burma Frontier Force and Military Police, and including also the Military Nursing Services and Women's Auxiliary Services,

(3) Our faithful subjects and persons under Our protection in civil life, male and female, within, and members of the Naval, Military or Air Force belonging to, any other part of Our Dominions, Our Government whereof has signified its desire that the Cross should be awarded under the provisions of this Our Warrant, and any Territory being administered by Us in such Government.

The Cross is intended primarily for civilians and award in Our military services is to be confined to actions for which purely military Honours are not normally granted.

Fourthly: It is ordained that awards shall be made only on recommendation to Us, for civilians by Our Prime Minister and First Lord of the Treasury, and for Officers and members of Our Naval, Military or Air Forces, as described in the previous Clause of this Our Warrant, only on recommendation by Our First Lord of the Admiralty, Our Secretary of State for War or Our Secretary of State for Air, as the case may be.

Fifthly: It is ordained that the Cross shall be awarded only for acts of the greatest heroism or of the most conspicuous courage in circumstances of extreme danger, and that the Cross may be awarded posthumously.

Sixthly: It is ordained that every recommendation for the award of the Cross shall be submitted with such description and conclusive proof as the circumstances of the case will allow, and attestation of the act as the Minster or Ministers concerned may think requisite.

Seventhly: It is ordained that the Cross shall be worn by recipients on the left breast suspended from a ribbon one and a quarter inches in width, of dark blue, that it shall be worn immediately after the Victoria Cross and in front of the insignia of all British Orders of Chivalry, and that on those occasions when only the ribbon is worn, a replica in silver of the Cross in miniature shall be affixed to the centre of the ribbon.

Provided that when the cross is worn by a woman, it may be worn on the left shoulder, suspended from a ribbon of the same width and colour, fashioned into a bow.

Eighthly: it is ordained that the award of the George Cross shall entitle the recipient on all occasions when the use of such letters is customary, to have placed after his or her names the letters 'G.C.'

Ninthly: it is ordained that an action which is worthy of recognition by the award of the Cross, but is performed by one upon whom the Decoration has been conferred, may be recorded by the award of a Bar to be attached to the ribbon by which the Cross is suspended, that for each such additional award an additional Bar shall be added, and that for each bar awarded a replica in silver of the Cross in miniature, in addition to the emblem already worn, shall be added to the ribbon when worn alone.

Tenthly: It is ordained that the names of all those upon or on account of whom

We may be pleased to confer or present the Cross, or a Bar to the Cross, shall be published in the London Gazette, and that a Register of such names shall be kept in the Central Chancery of the Orders of Knighthood.

Eleventhly: It is ordained that from the date of this Our Warrant, the grant of the Medal of the Order of the British Empire for Gallantry, which was instituted and created by His late Majesty King George V, shall cease, and a recipient of that Medal, living at the date of this Our Warrant, shall return it to the Central Chancery of the Orders of Knighthood and become instead a holder of the George Cross: provided that there shall be a similar charge in relation to any posthumous grant of the Medal of the Order of the British Empire for Gallantry made since the commencement of the present war.

Twelfthly: It is ordained that reproductions of the Cross, known as a Miniature Cross, which may be worn on certain occasions by those to whom the Decoration is awarded, shall be half the size of the George Cross.

Thirteenthly: It is ordained that it shall be competent for Us, our Heirs and Successors by an Order under Our Sign Manual and on recommendation to that effect by or through Our Prime Minister and First Lord of the Treasury, Our First Lord of the Admiralty, Our Secretary of State for War, Our Secretary of State for Air, as the case may be, to cancel and annul the award to any person of the George Cross and that thereupon the name of such person in the Register shall be erased: provided that it shall be competent for Us, Our Heirs and Successors to restore the Decoration so forfeited when such recommendation has been withdrawn.

Lastly: We reserve to Ourself, Our Heirs and Successors, full power of annulling, altering, abrogating, augmenting, interpreting, or dispensing with these rules and ordinances, or any part thereof, by a notification under Our Sign Manual.

Given at Our Court at St James's, the twenty-fourth of September, one thousand nine hundred and forty, in the fourth year of Our Reign.

By His Majesty's Command.

## Amendments and Changes to the Warrant

It was less than a year before the first amendment was made to the warrant. On 8 May 1941 an amendment to Clause 7 ordained that the ribbon was now to be 1.5 inches wide. Another warrant dated 17 October 1942 amended the 3rd, 4th and 13th Clauses so that condominium awards, and direct submissions in the case of any of the Dominions, were now permitted.

A new warrant was issued on 9 April 1964, again amending Clauses 3, 4 and 13. Clause 3 had the words 'India' and 'Burma' removed and replaced with 'or under Our Jurisdiction jointly with another power'. Further references to India, the Indian States and Burma were omitted. In Clause 4 recommendations in the case of a member of the Commonwealth, other than the United Kingdom, were to be made by the appropriate Minister of State for the particular Commonwealth country. In Clause 13 provision was made for the cancelling and annulling of any award in Commonwealth countries, other than the United Kingdom, on the recommendation of the appropriate Minister of State of that country.

A further royal warrant dated 15 June 1965 added the following three Clauses:

Fourteenthly: It is ordained that every living recipient of the George Cross, who falls to be in this matter a responsibility of the United Kingdom Government, shall from the first day of April, one thousand nine hundred and sixty-five, be entitled to a special pension of one hundred pounds a year, for life, and that subsequently such recipients of the George Cross shall be entitled to the special pension from the date of the said act by which the Decoration has been gained, and for life.

Fifteenthly: It is ordained that should a recipient of the George Cross die before he has received a total of fifty pounds in respect of the special pension of one hundred pounds a year which is payable to holders of the George Cross by the United Kingdom Government, there should be credited to his estate a sum equal to the balance needed to complete fifty pounds. It is also ordained that when the George Cross is awarded posthumously and the matter is a responsibility of the United Kingdom Government, the sum of fifty pounds should be credited to the estate of the deceased recipient of the award.

Sixteenthly: It is ordained that, subject to such exceptions as We, Our Heirs and Successors may ordain, a citizen of a Member Country of the Commonwealth Overseas to whom the George Cross may be awarded, shall receive such special pension as may be provided from the revenues of that Country under regulations made by the said Country.

In 1995 the pension was increased to £1,300. The pension was increased again to British holders of the George Cross on 1 April 2002 to £1,495, to bring it in line with the Victoria Cross. Australians holders receive $A250, and Canadian holders receive $C3,000.

# CHAPTER THREE

# Roll of Honour:
# a Complete Chronological List of
# All George Cross Holders

The following is a complete chronological list of all George Cross holders. Where two or more have been awarded for the same day, I have put them in order of rank. Where the rank has also been the same, I have put them in alphabetical order. Although used extensively locally, the term Trooper did not officially come into being until 1923. If the award was for an extended period of time I have used the start date for the position in the list.

Each entry starts with its number in the list, followed by the recipient's rank or position (all ranks are at the time of the George Cross deed), and then their name, all in **bold**. If the GC is an exchange, then this is where I have noted from which award it was exchanged. This is followed by the date of the George Cross deed. Next comes the burial location; if this is not known I have indicated where they died, but 'killed' does not necessarily mean that they were killed during the George Cross deed. Also note that 'near' can mean up to 5 miles away. I have tried to give as much detail as possible about the burial location in order to make finding each grave easier. However, this is not always possible and if anyone can help to improve this, please write to me at my email address below. An unmarked grave does not mean that you cannot visit, as most churches/cemeteries should have a record of the grave location on their register. Graves are in England unless otherwise specified. Last but not least is the present location of the George Cross (or other award if not exchanged), in *italics*. 'Not publicly held' means that the medal is either still with the recipient's family or in a private collection. The Ashcroft Collection is now on permanent display at the Imperial War Museum, London.

Amazingly there are forty-one George Cross holders whose burial location remains unknown; if anyone has any information as to where they may be buried, please contact me at the email address below. Also there are still ten George Cross holders buried in unmarked graves, nine of them in the UK and Ireland. So if you live nearby, or are descended from a George Cross holder who is buried in an unmarked grave, why not start a campaign to raise money for a headstone? Write to your local authority, your MP, the recipient's regiment or organisation and your local newspaper. Try to persuade them to put a headstone on the grave. This has worked in many cases, not only for unmarked graves but for badly damaged headstones too. The VC&GC memorial appeal was set up to look into the replacing of headstones and can be contacted at Horse Guards, London, SW1A 2AX. After all, we should honour our heroes. If you are successful in this, I would very much like to hear from you. I can be contacted at kib1856@yahoo.co.uk

1.  **Mr THOMAS McCORMACK** (Albert Medal) 27 November 1908, buried in unmarked grave, Jarrow Cemetery, Section 5, Grave 632; Cemetery Road, Jarrow, Co. Durham. *GC location: not publicly held.*

2.  **Nurse HILDA WOLSEY** (Albert Medal) 11 June 1910, cremated Mortlake Crematorium, Kew Meadow Path, Townmead Road, Richmond, Surrey. *GC location: unknown.*

3.  **Reverend JOHN O'SHEA** (Empire Gallantry Medal) 18 March 1911, buried Ballyporeen Churchyard, Co. Tipperary, Ireland. *GC location: Mount Melleray Abbey, Lismore, Co. Waterford, Ireland.*

4.  **Major HERBERT 'DICK' BURTON** (Empire Gallantry Medal) 1 November 1914, probably buried in Beadnell, Northumberland. *GC location: Royal Engineers Museum, Gillingham, Kent.*

5.  **Chief Petty Officer MICHAEL KEOGH (born SULLIVAN)** (Albert Medal) 19 August 1915, ashes interred Vintners Park Crematorium, Plot CR28/825; Aldon Close, Maidstone, Kent. *GC location: not publicly held.*

6.  **Miner PERCY HAVERCROFT** (Edward Medal) 27 August 1915, buried Beighton Cemetery, Section B, Row C, Grave 2; School Road, Sheffield. *GC location: not publicly held.*

7.  **Mr RICHARD RICHARDS** (Albert Medal) 9 October 1915–20 March 1916, buried Port Lonsdale Cemetery, Anglican Section, Section 1c, Grave 147; Victoria, Australia. *GC location: Canterbury Museum, New Zealand.*

8.  **Air Mechanic First Class HARRIE HARWOOD** (Albert Medal) 3 January 1916, ashes interred Oxford Crematorium, Crescent 6, Rosebush 37; Bayswater Road, Oxford. *GC location: with recipient's family.*

9.  **Sergeant ALBERT FORD** (Albert Medal) 30 March 1916, cremated at Carmountside Crematorium, South-West Section; Leek Road, Milton, Stoke-on-Trent. *GC location: with recipient's family.*

10. **Acting Sergeant CHARLES HARRIS** (Edward Medal) 2 April 1916, buried in unmarked grave, Woodlands Cemetery, Section BE, Grave 2771; Woodlands Road, Gillingham, Kent. *EM location: on loan to the Royal Engineers Museum, Gillingham, Kent.*

11. **Acting Bombardier ARTHUR EDWARDS** (Edward Medal) 2 April 1916, cremated. *GC location: not publicly held.*

12. **Mr ARCHIBALD YOUNG** (Edward Medal) 20 June 1916, burial

location unknown. *GC location: National War Museum of Scotland, Edinburgh, Scotland.*

13. **Miss DOREEN ASHBURNHAM** (later **ASHBURNHAM-RUFFNER**) (Albert Medal) 23 September 1916, cremated Obispo, California, USA. *GC location: on loan to the Imperial War Museum, London.*

14. **Sergeant WILLIAM RHOADES** (Albert Medal) 14 October 1916, cremated Eastbourne Crematorium, Hide Hollow, Langley. *AM location: not publicly held.*

15. **Coxswain HENRY BLOGG** (Empire Gallantry Medal) 9 January 1917, buried Cromer New Cemetery, Green's Lane, Norfolk. *GC location: The RNLI Henry Blogg Museum, Cromer, Norfolk.*

16. **Sergeant ALBERT HUTCHISON** (sometimes misspelt **HUTCHINSON**) (Albert Medal) 2 April 1917, cremated. *GC location: The Royal Highland Fusiliers Museum, Glasgow, Scotland.*

17. **Lieutenant OLIVER BRYSON** (Albert Medal) 15 March 1917, cremated Guildford Crematorium, Surrey. *GC location: RAF Museum, Hendon, London.*

18. **Second Lieutenant RICHARD** (known as **R.L.**) **BROWN** (Albert Medal) 27 March 1917, burial location unknown, died in Annan, Dumfriesshire, Scotland. *GC location: King's Own Royal Regiment Museum, Lancaster.*

19. **Deckhand GEORGE ABBOTT** (Albert Medal) 14 September 1917, ashes scattered Downham Churchyard, Yorkshire. *AM location: his daughter gave it to a friend and its location is now unknown.*

20. **Ordinary Seaman RICHARD KNOWLTON** (Albert Medal) 14 September 1917, ashes interred London Road Cemetery, Section O, Grave 839; Salisbury. *AM location: with recipient's family.*

21. **Acting Mate ALBERT** (aka **ALFRED**) **NEWMAN** (Albert Medal) 10 October 1917, ashes scattered at Sussex & Surrey Crematorium, Balcombe Road, Crawley. *GC location: on loan to the National Maritime Museum, London.*

22. **Leading Seaman THOMAS DAVIS** (Albert Medal) 6 December 1917, buried at sea, English Channel. *GC location: Royal Navy Submarine Museum, Gosport, Hampshire.*

23. **Flight Lieutenant VICTOR WATSON** (Albert Medal) 22 December 1917, ashes scattered Golders Green Crematorium, Plot 3G; Hoop Lane, London. *AM location: not publicly held.*

24. **Deckhand JOHN STANNERS** (Albert Medal) 29 December 1917, burial location unknown, died Durham North. *AM location: not publicly held.*

25. **Lance Corporal SIDNEY WILLIAMS** (Albert Medal) 4 January 1918, ashes scattered South London Crematorium (aka Streatham Vale Crematorium), Glade 1, Tree 4; Rowan Road, Streatham Vale, London. *GC location: not publicly held.*

26. **Flight Sergeant HORACE CANNON** (Albert Medal) 26 January 1918,

ashes scattered Nab Wood Crematorium, Bingley Road, Shipley, Yorkshire. *GC location: RAF Museum, Hendon, London.*

27. **Acting Flight Commander PAUL ROBERTSON** (Albert Medal) 28 February 1918, ashes interred Purewa Cemetery, Block X, Row 20, Plot 040; Auckland, New Zealand. (His headstone is unusual in that the letters GC do not appear after his name.) *GC location: not publicly held.*

28. **Sub Lieutenant ARTHUR BAGOT** (Albert Medal) 12 April 1918, ashes interred North Road Church of England Cemetery, Bagot family plot; Collingswood, Adelaide, South Australia. *GC location: not publicly held.*

29. **Lieutenant RANDOLPH RIDLING** (Albert Medal) 19 April 1918, ashes scattered Karori Cemetery, Returned Services Section; Wellington, New Zealand. *AM location: National Army Museum, State Highway 1, Waiouru, New Zealand.*

30. **Drawer JOHN McCABE** (Edward Medal) 9 July 1918, buried St Joseph's Cemetery, Dykehead Road, Airdrie, Lanarkshire, Scotland. *GC location: not publicly held.*

31. **Lieutenant BERNARD ELLIS** (Albert Medal) 21 August 1918, buried All Saints Churchyard, Willian Church Road, Willian, near Letchworth Garden City, Hertfordshire. *GC location: National Army Museum.*

32. **Sub Lieutenant DAVID EVANS** (Albert Medal) 16 September 1918, probably buried in Yorkshire. *GC location: with recipient's family.*

33. **Staff Nurse HARRIET FRASER** (later **BARRY**) (Albert Medal) 1 October 1918, burial location unknown. *GC location: held by the Home Office.*

34. **Second Lieutenant GEOFFREY RACKHAM** (Albert Medal) 27 October 1918, ashes scattered at West Herts Crematorium, High Elms Lane, Watford. *GC location: RLC Museum, Deepcut, Camberley, Surrey.*

35. **Acting Lieutenant HARRY 'WINGS' DAY** (Albert Medal) 9 November 1918, buried Ta Braxia International Cemetery, Malta. *GC location: Royal Marines Museum, Southsea, Portsmouth.*

36. **Fireman CHRISTOPHER FEETHAM** (Albert Medal) 10 November 1918, cremated Putney Vale Crematorium, Stag Lane, London. *GC location: not publicly held.*

37. **Lieutenant EDMUND 'BILL' ABBOTT** (Albert Medal) 5 August 1919, ashes scattered Easthampstead Park Crematorium, Plot 5; South Road, Bracknell. *GC location: National War Museum of Scotland, Edinburgh, Scotland.*

38. **Mr WALTER CLEALL** (Albert Medal) 11 August 1919, cremated Llwydcoed Crematorium, Heads of the Valleys Road, Aberdare, Mid-Glamorgan, Wales. *GC location: RLC Museum, Deepcut, Camberley, Surrey.*

39. **Mate HENRY BUCKLE** (Albert Medal) 27 August 1919, buried St Peter's Churchyard, Church Road, Pimperne, Dorset. *AM location: with recipient's family.*

40. **Fire Officer JOHN** (incorrectly named as **JAMES** on his citation) **BURKE** (Empire Gallantry Medal) 26 November 1919 and 8 December 1924, buried in unmarked grave, Agecroft Cemetery (aka Northern

Cemetery), Plot 5, Grave 448; Langley Road, Salford, Manchester. *GC location: not publicly held.*

41. **Park Keeper ALBERT WATERFIELD** (Empire Gallantry Medal) 10 May 1921, cremated Mortlake Crematorium, Kew Meadow Path, Townmead Road, Richmond, Surrey. *GC location: not publicly held.*

42. **Assistant Surgeon GEORGE RODRIGUES** (sometime spelt **RODRIQUES**) (Empire Gallantry Medal) 24 September 1921, buried Bangalore, India. *GC location: not publicly held.*

43. **Sergeant WILLIAM HAND** (Empire Gallantry Medal) 24 September 1921, buried St Nicholas Parish Churchyard, Winterslow Road, Porton, near Salisbury. *GC location: The Keep Military Museum, Dorchester.*

44. **Private FREDERICK CHANT** (Empire Gallantry Medal) 24 September 1921, buried St John the Baptist Churchyard, Row D, Grave 1117; Church Lane, Boldre, Hampshire. *GC location: not publicly held.*

45. **Private THOMAS MILLER** (Empire Gallantry Medal) 24 September 1921, ashes scattered Robin Hood Crematorium, Lawn D; Streetsbrook Road, Shirley, Solihull. *GC location: not publicly held.*

46. **Private FREDERICK TROAKE** (Empire Gallantry Medal) 24 September 1921, ashes interred Rockwell Green Cemetery, Grave 186; Hilly Head, Wellington, Somerset. *GC location: not publicly held.*

47. **Special Constable SAMUEL ORR** (Empire Gallantry Medal) 1922, buried in unmarked grave, Faughanvale Burial Ground, Eglinton, near Londonderry, Northern Ireland. *GC location: not publicly held.*

48. **Mr JOHN 'JACK' CHALMERS** (Albert Medal) 4 February 1922, ashes scattered at sea. *GC location: not publicly held.*

49. **Coxswain WILLIAM 'PINGO' or 'JUMBO' FLEMING** (Empire Gallantry Medal) 19–22 October 1922, buried Gorleston Old Ground, Area U, Grave 183; Magdalen Way, Gorleston-on Sea, Norfolk. *GC location: The RNLI Heritage Trust, Poole, Dorset.*

50. **Mr THOMAS WHITEHEAD** (Edward Medal) 22 March 1922, buried Larne Cemetery, Larne, Northern Ireland. *EM location: not publicly held.*

51. **Miner BERT** (born **BERTIE**) **CRAIG** (Edward Medal) 14 November 1922, ashes interred Llwydcoed Crematorium, Plot 918, Cedar Lawn; Heads of the Valleys Road, Aberdare, Mid-Glamorgan, Wales. *GC location: National Museum and Gallery Wales, Cardiff, Wales.*

52. **Mill Foreman ALFRED MORRIS** (Edward Medal) 29 May 1923, burial location unknown, died in Bulawayo, Zimbabwe. *GC location:*

53. **Constable FRANCIS MORTESHED** (Empire Gallantry Medal) 7 March 1924, buried in Zimbabwe. *GC location: not publicly held.*

54. **Miner HARRY WILSON** (Edward Medal) 10 March 1924, cremated Bradwell Crematorium, Chatterley Lane, Newcastle. *GC location: Imperial War Museum, London.*

55. **Chauffeur FREDERICK MARCH** (Empire Gallantry Medal) 19

November 1924, buried Khartoum War Cemetery, Plot 13, Row C, Grave 5; Sudan. *GC location: not publicly held.*

56. **Mr KHALIFA MUHAMMAD** (Empire Gallantry Medal) 27 November 1924, buried near his home town of Farouq, Sudan. *GC location: with recipient's family.*

57. **Nafar MUHAMMAD ABDULLA MUHAMMAD** (Empire Gallantry Medal) 27/28 November 1924, burial location unknown, died in Khartoum, Sudan, probably cremated. *GC location: not publicly held.*

58. **Sol IBRAHIM NEGIB** (Empire Gallantry Medal) 27/28 November 1924, burial location unknown, probably cremated. *GC location: not publicly held.*

59. **Shawish TAHA EL JAK EFFENDI** (Empire Gallantry Medal) 27/28 November 1924, burial location unknown, probably cremated. *GC location: not publicly held.*

60. **Senior European Overseer JAMES JOHNSTON** (Edward Medal) 7 January 1925, ashes scattered Salisbury Crematorium, Barrington Road, Salisbury. *GC location: with recipient's family.*

61. **Petty Officer ROBERT CHALMERS** (Empire Gallantry Medal) 23 June 1925, ashes scattered at Warriston Crematorium, Edinburgh, Scotland. *GC location: not publicly held.*

62. **Mr ROBERT PEARSON** (Edward Medal) 11 July 1925, ashes scattered at Stockport Crematorium, Cheshire. *GC location: not publicly held.*

63. **Miner DONALD FLETCHER** (Edward Medal) 10 September 1925, ashes scattered at Markeaton Crematorium, Markeaton Lane, Derby. *GC location: not publicly held.*

64. **Leading Hand GEORGE LOCK** (often incorrectly spelt **LOCKE**) (Edward Medal) 8 October 1925, buried in unmarked grave, Dovercourt Cemetery, Grave 788; Main Road, Harwich, Essex. *GC location: not publicly held.*

65. **Staff Sergeant REGINALD MALTBY** (Empire Gallantry Medal) 5 June 1926, buried Charlton Cemetery, Plot SJ, Grave 14; Old Charlton Road, Dover, Kent. *GC location: with recipient's family.*

66. **Mr ROBERT WILD** (Empire Gallantry Medal) 10 July 1926, ashes interred in unmarked grave, Rochdale Cemetery, Plot VI; Bury Road, Rochdale, Lancashire. *GC location: not publicly held.*

67. **Prison Officer CYRIL TUTTON** (Empire Gallantry Medal) 15 November 1926, cremated Wakefield Crematorium, Standbridge Lane, Crigglestone, Yorkshire. *GC location: not publicly held.*

68. **Miner JOHN BEATTIE** (Empire Gallantry Medal) 19 November 1926, probably buried in Easington, Co. Durham, England. *GC location: with recipient's family.*

69. **Bricklayer JOSEPH CLARK** (Empire Gallantry Medal) 19 November 1926, cremated Durham Crematorium, South Road, Durham. *GC location: not publicly held.*

70. **Mr HERBERT HENDERSON** (Empire Gallantry Medal) 6 December 1926, cremated Vintners Park Crematorium, Aldon Close, Maidstone, Kent. *GC location: not publicly held.*

71. **Mr STANLEY GIBBS** (Albert Medal) 3 January 1927, ashes interred at Eastern Suburbs Memorial Park, Military Road, Matraville, New South Wales, Australia. (His headstone is unusual as the letters GC do not appear after his name.) *GC location: not publicly held.*

72. **Gunner JOHN FAIRCLOUGH** (Albert Medal) 27 April 1927, ashes interred at St Helens Crematorium, Section 2; Rainford Road, St Helens, Lancashire. *AM location: not publicly held.*

73. **Lieutenant GEORGE BAIN-SMITH** (Albert Medal) 3 June 1927, cremated Lancashire & Morecambe Crematorium, Powderhouse Lane, Lancaster. *GC location: not publicly held.*

74. **Petty Officer Stoker HERBERT MAHONEY** (Empire Gallantry Medal) July 1927, no known grave, lost in the Mediterranean Sea. *GC location: not publicly held.*

75. **Mr BERTRAM CROSBY** (Edward Medal) 9 September 1927, buried West Hampstead Cemetery, Grave S.4.3B; Fortune Green Road, London. *GC location: not publicly held.*

76. **Sub Foreman WILLIAM LLOYD** (Edward Medal) 3 October 1927, buried Newark Cemetery, Westside, Row B, Grave 412; London Road, Newark, Nottinghamshire. *GC location: not publicly held.*

77. **Lieutenant Colonel JAMES STEWART** (Empire Gallantry Medal) November 1927, ashes interred Denstone, Staffordshire. *GC location: not publicly held.*

78. **Lieutenant REGINALD ARMYTAGE** (Albert Medal) 23 May 1928, buried in his wife's family vault, All Saints Church, Holbeton, Devon. *AM location: with recipient's family.*

79. **Leading Seaman DICK OLIVER** (Albert Medal) 23 May 1928, cremated at Bournemouth Crematorium, Strouden Avenue, Bournemouth. *AM location: British Legion, Bargates, Christchurch, Dorset.*

80. **Principal Officer JOHN STOVES** (Empire Gallantry Medal) 12 June 1928, buried Durham St Nicholas, Block B, Section 1, Row A, Grave 5; Durham. *GC location: held by the Prison Officers Association.*

81. **Leading Aircraftman WALTER ARNOLD** (Empire Gallantry Medal) 20 June 1928, cremated South Essex Crematorium, Ockendon Road, Upminster, Essex. *GC location: not publicly held.*

82. **Flying Officer WALTER ANDERSON** (Empire Gallantry Medal) 10 December 1928, burial location unknown, died in Hythe, Hampshire. *GC location: not publicly held.*

83. **Corporal THOMAS McTEAGUE** (Empire Gallantry Medal) 10 December 1928, buried Miltown Cemetery, family grave, Grave VA320 B; Falls Road, Belfast, Northern Ireland. (His name does not appear on the headstone.) *GC location: not publicly held.*

84. **Sergeant REGINALD RIMMER** (Empire Gallantry Medal) 1929–1930, ashes scattered Bron y Nant Crematorium, Bron y Nant Road, Mochdre, Colwyn Bay, Wales. *GC location: not publicly held.*

85. **Mr ROBERT KAVANAUGH** (Albert Medal) 12 January 1929, buried Field of Mars Cemetery, Anglican Section, Lawn 4, Grave 2213; Quarry Road, Ryde, New South Wales, Australia. *GC location: not publicly held.*

86. **Pit Lad JOHN** (known as **TOM) BAKER** (Edward Medal) 17 May 1929, ashes interred Windmill Road Cemetery, Hilary Road, Coventry. (His headstone is unusual as the letters GC do not appear after his name.) *GC location: with recipient's family.*

87. **Pit Lad JAMES PURVIS** (Edward Medal) 17 May 1929, ashes scattered at Mountsett Crematorium, Dipton, Stanley, Co. Durham. *GC location: Imperial War Museum, London.*

88. **Flight Cadet WILLIAM McKECHNIE** (Empire Gallantry Medal) 20 June 1929, no known grave, killed over Pokarber, Germany. *GC location: not publicly held.*

89. **Lieutenant Commander ALEXANDER MAXWELL-HYSLOP** (Albert Medal) 26 July 1929, buried Sts Ciricius and Julitta Churchyard, Luxulyan, Cornwall. *GC location: presented to the Speaker of the House of Commons (unclear if it is still with the Speaker's Office).*

90 **Midshipman ANTHONY COBHAM** (Empire Gallantry Medal) 26 July 1929, ashes scattered Ashley Down Copse, near Portchester. *GC location: with recipient's family.*

91. **Able Seaman GEORGE NIVEN** (Empire Gallantry Medal) 26 July 1929, buried Yardley Cemetery, Section 58, Grave 66438; Yardley Road, Birmingham. *GC location: not publicly held.*

92. **Miner JOHN INGRAM GOUGH** (Edward Medal) 11 September 1929, ashes scattered St John's Churchyard, on the graves of the Gough and Ingram families, Newhall, Derbyshire. *GC location: with recipient's family.*

93. **Mr JOHN SHEPHERD** (Edward Medal) 16 October 1929, buried Jarrow Cemetery, Section 22, Grave 170; Cemetery Road, Jarrow, Co. Durham. *GC location: not publicly held.*

94. **Mr ALBERT TYLER** (Edward Medal) 19 October 1929, cremated Stopsley Crematorium, Luton. *GC location: not publicly held.*

95. **Pilot Officer SIDNEY WILTSHIRE** (Empire Gallantry Medal) 21 October 1929, ashes scattered, Hunterville, New Zealand. *GC location: not publicly held.*

96. **Mr GRANVILLE WASTIE** (Edward Medal) 25 November 1929, buried Christ Church Churchyard, Long Hanborough, Oxfordshire. *GC location: with recipient's family.*

97. **Sub Inspector GHULAM MOHI-ud-DIN** (Empire Gallantry Medal) 1930, burial location unknown, probably cremated. *GC location: with recipient's family.*

98. **Able Seaman GEORGE HARRISON** (Empire Gallantry Medal) 15

February 1930, cremated Portchester Crematorium, Upper Cornaway Lane, Fareham, Hampshire. *GC location: not publicly held.*

99. **Sergeant ARNOLD BARRACLOUGH** (Empire Gallantry Medal) 18/19 April 1930, ashes scattered at crematorium in Sussex. *GC location: not publicly held.*

100. **Trooper CLIVE BAYLEY** (Empire Gallantry Medal) 22 April 1930, drowned at sea, off the coast of Lagos, Atlantic Ocean. *GC location: not publicly held.*

101. **Pit Manager JOHN BELL** (Empire Gallantry Medal) 17 May 1930, buried Great Malvern Cemetery, Plot 6W, Grave 6822; Madresfield Road, Malvern Cemetery, Worcestershire. *GC location: not publicly held.*

102. **Shri JOSEPH BAPTISTA d'SOUZA** (Empire Gallantry Medal) 27 May 1930, buried Catholic Cemetery, Holy Trinity Church, Belgaum, Karnataka, India. *GC location: not publicly held.*

103. **Leading Aircraftman ROBERT DOUGLAS** (Empire Gallantry Medal) 13 June 1930, burial location unknown, died in Hackney, London. *GC location: National War Museum of Scotland, Edinburgh, Scotland.*

104. **Miner RICHARD KING** (Edward Medal) 29 September 1930, ashes scattered Mountsett Crematorium, Dipton, Stanley, Co. Durham. *GC location: Beamish Museum, Co. Durham.*

105. **Lance Sergeant THOMAS ALDER** (Empire Gallantry Medal) 16/17 November 1930, cremated Sunderland Crematorium, Chester Road, Tyne & Wear. *GC location: on loan to the Green Howards Museum, Richmond, Yorkshire.*

106. **Constable EL IMAM YEHIA** (Empire Gallantry Medal) 1931, burial location unknown, died in Omdurman, Sudan, probably cremated. *GC location: not publicly held.*

107. **Railway Flagman ARTHUR THOMAS** (Edward Medal) 14 January 1931, ashes scattered at Breakspear Crematorium, 36V; Breakspear Road, Ruislip, Middlesex. *EM location: not publicly held.*

108. **Sub Inspector BALDEV SINGH** (Empire Gallantry Medal) June and July 1931, burial location unknown, probably cremated. *GC location: not publicly held.*

109. **Sub Inspector BHIM SINGH YADAVA** (Empire Gallantry Medal) June 1931, burial location unknown, probably cremated. *GC location: not publicly held.*

110. **Assistant Store Keeper ALBERT MEADOWS** (Edward Medal) 18 September 1931, ashes scattered Chichester Crematorium, Westhampnett Road, Sussex. *GC location: not publicly held.*

111. **Assistant Surveyor SAMUEL TEMPERLEY** (Edward Medal) 20 November 1931, cremated Darlington Crematorium, Co. Durham. *GC location: not publicly held.*

112. **Miner RICHARD DARKER** (Edward Medal) 20 November 1931, ashes interred Rose Hill Crematorium, Cantley Lane, Doncaster. *GC location: with recipient's family.*

113. **Miner ERNEST ALLPORT** (Edward Medal) 20 November 1931, buried Arksey Lane Cemetery, Sheffield Road, Bentley, near Doncaster, Yorkshire. *GC location: not publicly held.*

114. **Miner OLIVER SOULSBY** (Edward Medal) 20 November 1931, cremated Rose Hill Crematorium, Cantley Lane, Doncaster. *GC location: not publicly held.*

115. **Miner FRANK SYKES** (Edward Medal) 20 November 1931, cremated Dewsbury Moor Crematorium, Heckmondwike Road, Dewsbury, Yorkshire. *GC location: not publicly held.*

116. **Miner PHILIP YATES** (Edward Medal) 20 November 1931, cremated Rose Hill Crematorium, Cantley Lane, Doncaster. *GC location: not publicly held.*

117. **Miss EMMA TOWNSEND** (Empire Gallantry Medal) 7 May 1932, burial location unknown, died in Wimbledon, Surrey. *GC location: not publicly held.*

118. **Flight Sergeant ERIC 'JOCK' BONAR** (Empire Gallantry Medal) 24 May 1932, cremated Croydon Crematorium, Surrey. *GC location: not publicly held.*

119. **Electrical Foreman OSMOND WILLIAMS** (Edward Medal) 15 July 1932, cremated Bangor Crematorium, Bangor, Caenarvonshire, Wales. *GC location: with recipient's family.*

120. **Mr MIRGHANY AHMED MUHAMMAD** (Empire Gallantry Medal) 18 September 1932, burial location unknown, probably cremated. *GC location: not publicly held.*

121. **Shawish TAHA IDRIS** (Empire Gallantry Medal) September 1933, burial location unknown, died in Omdurman, Sudan, probably cremated. *GC location: not publicly held.*

122. **Mr ABDUS SAMID ABDUL WAHID GOLANDAZ** (Empire Gallantry Medal) 16 September 1933, burial location unknown, probably cremated. *GC location: not publicly held.*

123. **Miner THOMAS THOMAS** (Edward Medal) 21 September 1933, burial location unknown, died in Carmarthen, Wales. *GC location: not publicly held.*

124. **Babu RANGIT SINGH** (Empire Gallantry Medal) 1934, burial location unknown, probably cremated. *GC location: not publicly held.*

125. **Major DOUGLAS BRETT** (Empire Gallantry Medal) 7 January 1934, ashes scattered at Portchester Crematorium, Upper Cornaway Lane, Upper Cornaway Lane, Fareham, Hampshire. *GC location: with recipient's family.*

126. **Captain RICHARD DEEDES** (Empire Gallantry Medal) 7 January 1934, ashes scattered at Shrewsbury Crematorium, Shrewsbury. *GC location: not publicly held.*

127. **Nursing Sister DOROTHY THOMAS** (Empire Gallantry Medal) 26 January 1934, ashes scattered at Chelmsford Crematorium, Lawn 1; Writtle Road, Chelmsford, Essex. *GC location: not publicly held.*

128. **Mr EDWARDO OMARA** (Empire Gallantry Medal) February and October 1934, buried Patongo, Uganda. *GC location: not publicly held.*

129. **Shri BHUPENDRA NARAYAN SINGH** (Empire Gallantry Medal) 8 May 1934, burial location unknown, probably cremated. *GC location: not publicly held.*

130. **Mr CHARLES TANDY-GREEN** (Empire Gallantry Medal) 8 May 1934, buried The Old Burial Ground, Plot K3; Cemetery Lane, off Kidmore Lane, Denmead, Hampshire. *GC location: not publicly held.*

131. **Captain PATRICK TAYLOR** (Empire Gallantry Medal) 15 May 1935, ashes scattered over Lion Island, Broken Bay, New South Wales, Australia. *GC location: with recipient's family.*

132. **Lance Naik MATA DIN** (Empire Gallantry Medal) 31 May 1935, burial location unknown, died in Gailoth Village, India, probably cremated. *GC location: not publicly held.*

133. **Private ROBERT SPOORS** (Albert Medal) 31 May 1935, cremated St Faiths Crematorium, Manor Road, Norwich. *GC location: not publicly held.*

134. **Nurse FLORENCE ALLEN** (Albert Medal) 31 May 1935, ashes scattered at Chilterns Crematorium, Whielden Lane, Amersham. *GC location: not publicly held.*

135. **Lieutenant JOHN COWLEY** (Albert Medal) 31 May/1 June 1935, ashes interred in St John the Baptist Churchyard, Church Lane, Boldre, Dorset. (His headstone is unusual as the letters GC do not appear after his name.) *GC location: Wellington College, Crowthorne, Berkshire.*

136. **Havildar AHMED YAR** (Empire Gallantry Medal) 31 May/1 June 1935, burial location unknown, died in Khushab, Pakistan, probably cremated. *GC location: not publicly held.*

137. **Naik NANDLAL THAPA** (Empire Gallantry Medal) 31 May/1 June 1935, burial location unknown, died in Dhaulagiri, Nepal, probably cremated. *GC location: The Gurkha Museum, Winchester, Hants.*

138. **Lance Corporal GEORGE HENSHAW** (Empire Gallantry Medal) 31 May/1 June 1935, ashes scattered at Eastbourne Crematorium, Area AR2; Hide Hollow, Langley. *GC location: unknown, stolen.*

139. **Private ARTHUR BROOKS** (Empire Gallantry Medal) 31 May/1 June 1935, burial location unknown. *GC location: Queen's Royal Surrey Regiment Museum, Stoughton Barracks, Surrey.*

140. **Private ERNEST ELSTON** (Empire Gallantry Medal) 31 May/1 June 1935, buried Northern Cemetery, Compartment 367, Grave 5; Kingston-upon-Hull. (His headstone is unusual as the letters GC do not appear after his name.) *GC location: Imperial War Museum, London.*

141. **Lance Sergeant ALFRED 'JOE' LUNGLEY** (Empire Gallantry Medal) 2 June 1935, ashes scattered Earlham Crematorium, Earlham Road, Norwich. *GC location: with recipient's family.*

142. **Private RICHARD BLACKBURN** (Empire Gallantry Medal) 7 June

1935, cremated Anfield Crematorium, Priory Road, Liverpool. *GC location: Imperial War Museum, London.*

143. **Colliery Agent NORMAN BASTER** (Edward Medal) 22/23 August 1935, ashes interred Featherstone Cemetery, Row 21, Grave Space 86; Alberta, Canada. *GC location: not publicly held.*

144. **Miner GEORGE BEAMAN** (Edward Medal) 22/23 August 1935, buried Inglewood Cemetery, Inglewood, Western Australia. *GC location: not publicly held.*

145. **Under Manager JAMES POLLITT** (Edward Medal) 22/23 August 1935, ashes interred St Wilfred's Churchyard, Standish, Lancashire. *GC location: not publicly held.*

146. **Yard Foreman EDWIN CROSSLEY** (Empire Gallantry Medal) October 1935, ashes scattered at Medway Crematorium, Woodland Glade 41; Robin Hood Lane, Blue Bell Hill, Chatham, Kent. *GC location: not publicly held.*

147. **Pit Manager GEORGE HESLOP** (Edward Medal) 17 December 1935, buried in unmarked grave, Saltburn Cemetery, Saltburn-by-the-Sea, Yorkshire. *EM location: not publicly held.*

148. **Yuzbashi El AMIN EFFENDI HEMEIDA** (sometimes spelt **HUMMEIDA**) (aka **AGABANI**) (Empire Gallantry Medal) 4 January 1936, burial location unknown, probably cremated. *GC location: with recipient's family.*

149. **European Shift Superintendent WILLIAM JAMIESON** (Empire Gallantry Medal) 7 January 1936, buried New Cemetery, Church Street, Wanlockhead, Lanarkshire, Scotland. *GC location: not publicly held.*

150. **Lance Corporal WILLIAM BARNETT** (Empire Gallantry Medal) 15 April–14 September 1936, buried Longton Cemetery, Block 123, Row 9, Grave 7; Longton, Stoke-on-Trent, Staffordshire. *GC location: not publicly held.*

151. **Inspector GEORGE ADAMSON** (Empire Gallantry Medal) 6 May 1936, ashes interred Beckenham Crematorium, Bed 11; Elmers End Road, Beckenham, Kent. *GC location: not publicly held.*

152. **Assistant River Surveyor CECIL KELLY** (Empire Gallantry Medal) 6 May 1936, buried Catholic Cemetery, family plot; Calcutta (now Kolkata), India. *GC location: not publicly held.*

153. **Begum ASHRA-un-NISA** (often incorrectly spelt **ASHRAF**) (Empire Gallantry Medal) 14 June 1936, burial location unknown, probably cremated. *GC location: unknown.*

154. **Private FRANK NAUGHTON** (Empire Gallantry Medal) 5 August 1936, cremated at Efford Crematorium, Efford Road, Plymouth, Devon. *GC location: with recipient's family.*

155. **Senior Shipwright Diver CHARLES 'POP' or 'FISTICUFFS' DUFFIN** (Empire Gallantry Medal) 19/20 August 1936, cremated Southampton Crematorium, Bassett Green Road, Southampton. *GC location: not publicly held.*

156. **Dr ROBERT SAUNDERS** (Edward Medal) 4/5 January 1937, ashes scattered St Athanasius Anglican Church, Shurugwi, Zimbabwe. *GC location: not publicly held.*

157. **Pilot Officer GERALD CLOSE** (Empire Gallantry Medal) 13 April 1937, buried Boulogne Eastern Cemetery,; Plot 13, Row A, Collective Grave 5–7; Rue de Dringhem, Boulogne, France. *GC location: RAF Museum, Hendon, London.*

158. **Naik BARKAT SINGH** (Empire Gallantry Medal) 2 May 1937, burial location unknown, died in Mansurpur, India, probably cremated. *GC location: not publicly held.*

159. **Lieutenant PATRICK HUMPHREYS** (Empire Gallantry Medal) 13 May 1937, buried Maidstone Cemetery, Plot CCI, Grave 108; Sutton Road, Maidstone, Kent. *GC location: not publicly held.*

160. **Miner DAVID BOOKER** (Edward Medal) 14 May 1937, buried Bloxwich Cemetery, Division Z, Section 1, Grave 315; Field Road, Bloxwich, West Midlands. *GC location: National Coal Mining Museum of England, Caphouse Colliery, Wakefield.*

161. **Miner SAMUEL BOOKER** (Edward Medal) 14 May 1937, buried Bloxwich Cemetery, Division AA, Section 1, Grave 111; Field Road, Bloxwich, West Midlands. (His name does not appear on the headstone.) *GC location: National Coal Mining Museum of England, Caphouse Colliery, Wakefield.*

162. **Overman (Rescue Brigade Captain) AZARIAH** (known as **EZRA**) **CLARKE** (Edward Medal) 2 July 1937, ashes scattered at Bradwell Crematorium, Kerb 22; Chatterey Close, Staffordshire. *GC location: The Borough Museum & Art Gallery, Newcastle-under-Lyme.*

163. **Aircraftman WILLIAM McALONEY** (Albert Medal) 31 August 1937, ashes interred Cheltenham Cemetery, Melbourne, Victoria, Australia. *GC location: not publicly held.*

164. **Private JOSEPH MOTT** (Empire Gallantry Medal) 25 December 1937, ashes scattered South Essex Crematorium, Area 4, Lawn 28; Ockendon Road, Upminster, Essex. *GC location: not publicly held.*

165. **Rais RASHID ABDUL FATTAH** (Empire Gallantry Medal) 1 and 4 March 1938, burial location unknown, probably cremated. *GC location: not publicly held.*

166. **Quarryman BENJAMIN JONES** (Edward Medal) 21 May 1938, ashes interred St Cynfran Churchyard, Pentregwyddel Road, Llysfaen, Wales. (His headstone is unusual in that the letters GC do not appear after his name.) GC *location: not publicly held.*

167. **Qaid YOUSEF HUSSEIN ALI BEY** (Arabic spelling **YOSEF BEY ALI**) (Empire Gallantry Medal) 5 July 1938, buried in a special room in Pikiin Village, Upper Galilee, Jordan. *GC location: not publicly held.*

168. **Chief Engine Room Artificer FREDERICK ANDERSON** (Empire Gallantry Medal) 25 July 1938, buried St Paul's (Hooton Parish)

Churchyard, Section F; Chester Road, Little Sutton, Wirral. *GC location: with recipient's family.*

169. **Pit Deputy FRED HALLER** (born **HAWLER**) (Edward Medal) 8 October 1938, ashes scattered Rosehill Crematorium, Cantley Lane, Doncaster. *GC location: not publicly held.*

170. **Mr ERNEST KENT** (Edward Medal) 25/26 October 1938, cremated Southend Crematorium, Sutton Road, Southend, Essex. *GC location: with recipient's family.*

171. **Fitter ROBERT LITTLE** (Edward Medal) 11 January 1939, ashes scattered Landican Crematorium, Bed 21; Arrowe Park Road, Wirral, Merseyside. *GC location: not publicly held.*

172. **Assistant Civil Engineer HAROLD CHARRINGTON** (Empire Gallantry Medal) 3 February 1939, cremated Chilterns Crematorium, Whielden Lane, Amersham. *GC location: RAF Museum, Hendon, London.*

173. **Mr JOHN** (known as **JACK) DIXON** (Edward Medal) 16 February 1939, ashes scattered at Lincoln Crematorium, Washingborough Road, Lincoln. *GC location: with recipient's family.*

174. **Mulazim THEODORE 'BOG' BOGDANOVITCH** (sometimes spelt **BOGDANOVICH**) (Empire Gallantry Medal) 11 March 1939, buried English Cemetery, Nicosia, Cyprus. *GC location: Gordon Highlanders Museum, Aberdeen, Scotland.*

175. **Corporal THOMAS ATKINSON** (Empire Gallantry Medal) 15 March 1939, buried Portland Cemetery, Section F, Grave 192; Weston Road, Weston, Portland, Dorset. *GC location: The Green Howards Museum, Richmond, Yorkshire.*

176. **Private THOMAS McAVOY** (Empire Gallantry Medal) 15 March 1939, cremated Maryhill Crematorium, Glasgow, Scotland. *GC location: The Green Howards Museum, Richmond, Yorkshire.*

177. **Mr FREDERICK CHILD** (Empire Gallantry Medal) 29 March 1939, cremated Mortlake Crematorium, Kew Meadow Path, Townmead Road, Richmond, Surrey. *GC location: not publicly held.*

178. **Jib Crane Driver BERNARD FISHER** (Edward Medal) 26 April 1939, cremated. *GC location: not publicly held.*

179. **Radio Officer JAMES TURNER** (Empire Gallantry Medal) 6 September 1939, burial location unknown. *GC location: with recipient's family.*

180. **Flying Officer REGINALD GRAVELEY** (Empire Gallantry Medal) 20 September 1939, cremated at Ryecroft Crematorium; his ashes were then scattered from an aircraft. *GC location: RAF Museum, Hendon, London.*

181. **Commander RICHARD JOLLY** (Empire Gallantry Medal) 16 October 1939, ashes interred St Peter Churchyard, Grave 602; Church Hill, Boughton Monchelsea, Kent. *GC location: not publicly held.*

182. **Research Officer CHARLES 'JACK' HOWARD (Earl of Suffolk and Berkshire)**, 1939–12 May 1941, buried St John the Baptist Churchyard, Park Street, Charlton, near Malmesbury, Wiltshire. (His headstone is

unusual in that instead of the letters GC he has the words George Cross after his name.) *GC location: not publicly held.*

183. **Acting Wing Commander JOHN ROWLANDS**, 1940–1943, cremated Hutcliffe Wood Crematorium, Periwood Lane, Sheffield. *GC location: not publicly held.*

184. **Miner CHARLES SMITH** (Edward Medal) 3 January 1940, ashes interred Blaydon Cemetery, Division W, Grave 35; Shibdon Road, Blaydon, Co. Durham. *GC location: not publicly held.*

185. **Miner MATTHEW THOMPSON** (Edward Medal) 3 January 1940, cremated Pontefract Crematorium, Wakefield Road, Pontefract. *EM location: not publicly held.*

186. **Corporal JOHN McCLYMONT** (Empire Gallantry Medal) 18 January 1940, ashes interred Bethesda United Church Cemetery, Ancaster, Ontario, Canada. *GC location: RAF Museum, Hendon, London.*

187. **Explosive Worker LEO O'HAGEN** (sometimes spelt **O'HAGAN**) (Empire Gallantry Medal) 18 January 1940, cremated at Colchester Crematorium, Essex. *GC location: not publicly held.*

188. **Explosive Worker STANLEY SEWELL** (Edward Medal) 18 January 1940, burial location unknown, died in Enfield, Middlesex. England. *GC location: not publicly held.*

189. **Explosive Worker WILLIAM SYLVESTER** (Empire Gallantry Medal) 18 January 1940, cremated Wrexham Crematorium, Wrexham, Pentre Bychan Road, Wrexham, Wales. *GC location: Royal Gunpowder Mills, Waltham Abbey, Essex.*

190. **Jemadar Badragga (Escort) PIR KHAN** (Empire Gallantry Medal) 3 February 1940, buried Makeen Graveyard, Makeen, India. *GC location: with recipient's family.*

191. **Flight Lieutenant JOHN DOWLAND** (born **DOWLAND-RYAN**), 11 February 1940, buried Malta (Capuccini) Naval Cemetery, Protestant Section (Officers), Plot E, Collective Grave 14; Trig Santa Rokku, Kalkara, Malta. *GC location: RAF Museum, Hendon, London.*

192. **Civilian Armament Instructor LEONARD HARRISON**, 11 February 1940, ashes interred Eltham Crematorium, Section R; Crown Woods Way, London. *GC location: not publicly held.*

193. **Mine Agent THOMAS JAMESON** (Edward Medal) 14/15 February 1940, ashes scattered Wrexham Crematorium, Plot 4; Pentre Bychan Road, Wrexham. *GC location: not publicly held.*

194. **Overman CARL SCHOFIELD** (Edward Medal) 14/15 February 1940, ashes scattered St Helens Crematorium, Section 4; Rainford Road, Windle, Lancashire. *GC location: not publicly held.*

195. **Flying Officer ANTHONY TOLLEMACHE** (Empire Gallantry Medal) 11 March 1940, buried St Mary's Churchyard, Helmingham Road, Helmingham, Suffolk. *GC location: with recipient's family.*

196. **Leading Aircraftman MICHAEL 'MICK' CAMPION** (Empire Gallantry

Medal) 12 March 1940, lost at sea off the coast of Azores, Atlantic Ocean. *GC location: not publicly held.*

197. Aircraftman **ERNEST 'CHRIS' FROST** (Empire Gallantry Medal) 12 March 1940, buried Lakeview Cemetery, Ontario, Canada. *GC location: Canadian War Museum, Ottawa, Ontario, Canada.*

198. Sub Lieutenant **ALEXANDER 'SANDY' HODGE** (Empire Gallantry Medal) 14 March 1940, cremated Warriston Crematorium, Warriston Road, Edinburgh, Scotland. *GC location: not publicly held.*

199. Mr **GERALD WINTER** (Empire Gallantry Medal) 21 March 1940, burial location unknown, died in Lewes, Sussex. *GC location: not publicly held.*

200. Assistant Foreman **JOHN McCABE** (Empire Gallantry Medal) 2 April 1940, buried Shewalton Cemetery, Grave A326; Ayr Road, Irvine, Scotland. (His headstone incorrectly states he is an OBE.) *GC location: not publicly held.*

201. Lieutenant **JOHN LOW** (Empire Gallantry Medal) 29 April 1940, no known grave, lost in the North Sea. *GC location: not publicly held.*

202. Able Seaman **HENRY 'DUSTY' MILLER** (Empire Gallantry Medal) 29 April 1940, no known grave, lost in the North Sea. *GC location: with recipient's family.*

203. Captain **JENKIN** (aka **J.R.O.**) **THOMPSON**, May 1940–23/24 January 1944, no known grave, lost in the Mediterranean Sea. *GC location: Army Medical Services Museum, Keogh Barracks, Mytchett.*

204. Corporal **JOAN PEARSON** (Empire Gallantry Medal) 31 May 1940, cremated at The Necropolis, Princess Hwy, Springvale, Australia. *GC location: Imperial War Museum, London.*

205. Captain **ROBERT JEPHSON-JONES**, June–November 1940, ashes interred All Saints Churchyard, Church Lane, West Parley, Dorset. *GC location: RLC Museum, Deepcut, Camberley, Surrey.*

206. Lieutenant **WILLIAM EASTMAN**, June–November 1940, buried Ta Braxia International Cemetery, Malta. *GC location: RLC Museum, Deepcut, Camberley, Surrey.*

207. The Island of **MALTA**, June 1940–October 1942, *GC location: National War Museum, Fort Saint Elmo, Valletta, Malta.*

208. Pilot Officer **EDWARD PARKER** (Empire Gallantry Medal) 8 June 1940, buried Berlin 1939–1945 War Cemetery, Plot 1, Row F, Grave 3; Berlin, Germany. *GC location: not publicly held.*

209. Foundryman **JOHN FARR** (Empire Gallantry Medal) 12 June 1940, ashes scattered at Slough Crematorium, Grid Ref K8; Stoke Road, Slough. *GC location: not publicly held.*

210. Aircraftman 1st Class **VIVIAN 'BOB' HOLLOWDAY**, 2 July and August 1940, cremated Bedford Crematorium, Norse Road Cemetery, Norse Road, Bedford. (His ashes may have been scattered on his mother's grave.) *GC location: RAF Museum, Hendon, London.*

211. Lieutenant **EDWARD REYNOLDS** (Empire Gallantry Medal) 17

August and 3 September 1940, buried in unmarked grave, St Peter's Churchyard, Grave ref. B19, but his name is on his parents' headstone (B47); Harborne, Birmingham. *GC location: on loan to the Imperial War Museum, London.*

212. **Lance Sergeant WILLIAM BUTTON** (Empire Gallantry Medal) 18 August 1940, ashes scattered Haycombe Cemetery, Bath. *GC location: with recipient's family.*

213. **Second Lieutenant ELLIS TALBOT** (Empire Gallantry Medal) 24/25 August 1940, buried Catania War Cemetery, Collective Grave Plot I, Row H, Grave 19; Stradale Passo del Feco, Sicily. *GC location: Royal Engineers Museum, Gillingham, Kent.*

214. **Second Lieutenant WALLACE ANDREWS** (Empire Gallantry Medal) 26 August 1940, buried St Mary's Cemetery, Grave 2/4242; Taunton, Somerset. *GC location: not publicly held.*

215. **Acting Squadron Leader ERIC MOXEY**, 27 August 1940, buried St Peter and St Paul Churchyard, Section NN, Grave 26; Cudham Lane South, Cudham, Kent. *GC location: with recipient's family.*

216. **Acting Major HERBERT BAREFOOT**, September–October 1940, buried Ipswich New Cemetery, Ref XJ-2, Grave 49; Cemetery Lane, Ipswich, Suffolk. *GC location: Imperial War Museum, London.*

217. **Temporary Lieutenant ROBERT** (known as **SELBY) ARMITAGE**, September–October 1940, ashes interred St Bartholomew's Churchyard, High Street, Nettlebed, Oxfordshire. *GC location: Imperial War Museum, London.*

218. **Acting Flight Lieutenant WILSON 'BOMBS' CHARLTON**, September–October 1940, burial location unknown, died in St Mary's Hospital, Roehampton, Surrey. *GC location: not publicly held.*

219. **Acting Lieutenant BERTRAM 'ARCHIE' ARCHER**, 2 September 1940, still living. *GC location: with recipient.*

220. **Hospital Porter ALBERT DOLPHIN**, 7 September 1940, burial location unknown, died in South Eastern Hospital, London. *GC location: with recipient's family.*

221. **Doctor ARTHUR MERRIMAN**, 11 September 1940, buried Streatham Park Cemetery, Square 33, Grave 60174; Rowan Road, Streatham Vale, London. *GC location: not publicly held.*

222. **Temporary Lieutenant ROBERT 'JOCK' DAVIES**, 12 September 1940, cremated Northern Suburbs Crematorium, Delhi Road, Ryde, Sydney, New South Wales, Australia. *GC location: Imperial War Museum, London.*

223. **Sapper GEORGE WYLLIE** (sometimes misspelt **WYLIE**), 12 September 1940, cremated. *GC location: St Paul's Cathedral, London.*

224. **Detachment Leader THOMAS ALDERSON**, 15–20 September 1940, ashes scattered Woodlands Crematorium, East Section of the Garden of

Remembrance, Ref: 3358; Scarborough, Yorkshire. *GC location: on loan to the Imperial War Museum, London.*

225. **Lieutenant Commander RICHARD RYAN**, 16–21 September 1940, buried Haslar Royal Naval Cemetery, Plot G, Row 8, Grave 24; Clayhall Road, Gosport, Hampshire. *GC location: not publicly held.*

226. **Temporary Sub Lieutenant RICHARD MOORE**, 16–21 September 1940, ashes scattered at Walton Lea Crematorium, Autumn Section; Chester Road, Warrington, Cheshire. *GC location: not publicly held.*

227. **Chief Petty Officer REGINALD ELLINGWORTH**, 16–21 September 1940, buried Milton Cemetery, Plot Y, Row 18, Grave 11; Portsmouth. *GC location: on loan to the Imperial War Museum, London.*

228. **Auxiliary Fireman HARRY ERRINGTON**, 17 September 1940, buried Western Synagogue Cemetery, Row P, Grave 322; Bulls Cross Ride, Cheshunt, Hertfordshire. *GC location: Jewish Military Museum, London.*

229. **Chief Combustion Officer ROY HARRIS**, 18 September 1940, ashes scattered Bushbury Crematorium, Square 8.2, Marker 55M; Underhill Lane, Wolverhampton. *GC location: not publicly held.*

230. **Acting Captain MICHAEL 'MAX' BLANEY**, 18 September, 20 October and 13 December 1940, buried Old Chapel (St Mary's) RC Cemetery (Old Ground), Chapel Street, Newry, Co. Down, Northern Ireland. (His headstone is unusual in that the letters GC do not appear after his name.) *GC location: with recipient's family.*

231. **Lieutenant JOHN PATTON**, 21 September 1940, buried Christ Church Churchyard, Warwick, Bermuda. *GC location: not publicly held.*

232. **Sub Lieutenant GEOFFREY TURNER**, 21 December 1940, cremated Cambridge Crematorium, Huntingdon Road, Cambridge. *GC location: not publicly held.*

233. **ARP Warden LEONARD MILES**, 21/22 September 1940, ashes scattered at City of London Crematorium, Ref: 4323; Aldersbrook Road, Manor Park, London. *GC location: Held by the Worshipful Company of Skinners, Skinners Hall, City of London.*

234. **Temporary Sub Lieutenant JOHN MILLER** (later **DUPPA-MILLER**), 23 September 1940, ashes scattered off the coast of South Africa. *GC location: with recipient's family.*

235. **Able Seaman STEPHEN TUCKWELL**, 23 September 1940, burial location unknown, died in Sompting, Lancing, Sussex. *GC location: not publicly held.*

236. **Shunter NORMAN TUNNA**, 26 September 1940, ashes scattered Landican Crematorium, Bed 12; Arrowe Park Road, Wirral, Merseyside. *GC location: not publicly held.*

237. **Temporary Sub Lieutenant WILLIAM TAYLOR**, 26 September–17 October 1940, cremated Aberdeen Crematorium, Skene Road, Scotland. *GC location: with recipient's family.*

238. **Acting Second Hand JOHN MITCHELL** (Albert Medal) 27 September

1940, burial location unknown, died in Wandsworth, London. *GC location: not publicly held.*

239. **Wing Commander LAURENCE 'LAURIE' SINCLAIR** 30 September 1940, buried St Mary the Virgin Churchyard, Hatfield Broad Oak, Essex. *GC location: Imperial War Museum, London.*

240. **Temporary Sub Lieutenant JOHN BABINGTON**, autumn 1940, ashes scattered Oxford Crematorium, Plot M; Bayswater Road, Oxfordshire. *GC location: on loan to the Imperial War Museum, London.*

241. **Section Commander GEORGE INWOOD**, 15/16 October 1940, buried Yardley Cemetery, Grave 46739; Yardley Road, Birmingham. *GC location: Birmingham Museum and Art Gallery, Birmingham.*

242. **Second Lieutenant ALEXANDER 'SANDY' CAMPBELL**, 17 October 1940, buried Coventry (London Road) Cemetery, Square 348, Collective Grave 46 (next to Michael Gibson); London Road, Coventry. *GC location: Royal Engineers Museum, Gillingham, Kent.*

243. **Temporary Sub Lieutenant JACK EASTON**, 17 October 1940, ashes scattered Chichester Crematorium, Westhampnett Road, Sussex. *GC location: stolen in 1945, official replacement issued. The original GC came up for auction years later, and it was decided that the seller had bought it in good faith and was allowed to sell it. It was bought by Jack Easton's son Michael. Both crosses are now with recipient's family.*

244. **Sergeant MICHAEL GIBSON**, 17 October 1940, buried Coventry (London Road) Cemetery, Square 348, Collective Grave 46 (next to Alexander Campbell); London Road, Coventry. *GC location: not publicly held.*

245. **Ordinary Seaman BENNETT SOUTHWELL**, 17 October 1940, buried Gilroes Cemetery, Section K, Grave 286; Groby Road, Leicester. *GC location: with recipient's family.*

246. **Special Constable BRANDON MOSS**, 20/21 October 1940, cremated Canley Crematorium, London Road, Coventry. *GC location: The Ashcroft Collection.*

247. **Sub Lieutenant PETER DANCKWERTS**, late 1940, cremated Cambridge Crematorium, Huntingdon Road, Cambridge. *GC location: not publicly held.*

248. **Sergeant RAYMOND LEWIN**, 3 November 1940, buried Kettering Cemetery, Row 00, Grave 9; London Road, Kettering, Northamptonshire. *GC location: not publicly held.*

249. **Temporary Lieutenant HAROLD NEWGASS**, 28 November 1940, ashes scattered in West Stafford Cemetery, Dorchester. *GC location: Imperial War Museum, London.*

250. **Sub Lieutenant FRANCIS BROOKE-SMITH**, December 1940, buried Hasketon Churchyard, Church Road, near Woodbridge, Suffolk. *GC location: on loan to the Imperial War Museum, London.*

251. **Able Seaman ALFRED MILES** (Albert Medal) 1 December 1940, buried

Woodlands Cemetery, Section CJ, Grave 85; Woodlands Road, Gillingham, Kent. *GC location: National Maritime Museum, London.*

252. **Station & Rescue Officer WILLIAM MOSEDALE**, 12 December 1940, ashes scattered Arnos Vale Crematorium, Garden of Rest No 1; Bath Road, Bristol, Avon. *GC location: Birmingham Museum and Art Gallery, Birmingham.*

253. **Pit Manager THOMAS HULME** (Edward Medal) 23 January 1941, ashes scattered St Helens Crematorium, Section 8; Rainford Road, Windle, Lancashire. *GC location: not publicly held.*

254. **Cadet DAVID HAY** (Albert Medal) 29 January 1941, buried Gifford Churchyard, High Street, Gifford, East Lothian, Scotland. *AM location: on loan to the Imperial War Museum, London.*

255. **Corporal JAMES SCULLY**, 8 March 1941, buried Streatham Cemetery, Block R, Grave 466; Garratt Lane, London. *GC location: not publicly held.*

256. **Temporary Lieutenant ERNEST 'MICK' GIDDEN**, 17 April 1941, ashes scattered at Golders Green Crematorium, Ref: 166569, Plot 4; Hoop Lane, London. *GC location: not publicly held.*

257. **Ordinary Seaman ALBERT HOWARTH** (Albert Medal) 9 May 1941, ashes scattered Burnley Crematorium, Summer Section; Accrington Road, Burnley, Lancashire. *GC location: with recipient's family.*

258. **Mr PERCY WELLER** (Edward Medal) 16 May 1941, buried St Bartholomew Churchyard, Leigh, Surrey. *GC location: not publicly held.*

259. **Lieutenant HUGH 'HUGHIE' SYME**, 19 May 1941–25 December 1942, cremated Springvale Crematorium, Melbourne, Victoria, Australia. *GC location: Australian War Memorial, Canberra, Australia.*

260. **Squadron Leader the Reverend HERBERT PUGH**, 5 July 1941, no known grave, lost in the Atlantic Ocean. *GC location: not publicly held.*

261. **Mr WILLIAM BAXTER** (Edward Medal) 8 July 1941, ashes scattered Woodlands Crematorium, Plot 3/4 West, Woodlands Drive, Scarborough, North Yorkshire. *GC location: not publicly held.*

262. **Corporal JAMES 'SCOTTY' HENDRY**, 13 June 1941, buried Brookwood Military Cemetery, Canadian Section, Plot 31, Row F, Grave 9; Pirbright Road, Woking, Surrey. *GC location: Canadian War Museum, Ottawa, Ontario, Canada.*

263. **Bombardier HENRY** (aka **HERBERT**) **REED**, 20/21 June 1941, buried Bishopwearmouth Cemetery, Ward 34, Section CC, Grave 939; Chester Road, Sunderland, Tyne & Wear. *GC location: National Army Museum, London.*

264. **Acting Lieutenant Commander WILLIAM HISCOCK**, September 1941, buried Malta (Capuccini) Naval Cemetery, Protestant Section (Officers), Plot E, Collective Grave 16; Trig Santa Rokku, Kalkara, Malta. *GC location: not publicly held.*

265. **Temporary Lieutenant JOHN GIBBONS** (Albert Medal) 22 September 1941, ashes scattered off the coast of Ischia, Mediterranean Sea. *AM location: unknown, stolen in the 1950s.*

266. **Leading Aircraftman ALBERT 'MATT' OSBORNE**, November

1941–1 April 1942, buried Malta (Capuccini) Naval Cemetery, Protestant Section (Men's), Plot F, Grave 96; Trig Santa Rokku, Kalkara, Malta. *GC location: not publicly held.*

267. **Leading Aircraftman KARL GRAVELL**, 10 November 1941, buried Mountain View Cemetery, Block 4, Plot 7, Lot 2; Vancouver, British Columbia, Canada. (His headstone is unusual as the letters GC do not appear after his name.) *GC location: 1 Wing HQ, Winnipeg, Canada.*

268. **Lieutenant JOHN 'MOULDY' MOULD**, 14 November 1941–30 June 1942, cremated Northern Suburbs Crematorium, Delhi Road, Ryde, Sydney, New South Wales, Australia. *GC location: not publicly held.*

269. **Captain MATEEN** (often incorrectly spelt **MATREEN**) **AHMED ANSARI**, 1942–19 or 29 October 1943, buried Stanley Military Cemetery, Plot I, Row E, Grave 1; Hong Kong, China. *GC location: Pakistan Army Museum, Rawalpindi, Pakistan.*

270. **Assistant Attorney General JOHN FRASER** (sometimes spelt **FRAZER**), 1942–29 October 1943, buried Stanley Military Cemetery, Plot I, Row C, Collective Grave 1–11; Hong Kong, China. *GC location: not publicly held.*

271. **Flight Lieutenant HECTOR 'DOLLY' GRAY**, December 1941–18 December 1943, buried Stanley Military Cemetery, Plot I, Row A, Grave 59; Hong Kong, China. *GC location: not publicly held.*

272. **Captain MAHMOOD** (or **MAHMUD**) **KHAN DURRANI**, 1942–1944, burial location unknown, died in Pakistan, probably cremated. *GC location: Imperial War Museum, London.*

273. **Temporary Lieutenant GEORGE 'GRANNY' GOODMAN**, 15 January–27 March 1942, buried Westduin General Cemetery, Row 5, Grave 100; The Hague, Holland. *GC location: with recipient's family.*

274. **Captain LIONEL 'THE DUKE' MATTHEWS**, August 1942–2 March 1944, buried Labuan War Cemetery, Plot J, Row B, Grave 15; Cantonment Road, Near Victoria Township, on an island in Brunei Bay, Borneo, Malaysia. *GC location: with recipient's family.*

275. **Lieutenant DENNIS COPPERWHEAT**, 22 March 1942, buried Weekley Parish Churchyard, Church Walk, Weekley, Kettering, Northamptonshire. *GC location: not publicly held.*

276. **Apprentice (Merchant Navy) DONALD CLARKE**, 8/9 August 1942, lost at sea off the coast of Trinidad. *GC location: Chester-le-Street District Council, Co. Durham.*

277. **Captain DUDLEY MASON**, 12–15 August 1942, ashes scattered at his home, The Mill Cottage, off Station Road, Sway, Hampshire. *GC location: HQS Wellington, Thames River, London.*

278. **Apprentice JOHN GREGSON** (Albert Medal) 12 August 1942, still living. *AM location: with recipient.*

279. **Petty Officer Cook CHARLES WALKER** (Albert Medal) 13 August

1942. Cremated Llanelli Crematorium, Wales. His ashes were scattered at sea from HMS *Ledbury*. *GC location: with recipient's family.*

280. **Lieutenant WILLIAM FOSTER**, 13 September 1942, buried St Mary's Churchyard, Plot 164, New Ground; Lights Lane, Alderbury, Wiltshire. *GC location: St Mary's Church, Alderbury, Wiltshire.*

281. **Chief Officer JAMES REEVES** (Albert Medal) 14 September 1942, ashes interred St Cuthberts Churchyard, Darwen, Lancashire. *GC location: with recipient's family.*

282. **Sergeant GRAHAM PARISH**, 16 September 1942, buried Khartoum War Cemetery, Plot 11, Row C, Grave 7; Khartoum, Sudan. *GC location: not publicly held.*

283. **Acting Leading Seaman WILLIAM GOAD** (Albert Medal) 20/21 September 1942, ashes scattered at Maddingly Crematorium, Cambridge. *AM location: with recipient's family.*

284. **Assistant Works Manager Dr WILSON BALDWIN** (Edward Medal) 20 November 1942, ashes scattered in the wildfowl area, Great Oakley, Essex. *EM location: Imperial War Museum, London.*

285. **Lieutenant FRANCIS 'TONY'** or **'JIMMY' FASSON**, 30 October 1942, lost at sea in the Mediterranean. *GC location: National War Museum of Scotland, Edinburgh, Scotland.*

286. **Able Seaman COLIN GRAZIER**, 30 October 1942, lost at sea in the Mediterranean. *GC location: National War Museum of Scotland, Edinburgh, Scotland.*

287. **Boatswain WILLIAM 'MAC' McCARTHY** (Albert Medal) 3 January 1943, cremated Portchester Crematorium, Upper Cornaway Lane, Upper Cornaway Lane, Fareham, Hampshire. *GC location: on permanent loan to the Imperial War Museum, London.*

288. **Acting Able Seaman EYNON HAWKINS** (Albert Medal) 10 January 1943, cremated Coychurch Crematorium, Bridgend, Wales. *GC location: not publicly held.*

289. **Temporary Major CYRIL MARTIN**, 17/18 January 1943, buried St Thomas A Becket Churchyard, Church Road, South Cadbury, Somerset. *GC location: with recipient's family.*

290. **Temporary Major HUGH SEAGRIM**, February 1943–22 September 1944, buried Rangoon War Cemetery, Plot IV, Row A, Grave 11–20; Pyi Road, Burma. *GC location: on loan from the family to the Imperial War Museum, London.*

291. **Wing Commander FOREST** (known as **TOMMY**) **'The White Rabbit' YEO-THOMAS**, February 1943–1945, ashes interred Brookwood Cemetery, Glades of Remembrance, Pine Glade; Cemetery Pales, Woking, Surrey. *GC location: Imperial War Museum, London.*

292. **Lieutenant Commander PATRICK O'LEARY** (real name **ALBERT-MARIE EDMOND GUERISSE**), March 1943–May 1945, burial location unknown, died in Waterloo, Belgium. *GC location: not publicly held.*

293. **Chief Officer GEORGE STRONACH**, 19 March 1943, buried

Acharacle Parish Churchyard, Acharacle, Ardnamurchan, Scotland. (His headstone is unusual as that the letters GC do not appear after his name.) *GC location: not publicly held.*

294. **Second Engineer Officer GORDON BASTIAN** (Albert Medal) 30 March 1943, buried Barrie Union Cemetery, Section E, Plot 220, Grave 4 &5; Ontario, Canada. (His headstone is unusual as the letters GC do not appear after his name.) *GC location: on loan to the Imperial War Museum, London.*

295. **Mrs ODETTE SANSOM** (Née **BRAILLY,** then **CHURCHILL**, later **HALLOWES**), April 1943–May 1945, ashes interred Burvale Cemetery, Grave 3506; Burwood Road, Hersham, Surrey. *GC location: Imperial War Museum, London.*

296. **Boilerman FREDERICK CRADOCK (or CRADDOCK)**, 4 May 1943, buried in unmarked grave, St Mary's Churchyard, Hawkedon, Suffolk. *GC location: with recipient's family.*

297. **Leading Aircraftman KENNETH SPOONER**, 14 May 1943, buried Hillcrest Cemetery, Plot 225, Row 15; Smith's Falls, Ontario, Canada. *GC location: Canadian War Museum, Ottawa, Ontario, Canada.*

298. **Temporary Lieutenant LEON 'FICKY' GOLDSWORTHY**, 12 June 1943–10 April 1944, cremated Karrakatta Crematorium, Railway Road, Hollywood, Perth, Western Australia. *GC location: not publicly held.*

299. **Private CHARLES DUNCAN**, 10 July 1943, buried Enfidaville (Enfida) War Cemetery, Plot III, Row B, Grave 28; Tunisia. *GC location: Airborne Forces Museum, Duxford.*

300. **Temporary Colonel LANCERAY** (known as **LANCE** or **LAN**) **NEWNHAM**, 10 July–18 December 1943, buried Stanley Military Cemetery, Plot I, Row A, Grave 58; Hong Kong, China. *GC location: Imperial War Museum, London.*

301. **Captain DOUGLAS FORD**, 10 July–18 December 1943, buried Stanley Military Cemetery, Plot I, Row B, Grave 41; Hong Kong, China. *GC location: Royal Scots Regimental Museum, Edinburgh, Scotland.*

302. **Temporary Major ANDRE KEMPSTER** (formerly **ANDRE GILBERTO COCCIOLETTI**), 21 August 1943, buried Bone War Cemetery, Plot II, Row D, Grave 1; Annaba, Algeria. *GC location: not publicly held.*

303. **Temporary Lieutenant JOHN BRIDGE**, 30 August–2 September 1943, ashes believed to be interred at St Andrew's Parish Churchyard, Talbot Road, Roker, Tyne & Wear. *GC location: Imperial War Museum, London.*

304. **Assistant Section Officer NOOR-UN-NISA** (wrongly gazetted as **NORA**) **INAYAT-KHAN**, September 1943–12 September 1944, no known grave, killed at Dachau Concentration Camp, Germany. *GC location: not publicly held.*

305. **Acting Brigadier ARTHUR NICHOLLS**, October 1943–January 1944, buried in mass grave near headstone, Tirana Park Memorial Cemetery, Tirana, Albania. *GC location: Guards Museum, London.*

306. Warrant Electrician **ERNEST WOODING** (Albert Medal) 13 October 1943, still living. *AM location: with recipient.*

307. Acting Sergeant **JOHN 'JOCK' RENNIE**, 29 October 1943, buried Brookwood Military Cemetery, Canadian Section, Plot 47, Grave D.8; Pirbright Road, Woking, Surrey. *GC location: with recipient's family.*

308. Private **JOSEPH SILK** (born **KIBBLE**), 4 December 1943, buried Taukkyan War Cemetery, Plot 10, Row K, Grave 22; Rangoon, Burma. *GC location: Somerset Military Museum, Taunton Castle, Taunton, Somerset.*

309. Mr **JOHN WELLER** (often mistakenly called **WELLER-BROWN**) (Edward Medal) 4 February 1944, buried in Richmond, Yorkshire. *GC location: not publicly held.*

310. Deputy Party Leader **LESLIE FOX**, 20/21 February 1944, ashes scattered at Portchester Crematorium, at posts nos 64–65; Upper Cornaway Lane, Fareham, Hampshire. *GC location: not publicly held.*

311. Factory Development Officer **RICHARD** (known as **ARTHUR**) **BYWATER**, 22 February 1944, buried Scone Lawn Cemetery, Section B, Grave 382; New South Wales, Australia. *GC location: not publicly held.*

312. Mr **ANTHONY SMITH**, 23 February 1944, buried North Sheen Cemetery, Plot SC, Grave 478; Lower Richmond Road, Surrey. *GC location: not publicly held.*

313. Subadar **SUBRAMANIAN**, 24 February 1944, ashes interred Sangro River Cremation Memorial, Italy. *GC location: not publicly held.*

314. Ensign **VIOLETTE SZABO** (née **BUSHELL**), April 1944–between 25 January and 5 February 1945, no known grave, killed at Ravensbruck Concentration Camp, Germany. *GC location: not publicly held.*

315. Pit Deputy **FRANK NIX** (Edward Medal) 18 April 1944, buried St Mary's Churchyard, Church Street, Pilsley, Derbyshire. *EM location: with recipient's family.*

316. Mr **GEOFFREY RILEY** (Albert Medal) 29 May 1944, cremated Huddersfield Crematorium, Yorkshire. *GC location: not publicly held.*

317. Engine Driver **BENJAMIN GIMBERT**, 2 June 1944, buried Eastwood Cemetery, Section A; Upwell Road, March, Cambridgeshire. *GC location: on permanent loan to the March Museum, March, Cambridgeshire.*

318. Fireman **JAMES NIGHTALL** (misspelt **KNIGHTALL** on his headstone), 2 June 1944, buried Littleport Cemetery, Section E, Grave 292; Parson's Lane, Littleport, Cambridgeshire. *GC location: Soham College, Soham Village, Cambridgeshire.*

319. Mr **HARWOOD FLINTOFF** (Edward Medal) 23 June 1944, still living. *GC location: unknown, stolen.*

320. Air Commodore **ARTHUR** (known as **DWIGHT**) **ROSS**, 28 June 1944, buried Cataraqui Cemetery, Kingston, Ontario, Canada. *GC location: Canadian War Museum, Ottawa, Ontario, Canada.*

321. Lieutenant **ST JOHN YOUNG**, 23/24 July 1944, buried Arezzo War Cemetery, Plot VI, Row B, Grave 8; Italy. *GC location: with recipient's family.*

322. **Sowar DITTO RAM**, 23/24 July 1944, no known grave. *GC location: not publicly held.*

323. **Private BENJAMIN HARDY**, 5 August 1944, buried Cowra War Cemetery, Plot D, Row D, Grave 11; New South Wales, Australia. *GC location: Australian War Memorial, Canberra, Australia.*

324. **Private RALPH JONES**, 5 August 1944, buried Cowra War Cemetery, Plot D, Row D, Grave 10; New South Wales, Australia. *GC location: Cowra Shire Council, New South Wales, Australia.*

325. **Corporal KENNETH HORSFIELD**, 18 August 1944, buried Bari War Cemetery, Plot XI, Row E, Grave 27; Italy. *GC location: held by the Manchester Regiment.*

326. **Flying Officer RODERICK 'CY' GRAY**, 27 August 1944, lost at sea in the Atlantic Ocean. *GC location: Canadian War Museum, Ottawa, Ontario, Canada.*

327. **Sergeant ARTHUR BANKS**, 27 August–20 December 1944, buried Argenta Gap War Cemetery, Plot III, Row A, Grave 7; Italy. *GC location: not publicly held.*

328. **Captain SIMMON LATUTIN**, 29 December 1944, buried Nairobi War Cemetery, Plot I, Grave 3; Ngong Road, Nairobi, Kenya. *GC location: Somerset Military Museum, Taunton Castle, Taunton, Somerset.*

329. **Signalman KENNETH SMITH**, 10 January 1945, buried Belgrade War Cemetery, Plot VI, Row D, Grave 9; Belgrade, Yugoslavia. *GC location: Royal Signals Museum, Blandford.*

330. **Constable 1st Class ERIC BAILEY**, 12 January 1945, buried Rookwood Cemetery, Rookwood, Sydney, Australia. (His headstone is unusual as the letters GC do not appear after his name.) *GC location: not publicly held.*

331. **Flight Sergeant STANLEY WOODBRIDGE**, 31 January–7 February 1945, buried Rangoon War Cemetery, as an unknown British airman, Plot III, Row F, Grave 6–9; Pyi Road, Burma. *GC location: RAF Museum, Hendon, London.*

332. **Lance Corporal DAVID RUSSELL**, 22–28 February 1945, buried Udine War Cemetery, Plot IV, Row D, Grave 2; Italy. *GC location: National Army Museum, State Highway 1, Waiouru, New Zealand.*

333. **Section Leader EDWARD HEMING** (spelt **HEMMING** on his citation), 2 March 1945, ashes interred St Peter and St Paul Churchyard, Cudham Lane South, Cudham, Kent. *GC location: not publicly held.*

334. **Lance Naik ISLAM-un-DIN**, 12 April 1945, burial location unknown, died in Pyawbwe, Burma, probably cremated. *GC location: not publicly held.*

335. **Lieutenant GEORGE GOSSE**, 8–19 May 1945, ashes interred Centennial Park Crematorium, Wall 134, Niche J/8; Adelaide, South Australia. *GC location: put up for sale in 2005 but did not sell; however, the Royal Australian Navy was trying to raise the money to buy it.*

336. **Mr WILLIAM WATERSON** (Edward Medal) 18 August 1945, ashes

scattered Sutton Crematorium, Plot 4; Tamworth Road, Birmingham. *GC location: not publicly held.*

337. **Fireman FREDERICK DAVIES**, 22 August 1945, buried Kensal Green Cemetery, Square III, Row 3, Grave 51668; Harrow Road, London. (His headstone does not bear the letters GC, but at the end of the grave there is an additional footstone which does.) *GC location: London Fire Brigade Museum, London.*

338. **Naik KIRPA RAM**, 12 September 1945, burial location unknown, died in Thondebhavi, India, probably cremated. *GC location: stolen. It came up for sale in 2009, but was withdrawn when his widow laid claim to it. This matter is still under investigation.*

339. **Major KENNETH BIGGS**, 2 January 1946, ashes scattered at Guildford Crematorium, Surrey. *GC location: not publicly held.*

340. **Acting Staff Sergeant SYDNEY** (sometimes spelt **SIDNEY)** **ROGERSON**, 2 January 1946, ashes scattered at Thanet Crematorium, Manston Road, Margate, Kent. *GC location: RLC Museum, Deepcut, Camberley, Surrey.*

341. **Havildar RAHMAN** (sometimes spelt **REHMAN) ABDUL**, 22 February 1946, no known grave, died shortly after his GC deed, probably cremated. *GC location: not publicly held.*

342. **Driver JOSEPH HUGHES**, 21 March 1946, buried Government Cemetery (formerly Hong Kong Colonial Cemetery); Section 16D, Grave 10625; Hong Kong, China. *GC location: not publicly held.*

343. **Squadron Leader HUBERT DINWOODIE**, 20–23 August 1946, cremated Bournemouth Crematorium, Strouden Avenue, Bournemouth. *GC location: RAF Museum, Hendon, London.*

344. **Temporary Lieutenant ERIC WALTON** (Albert Medal) 24 August 1946, burial location unknown, died in Malvern, Worcestershire. *AM location: with recipient's family.*

345. **Overman DAVID BROWN** (Edward Medal) 10 January 1947, buried Burngrange Cemetery, Burngrange Cottages, West Calder, Scotland. *GC location: with recipient's family.*

346. **Able Seaman THOMAS KELLY**, 18 March 1947, lost at sea in the Bay of Biscay, off the coast of France. *GC location: with recipient's family.*

347. **Sergeant JOHN BECKETT**, 28 March 1947, buried Khayat Beach War Cemetery, Plot D, Row C, Grave 4; Israel. *GC location: not publicly held.*

348. **Pit Deputy JOHN DANIEL CHARLTON** (Edward Medal) 30 March 1947, cremated Sunderland Crematorium, Chester Road, Tyne & Wear. *GC location: not publicly held.*

349. **Shotfirer SYDNEY BLACKBURN** (Edward Medal) 7 May 1947, ashes scattered at Barnsley Crematorium, North Glade, Yorkshire. *GC location: with recipient's family.*

350. **Leading Seaman PHILLIP MAY** (Albert Medal) 20 June 1947, ashes

scattered at Thanet Crematorium, Manston Road, Margate, Kent. *GC location: not publicly held.*

351. **Dr ARTHUR 'DICK' BUTSON** (Albert Medal) 26/27 July 1947, still living. *GC location: with recipient.*

352. **Pit Deputy HARRY ROBINSON** (Edward Medal) 22/23 August 1947, buried Stanley Cemetery, Section 23, Grave 238; Stanley, Co. Durham. *GC location: not publicly held.*

353. **Pit Deputy JOSEPH SHANLEY** (Edward Medal) 22/23 August 1947, cremated Rainworth Crematorium, Mansfield, Nottinghamshire. *GC location: not publicly held.*

354. **Pit Deputy WILLIAM YOUNGER** (Edward Medal) 22/23 August 1947, ashes scattered at Derwentside Crematorium, Medomsley Road, Consett, Co. Durham. *GC location: not publicly held.*

355. **Overman JOHN HUTCHINSON** (Edward Medal) 22/23 August 1947, cremated. *GC location: not publicly held.*

356. **Pit Worker WALTER LEE** (Edward Medal) 11 November 1947, ashes scattered at Ardsley Crematorium, Doncaster Road, Ardsley, Yorkshire. *GC location: not publicly held.*

357. **Chief Petty Officer JOSEPH LYNCH** (Albert Medal) 26 February 1948, cremated Landican Crematorium, Arrowe Park Road, Wirral, Merseyside. *GC location: with recipient's family.*

358. **Mr DAVID WESTERN** (Albert Medal) 27 February 1948, cremated Weston Mill Crematorium; Ferndale Road, Plymouth; his ashes were scattered at sea. *GC location: Royal Naval Museum, Portsmouth.*

359. **Constable KENNETH FARROW** (Albert Medal) 21 June 1948, cremated Thornhill Crematorium, Thornhill Road, Cardiff, Wales. *GC location: not publicly held.*

360. **Boy 1st Class ALFRED LOWE** (Albert Medal) 17 October 1948, still living. *GC location: with recipient.*

361. **Miss MARGARET VAUGHAN** (later **PURVES**) (Albert Medal) 28 May 1949, still living. *GC location: with recipient.*

362. **Miner THOMAS MANWARING** (Edward Medal) 30 June 1949, cremated Forest of Dean Crematorium, Yew Tree Brake, Speech House Road, near Cinderford. *GC location: not publicly held.*

363. **Mr CHARLES WILCOX** (Edward Medal) 23 August 1949, cremated Lodge Hill Crematorium, Selly Oak, Birmingham. *GC location: with recipient's family.*

364. **Mr ROBERT 'TIGER' TAYLOR**, 13 March 1950, cremated Arnos Vale Crematorium, Bath Road, Bristol, Avon. *GC location: on loan to the Imperial War Museum, London.*

365. **Aircraftman First Class IVOR GILLETT**, 26 March 1950, buried Kranji Military Cemetery, Plot III, Row D, Grave 6; Singapore, Malaya. *GC location: not publicly held.*

366. **Vulcanologist GEORGE** (aka **TONY**) **TAYLOR**, 21 January–1 April

1951, ashes interred St John's Church, corner of Constitution Avenue and Anzac Park West, Canberra, Australia. *GC location: not publicly held.*

367. **Lieutenant TERENCE WATERS**, 22 April–September/October 1951, no known grave, died in Korea, shortly after his GC deed. *GC location: Soldiers of Gloucestershire Museum, Gloucester.*

368. **Private HORACE MADDEN**, 24 April–6 November 1951, buried UN Military Cemetery, Plot 36, Row 9, Grave 2978; Tanggok, Pusan, Korea. *GC location: on loan to the Australian War Memorial, Canberra, Australia.*

369. **Fusilier DEREK KINNE**, 25 April 1951–10 August 1953, still living. *GC location: with recipient.*

370. **Sub Officer GEORGE HENDERSON**, 27 April 1951, buried North Front Cemetery, Grave ref. 1386, Gibraltar. (His headstone is unusual as the letters GC do not appear after his name.) *GC location: not publicly held.*

371. **Tracker AWANG anak RAWENG** (sometimes spelt **RAWANG**), 27 May 1951, still living. *GC location: original stolen while in London; official replacement with recipient.*

372. **Flight Lieutenant JOHN** (aka **JACK**) **QUINTON**, 13 August 1951, buried St Augustine Churchyard, Leeming Bar, Yorkshire. *GC location: on loan to the Imperial War Museum, London.*

373. **Mr JOHN** (aka **JACK**) **BAMFORD**, 19 October 1952, still living. *GC location: with recipient.*

374. **Detective Constable FREDERICK FAIRFAX**, 2 November 1952, ashes interred St James the Great Churchyard, Church Lane, Longburton, Dorset. (His headstone is unusual as the letters GC do not appear after his name.) *GC location: not publicly held.*

375. **Radio Officer DAVID BROADFOOT**, 31 January 1953, lost at sea, off the coast of Larne, Northern Ireland. *GC location: Stranraer Museum, Stranraer, Dumfries & Galloway, Scotland.*

376. **Train Driver JOHN AXON**, 9 February 1957, ashes scattered at Stockport Crematorium, Cheshire. *GC location: on loan to National Railway Museum, York.*

377. **Second Lieutenant MICHAEL BENNER**, 1 July 1957, buried in unmarked grave, St Rupert Churchyard, Kals, Austria. *GC location: unknown, stolen.*

378. **Constable HENRY STEVENS**, 29 March 1958, still living. *GC location: with recipient.*

379. **Tram Conductor RAYMOND 'PUDDIN' DONOGHUE**, 29 April 1960, buried Carnelian Bay Cemetery, Protestant Section; Hobart, Tasmania, Australia. *GC location: Tasmanian Museum and Art Gallery, Hobart, Tasmania.*

380. **Chief Petty Officer JONATHAN 'BUCK' ROGERS**, 10 February 1964, lost at sea in Jervis Bay, Australia. *GC location: on loan to the Australian War Memorial, Canberra, Australia.*

381. **Mr MICHAEL MUNNELLY**, 25 December 1964, buried at Sligo, Ireland. *GC location: not publicly held.*

382. **Mr BRIAN SPILLETT**, 9 January 1965, buried Cheshunt Cemetery, Grave IKR; Bury Green Road, Cheshunt, Hertfordshire. *GC location: held by his unit and sent to Woolwich with the regimental silver, but when a request was made for the return of the silver, there was no medal.*

383. **Train Driver WALLACE OAKES**, 5 June 1965, buried in unmarked grave, St Matthews Churchyard, Block F, Row 3, Grave 4; Haslington, Church View, Crewe. *GC location: not publicly held.*

384. **Constable TONY GLEDHILL**, 25 August 1966, still living. *GC location: on loan to the Imperial War Museum, London.*

385. **Air Stewardess BARBARA** (known as **JANE**) **HARRISON**, 8 April 1968, buried Fulford Cemetery, Plot 21, Grave 16W; Fordlands Road, York. *GC location: held by British Airways.*

386. **The ROYAL ULSTER CONSTABULARY** (now **The POLICE SERVICE of NORTHERN IRELAND**), 1969–1999. *GC location: RUC Museum, Belfast, Northern Ireland.*

387. **District Commissioner ERROL** (known as **JACK**) **EMANUEL**, July 1969–19 August 1971, buried Rabaul European Cemetery, East New Britain, Papua New Guinea. All the headstones have since been destroyed by an eruption. *GC location: National Museum, Port Moresby, Papua New Guinea.*

388. **Sergeant MICHAEL WILLETTS**, 25 May 1971, buried St Mary of the Purification, Blidworth, Nottinghamshire. *GC location: National Army Museum, London.*

389. **Superintendent GERALD 'GERRY' RICHARDSON**, 23 August 1971, buried Layton Cemetery, Section Z, Grave 2; Talbot Road, Blackpool. *GC location: Imperial War Museum, London.*

390. **Constable CARL WALKER**, 23 August 1971, still living. *GC location: with recipient.*

391. **Major STEPHEN** (known as **GEORGE**) **STYLES**, 20 and 22 October 1971, buried in Crawley, Sussex. *GC location: Imperial War Museum, London.*

392. **Security Officer JAMES KENNEDY**, 21 December 1973, cremated at Clydebank Crematorium; it is said that the ashes were interred in Hillfoot Cemetery, Glasgow, Scotland, but there are no records of this at the cemetery. *GC location: not publicly held.*

393. **Sergeant MURRAY 'KINA'** or **'HUDDY' HUDSON**, 13 February 1974, buried Opotiki Cemetery, Returned Service Association Section; Waioeka Road, State Highway 2, Opotiki, North Island, New Zealand. *GC location: National Army Museum, State Highway 1, Waiouru, New Zealand.*

394. **Inspector JAMES** (known as **JIM**) **BEATON**, 20 March 1974, still living. *GC location: with recipient.*

395. **Captain ROGER GOAD**, 29 August 1975, ashes interred at The Park Crematorium, Plot 79, Row 181; Guildford Road, Aldershot. *GC location: not publicly held.*

396. **Schoolmaster JOHN CLEMENTS**, 12 April 1976, ashes scattered at Stopsley Crematorium, Welwyn, Hertfordshire. *GC location: not publicly held.*

397. **Constable MICHAEL PRATT**, 4 June 1976, still living. *GC location: with recipient.*

398. **Captain ROBERT NAIRAC**, 14/15 May 1977, no known grave, murdered in Ireland by the IRA. *GC location: Grenadier Guards RHQ, Wellington Barracks, London.*

399. **Warrant Officer Class I BARRY JOHNSON** (born **HAMILTON WELCH**), 7 October 1989, still living. *GC location: with recipient.*

400. **Sergeant STEWART** (known as **STU) GUTHRIE**, 13 November 1990, ashes scattered off Aramoana, at the entrance to Otago Harbour, New Zealand. *GC location: with recipient's family.*

401. **Trooper CHRISTOPHER FINNEY**, 28 March 2003, still living. *GC location: with recipient.*

402. **Captain PETER NORTON**, 30 April, 9 May, 23 June and 24 July 2005, still living. *GC location: with recipient.*

403. **Corporal MARK WRIGHT**, 6 September 2006, cremated Mortonhall Crematorium, Howden Hall Road, Edinburgh, Scotland. *GC location: on loan from the family to the National War Museum of Scotland, Edinburgh, Scotland.*

404. **Lance Corporal MATTHEW CROUCHER**, 9 February 2008, still living. *GC location: on loan to the Imperial War Museum, London.*

405. **Staff Sergeant KIM HUGHES**, 16 August 2009, still living. *GC location: with recipient.*

406. **Staff Sergeant OLAF 'OZ' SCHMID**, June 2009–31 October 2009, cremated Penmount Crematorium, Newquay Road, Truro, Cornwall. *GC location: on loan to the Imperial War Museum, London.*

CHAPTER FOUR

# George Crosses (Exchanges) Awarded before the First World War

**Mr THOMAS McCORMACK** (Albert Medal)
*JARROW DRY DOCK, CO. DURHAM, England*
27 November 1908

McCormack was 21 years old and working at Jarrow Shipbuilders when workmen were engaged in painting the inside of a tank in the hold of the SS *Cairngorm*. Owing to the very strong fumes being given off by the anti-corrosive paint used, the men worked in ten- to fifteen-minute relays.

When a workman named Graham was overcome by the fumes, the chargeman, Archibald Wilson, attempted to extract him, but was unsuccessful, he himself being overcome and sacrificing his life in the attempt. McCormack, who had already been affected by the fumes while working in the tank, went to Wilson's assistance, but was rendered insensible, and was himself rescued by James Chapman, the Works Manager, who, having pulled McCormack out, re-entered the tank and endeavoured to save Graham, but was himself overcome by the fumes. The rescue of Chapman and Graham was eventually effected from the top of the tank.

McCormack and Chapman were immediately awarded the AM, Wilson's being awarded later posthumously. Only McCormack lived to exchange his AM for the GC.

He died on 6 March 1973.

**Nurse HILDA WOLSEY** (Albert Medal)
*HANWELL ASYLUM, MIDDLESEX, England*
11 June 1910

She was 22 years old and working as a nurse when a female patient was exercising in one of the airing courts. The patient then climbed over the wire covering one of the fire-escape staircases; reaching the roof of the laundry ward, she ran

39

along the narrow guttering at the edge of the roof for some 60 or 70ft. Nurse Wolsey followed her over the wire covering the staircase and along the narrow guttering, which was about 25ft above the ground, making her way by leaning with one hand against the sloping roof; on reaching the patient, she held her, at great personal risk, until ropes and ladders could be procured and she was lowered to safety.

She died on 15 March 1974.

### Reverend JOHN O'SHEA (Empire Gallantry Medal)
*ARDMORE BAY, Ireland*
18 March 1911

The Reverend O'Shea was 40 years old and was the parish priest of Ardmore when the schooner *Teaser* was driven ashore in a fierce gale. After attempts to summon the nearest lifeboat failed, the coastguard fired rocket lines over the vessel. However, the crew were so exhausted they could not make use of them.

It was then that O'Shea remembered that there was a fisherman's boat nearly a mile away. He gathered a willing band of volunteers who went with him to get the boat, and it was drawn by horse over rough ground to the scene of the wreck. With a crew of seven men and O'Shea in command, the little boat put to sea. Upon reaching the wreck, however, they found that two men were beyond aid and the other succumbed soon afterwards. O'Shea administered the last rites.

He died on 11 September 1942.

### Major HERBERT 'DICK' BURTON (Empire Gallantry Medal)
*off the coast of WHITBY, England*
1 November 1914

He was 50 years old and serving in the Tynemouth motor lifeboat when the hospital steamer *Rohilla* ran aground on Saltwick Nab near Whitby. Attempts by the Whitby and Upgang lifeboats both failed to reach the *Rohilla*, due to the overpowering seas, so the Tynemouth boat was called. Coxswain Robert Smith and Major Herbert Burton steered the *Henry Vernon* 44 miles through the night amid the storm, unaided by coast lights. The lifeboat was able to reach the wreck, which had run aground two days before, and after all other efforts had failed, rescued fifty people. Both men were awarded the Empire Gallantry Medal but Smith died before his EGM could be exchanged for the GC.

Burton served in the Boer War and both world wars. He died on 4 December 1944.

# CHAPTER FIVE

# George Crosses (Exchanges) Awarded during the First World War

**Chief Petty Officer MICHAEL KEOGH** (born **SULLIVAN**) (Albert Medal)
*ISLAND of IMBROS, Turkey*
19 August 1915
Keogh was 26 years old and serving in the Royal Naval Air Service. An aircraft was taking off from Imbros airfield when, at a height of 150ft, the engine stopped and the aircraft fell vertically to the ground, where it burst into flames. Keogh at once made an attempt to save the pilot, Captain Charles Collet, by dashing into the burning wreckage. He had nearly succeeded in dragging Collet clear of the flames when he was himself overcome by burns, caused by the blazing petrol. Collet later died from his injuries.

Keogh also served in the Second World War. He died on 22 July 1983.

**Miner PERCY HAVERCROFT** (Edward Medal)
*SHEFFIELD, England*
27 August 1915
He was 32 years old and working at Waleswood Colliery when a descending cage containing ten men collided with an empty ascending cage. The impact was extremely violent, severely injuring all the men and breaking the winding ropes. The cages were, however, wedged together in the shaft so that neither of them fell to the bottom, though there was serious danger that they might do so at any moment. A hoppit manned by Havercroft, Albert Tomlinson and John Walker was at once sent down to effect the rescue of the trapped men. All the men were carried from the damaged cage along a girder to the hoppit, which made five descents altogether, the rescue taking two hours. During the whole of this time Havercroft, Tomlinson and Walker were exposed to great danger, either from the hoppit being upset by the winding ropes swinging in the shaft, or from the damaged cage breaking loose and falling down the shaft.

Meanwhile, Edward Wingfield, one of the occupants of the descending cage, who had both legs fractured and had received a severe wound to his thigh and a wound to the head, seized hold of another man who had fallen half-way through the bottom of the cage, and held on to him until he was rescued. During the whole time he displayed the greatest coolness and bravery, despite his own severe injuries, and insisted on all his fellow workmen being removed before allowing himself to be taken to the surface. Havercroft, Tomlinson, Walker and Wingfield were all awarded the EM, but only Havercroft lived to exchange his medal for the GC.

Havercroft died on 15 July 1976.

### Mr RICHARD RICHARDS (Albert Medal)
*Antarctica*
9 October 1915–20 March 1916

He was 19 years old and serving as a member of the Ross Sea Party of the Shackleton Trans-Antarctic Expedition. The expedition had as its object the crossing of the Antarctic, a distance of some 1,700 miles. As sufficient supplies for the whole journey could not be carried, it was necessary to establish a chain of depots on the Ross Sea side as far south as possible.

With this in mind the *Aurora* was sent to McMurdo Sound at the southern end of the Ross Sea, as it was intended that only part of the stores and equipment were to be unloaded. In May the *Aurora* was blown out to sea by a blizzard and was unable to return. The ten crew members ashore were stranded. However, realising that failure to establish the depots would undoubtedly result in the loss of the main body of the expedition, they resolved, in spite of the grave shortage of supplies, to carry out their allotted task.

Eight men, including Mr Ernest Joyce, Mr Richards, Mr Victor Hayward, the Reverend A. Spencer-Smith, Petty Officer Harry Wild and Lieutenant A. Mackintosh, set out in October with two sledges and four dogs, and 162 days elapsed before they returned, having covered a distance of 950 miles. Spencer-Smith had to be dragged on a sledge for forty-two days. Lieutenant Mackintosh collapsed with 100 miles remaining, imposing an additional burden on the active members of the party, who were all suffering from scurvy and snow blindness and were so enfeebled by their labours that at times they were unable to cover more than 2 or 3 miles in fifteen hours. The Reverend Spencer-Smith died when only 19 miles remained to be covered, Lieutenant Mackintosh and Mr Hayward died later. However, the mission was completed. But all their efforts were in vain as Shackleton failed in this part of the expedition.

Joyce, Hayward and Wild were also awarded the AM, but died before their medals could be exchanged. In the original citation Richards is referred to as ex-Petty Officer William Rayment Richards. He died on 8 May 1986.

### Air Mechanic First Class HARRIE HARWOOD (Albert Medal)
*ST OMER, France*
3 January 1916

42

He was 31 years old and serving in the RFC when a fire broke out inside a large bomb store. The store contained nearly two thousand high explosive bombs and some incendiary bombs which were burning freely. Major Newall at once took all necessary precautions, and then, assisted by Air Mechanic Alfred Simms, poured water into the store through a hole made by the fire. He sent for the store key, and with Harwood, Simms and Corporal Henry Hearne entered the store and succeeded in putting out the fire. The wooden cases containing the bombs were burnt and some of them were charred to a cinder. Simms and Hearne were also awarded the AM, but did not live to exchange it for the GC.

Harwood also served in the Second World War. He died on 13 November 1975.

### Sergeant ALBERT FORD (Albert Medal)
*GORRE, France*
30 March 1916
He was 22 years old and serving in the 17th Battalion, Royal Welch Fusiliers. He was acting as instructor for a bombing class when a member of the class threw his bomb too weakly and it hit the traverse in front of him, so that the smoking bomb fell into the trench. The man immediately ran away, knocking down Sergeant Ford. He at once recovered his feet, pushed past another man, and managed to pick up the bomb and throw it clear. It exploded immediately it left his hand.

He died on 27 July 1976.

### Acting Sergeant CHARLES HARRIS (Edward Medal)
*FAVERSHAM, KENT, England*
2 April 1916
He was 33 years old and serving in the Corps of Royal Engineers when there was an explosion in a store at the Faversham Powder Mills. The store contained 200 tons of TNT, and the factory site some 500 tons altogether. All the buildings were destroyed and a chain of explosions followed. Fires spread rapidly and the dead and injured lay all around.

Harris, Lieutenant John Stebbings, Acting Bombardier Arthur Edwards, Bombardier Bert Dugdale and Corporal Charles Ashley assisted in the rescue of the wounded, showing great courage, devotion to duty and disregard for their own safety. Not only did they prevent further explosions, but by their splendid example others who at first showed some diffidence at entering the danger area became willing helpers.

Explosions were constantly taking place, making the work particularly dangerous. A great crater about 40yds across and 20ft deep had been made by the initial explosion and, as fires raged on, some 400 to 500 tons of explosives remained in the vicinity. All of the men named above were awarded the EM, but only Harris and Edwards lived to be entitled to exchange.

Harris declined to exchange his EM for the GC. He died on 27 January 1972.

**Acting Bombardier ARTHUR EDWARDS** (Edward Medal)

*FAVERSHAM, KENT, England*

2 April 1916

He was 20 years old and serving in the Royal Field Artillery (later the Royal Artillery) when there was an explosion in a store at the Faversham Powder Mills. The store contained 200 tons of TNT, and the factory site some 500 tons altogether. All the building were destroyed and a chain of explosions followed. Fires spread rapidly and the dead and injured lay all around.

Edwards, Acting Sergeant Charles Harris, Lieutenant John Stebbings, Bombardier Bert Dugdale and Corporal Charles Ashley assisted in the rescue of the wounded, showing great courage, devotion to duty and disregard for their own safety. Not only did they prevent further explosions, but by their splendid example others who at first showed some diffidence at entering the danger area became willing helpers.

Explosions were constantly taking place, making the work particularly dangerous. A great crater about 40yds across and 20ft deep had been made by the initial explosion and, as fires raged on, some 400 to 500 tons of explosives remained in the vicinity. All of the men named above were awarded the EM, but only Harris and Edwards lived to be entitled to exchange.

Edwards died on 28 May 1984.

**Mr ARCHIBALD YOUNG** (Edward Medal)

*ROSLIN, MIDLOTHIAN, Scotland*

20 June 1916

He was 23 years old and working at the Roslin Explosives Factory when there was a small explosion in a building that was full of explosives. The building caught fire. William Morrison and George Sang, aware that four girls were inside it, at once ran towards it. As they approached, two of the girls came out and fell unconscious on the grass. The building was now burning furiously but Morrison and Sang, who knew the location of the explosives within, used buckets of water to keep the fire back. Morrison then went in, groping his way through the thick smoke; finding one of the girls, he passed her out to Archibald Young, who had just arrived to help. Morrison then went back for the last girl and brought her out while Young placed the other girl on a bogey, which he used to get her to a place of safety, before returning for the last girl. Sang meanwhile kept the fire down as far as possible. During the whole time small explosions were continually taking place within the building, and immediately after the last rescue a heavy explosion occurred, which flattened part of the building. All three men were awarded the EM but only Young lived long enough to exchange it for the GC.

He died on 7 November 1976.

**Miss DOREEN ASHBURNHAM** (later **ASHBURNHAM-RUFFNER**) (Albert Medal)

*COWICHAN LAKE, VANCOUVER ISLAND, Canada*
23 September 1916

She was 11 years old and a schoolgirl when she, with Anthony Farrer, aged 8, was attacked by a cougar. They were almost upon the animal before they saw it crouching in a path at a corner. Doreen was attacked first; the cougar sprang at her, and she was knocked down with her face to the ground, the animal being on her back. Anthony at once attacked the cougar with his fists and a riding bridle and drove the animal off. It then attacked him. Doreen, getting to her feet, came to his rescue, fighting with her clenched hands and bridle, and even putting her arm into the cougar's mouth to try to prevent it from biting Anthony. She succeeded in getting it off the boy, and it stood on its hindquarters and fought with her, but evidently was disturbed by some sound, for presently it slunk away and ran under a log, where it was afterwards killed. It measured over 7ft from nose to the tip of its tail. The children, though both injured, were able to make their own way home. Both received the AM, but Anthony died before he could exchange his for the GC. They were the youngest recipients of the AM.

Ashburnham-Ruffner died on 4 October 1991.

**Sergeant WILLIAM RHOADES** (Albert Medal)

*DROGLANDT France*
14 October 1916

He was 30 years old and serving in 6 Squadron RFC when a bomb accidentally exploded in the mouth of a bomb store dug-out. Two men were killed by the explosion and another man, who was severely injured, was thrown down into the store, which was full of bombs packed in wooden cases. Dense volumes of smoke issued from the dug-out and there was a risk of further explosions. Lieutenant Smith and Sergeant Rhoades immediately entered the dug-out and succeeded in rescuing the wounded man. Smith died before he could exchange his AM.

Rhoades also served in the Second World War. He declined to exchange his AM for the GC. He died on 4 March 1972.

**Coxswain HENRY BLOGG** (Empire Gallantry Medal)

*off the coast of CROMER, England*
9 January 1917

He was 40 years old and serving in the RNLI when the SS *Fernebo* was struck by a mine in a gale. The Cromer lifeboat, which had just returned from service to a Greek vessel, was immediately launched again. It was entirely due to the remarkable personality and great leadership qualities of Coxswain Blogg, which magnetised the tired men into relaunching. When the boat was put to sea again, it was the consummate skill with which he handled her and the encouragement he gave his crew which brought their efforts to such a successful conclusion.

Blogg's record in life-saving was unequalled in the lifeboat service, and he became a legend in his lifetime. During his career he was responsible for saving 873 lives. As well as the George Cross, he was awarded the BEM, the Medal for Conspicuous Gallantry, four RNLI Silver and three Gold Medals, and the Silver Medal of the Canine Defence League, while the Italian government awarded him a Silver Medal for his rescue of the crew of the *Monte Nevoso* in 1932. He died on 13 June 1954. His biography is called *Henry Blogg of Cromer, the Greatest of the Lifeboatmen.*

### Sergeant ALBERT HUTCHISON (sometimes misspelt HUTCHINSON) (Albert Medal)

*CURRAGH CAMP, Ireland*
2 April 1917

He was 25 years old and serving in the Highland Light Infantry (City of Glasgow Regiment) when, during bombing practice, a live grenade hit the parapet of the trench and fell at the feet of the thrower, who was too terrified to move. Hutchison, seeing what had happened, tried to pick up the grenade but was obstructed by the thrower. The fuse had already been burning for four seconds when Hutchison managed to push the man out of the way, pick up the bomb and throw it over the parapet, where it immediately exploded. But for his coolness and gallantry the man would undoubtedly have been killed.

Hutchison died on 4 January 1988.

### Lieutenant OLIVER BRYSON (Albert Medal)

*WYE AERODROME, KENT, England*
15 March 1917

He was 20 years old and serving in the RFC when his aircraft sideslipped and crashed in flames. Disentangling himself from the burning wreckage, he at once went back into the flames and dragged his observer, Lieutenant Hillebrandt, from the fire. Notwithstanding his own injuries, which were undoubtedly aggravated by his gallant efforts to rescue his crewman, he then endeavoured to extinguish Lieutenant Hillebrandt's burning clothes. However, he was unable to save his life and Hillebrandt died a few days later.

As well as the GC, Bryson was awarded the MC, and the DFC and Bar. He died on 27 March 1977.

### Second Lieutenant RICHARD (known as R.L.) BROWN (Albert Medal)

*MARQUAY France*
27 March 1917

He was 19 years old and serving in the King's Own Royal Regiment. He was instructing a class in firing rifle grenades when, owing to a defective cartridge, one of the grenades only lifted about 2in and then fell back into the cup. The safety catch had been released and the grenade was live. Lieutenant Brown at once ordered the men to take cover and, running forward, he picked up the rifle, seized it between his legs, grasped the grenade in his hands and endeavoured to throw it away. While he was doing so it exploded, blowing off his right hand and inflicting other wounds. Had he not seized the grenade there can be little doubt that several men would have been killed or severely injured.

He died on 25 September 1982.

### Deckhand GEORGE ABBOTT (Albert Medal)

*HORSEA ISLAND, PORTSMOUTH, England*

14 September 1917

He was 19 years old and serving in the Royal Naval Reserve when a seaplane collided with a Poulsen mast and remained wedged in it. The pilot, Acting Flight Commander E.A. de Ville, was thrown on to the aircraft wing and rendered unconscious. Abbott, with Ordinary Seaman Richard Knowlton and Seaman Nicholas Ruth, at once climbed 100ft up the mast, where Ruth, making use of a boatswain's chair, which moves up and down the inside of the mast, was hoisted up another 200ft to where the aircraft was lodged.

He then climbed out on to the plane and secured de Ville with a masthead gantline until the other men arrived, then they lowered him to the ground. The three men were well aware of the damage to the mast and the likelihood of the seaplane falling. All three were awarded the AM, but Ruth died before he could exchange his for the GC.

Abbott declined to exchange his AM for the GC. He died from bronchopneumonia on 10 June 1977.

### Ordinary Seaman RICHARD KNOWLTON (Albert Medal)

*HORSEA ISLAND, PORTSMOUTH, England*

14 September 1917

He was 18 years old and serving in the Royal Navy when a seaplane collided with a Poulsen mast and remained wedged in it. The pilot, Acting Flight Commander E.A. de Ville, was thrown on to the aircraft wing and rendered unconscious. Knowlton, with Deckhand George Abbott and Seaman Nicholas Ruth at once climbed 100ft up the mast, where Ruth, making use of a boatswain's chair, which moves up and down the inside of the mast, was hoisted up another 200ft to where the aircraft was lodged.

He then climbed out on to the plane and secured de Ville with a masthead gantline until the other men arrived, then they lowered him to the ground. The three men were well aware of the damage to the mast and the likelihood of the seaplane falling. All three were awarded the AM, but Ruth died before he could exchange his for the GC.

Knowlton declined to exchange his AM for the GC. He died on 24 August 1981.

**Acting Mate ALBERT (aka ALFRED) NEWMAN** (Albert Medal)
*HARWICH, England*
10 October 1917
He was 29 years old and serving in the Royal Navy when a fire alarm was sounded onboard HMS *Tetrarch*. Newman proceeded to the magazine as soon as he heard the alarm; seeing smoke issuing from a box of cordite, he opened the lid and passed the cartridges up to the upper deck, where they were thrown overboard. One cartridge in the middle of the box was very hot, and smoke was issuing from it. By his prompt action he saved the magazine from exploding, with the loss of many lives.
He died on 1 September 1984.

**Leading Seaman THOMAS DAVIS** (Albert Medal)
*HALIFAX HARBOUR, NOVA SCOTIA, Canada*
6 December 1917
He was 22 years old and serving in the Royal Naval Reserve aboard HMS *Highflyer* when the French steamer *Mont Blanc*, carrying high explosives, and the Norwegian steamer *Imo* collided. Fires broke out on the *Mont Blanc* and a few minutes later a tremendous explosion took place. The tug *Musquash* was seen to be on fire forward, and there was a danger of her drifting into another ship.
The captain of the *Highflyer* hailed a private tug and asked her captain to take the *Musquash* in tow, but his crew were unwilling to board the blazing tug, which was brought alongside the *Highflyer* instead. Davis and Able Seaman Stones volunteered to board the *Musquash*, and were transferred to the tug, which by this time had broken adrift; they secured a line from her stern and she was towed into midstream. When this line parted, they passed another line from *Musquash* to the pumping lighter *Lee*, which had now arrived.
Both men then went forward and succeeded in getting to the ammunition, which was by this time badly scorched; pulling it away from the flames, they threw it overboard. Next they broke open the door of the galley and a cabin, which were both on fire, to enable the *Lee* to play her hoses into the flames. Some two thousand people were killed and five thousand injured by the explosion and fires that followed, and large parts of Nova Scotia were destroyed. Both men were awarded the AM, but Stones died before he could exchange his for the GC.
Davis died on 18 October 1978.

**Flight Lieutenant VICTOR WATSON** (Albert Medal)
*JEVINGTON DOWN, SUSSEX, England*
22 December 1917
He was 19 years old and serving in the Royal Naval Air Service when the airship *SSZ7* crashed into the airship *SSZ10* in mid-air, and both burst into flames. Watson, the senior officer on the spot, immediately rushed up to the car of *SSZ10* under the impression that one of the crew was still inside, although he was well aware that there were bombs attached to the airship that could explode at any

time. Having satisfied himself that there was no one in the car, he turned away to render assistance elsewhere. At that moment one of the bombs exploded, shattering his right arm, which had to be amputated almost immediately.

In the same incident Air Mechanic 1st Grade Harold Robinson and Boy Mechanic Eric Steere were also awarded the AM for pulling from the wreckage the dead pilot and two injured crewmen, Hughes and Dodd. They then removed the bombs from the airship, although they were so hot their hands were burned. Both men died before they could exchange their AMs for the GC.

Watson declined to exchange his AM for the GC. He died on 2 October 1974.

### Deckhand JOHN STANNERS (Albert Medal)
*Trinidad*
29 December 1917
He was 26 years old and serving in the Royal Naval Reserve when the cotton waste stored in the magazine of *ML289* caught fire. On discovering the fire, Stanners, without hesitation, went down into the magazine and brought up a quantity of burning waste.

Leading Deckhand Rupert Bugg, who was on board *ML285*, which was alongside *ML289*, smelt burning, and on seeing Stanners with the burning cotton waste went to the magazine and extinguished the remainder of the fire.

The prompt action and high courage shown by these men in the face of very great danger averted a serious explosion and probably saved the lives of all those on board. Both men were awarded the AM, but Bugg died before he could exchange his.

Stanners declined to exchange his AM for the GC. He died on 23 February 1974.

### Lance Corporal SIDNEY WILLIAMS (Albert Medal)
*France*
4 January 1918
He was 30 years old and serving in the 1/6th Battalion, City of London Regiment when George Williams dropped a lighted match in a dug-out used as a gunpowder store. Although most of the gunpowder had been removed, there was still a considerable amount scattered on the floor, which caught fire. George was overcome by the fumes. In spite of the volume of smoke issuing from the dug-out, Sidney entered and rescued his friend, who was badly burned and unconscious. Sidney, who was also severely burned, had to carry his friend up twenty steps. But for his prompt action George would have lost his life.

John, Sidney's brother, was awarded the MM during the First World War. Sidney also served in the Second World War. He died on 12 October 1976.

**Flight Sergeant HORACE CANNON** (Albert Medal)
*SPITALGATE, GRANTHAM, England*
26 January 1918
He was 22 years old and serving in 50 Training Squadron RFC when an aircraft lost control and crashed, bursting into flames. Cannon and Flight Sergeant Albert Warne went to the rescue of the pilot at great personal risk to themselves, as one petrol tank blew up and another was on fire; moreover the aircraft was carrying a belt of live ammunition, which they dragged from the wreckage. They managed to extricate the pilot, who was strapped into the burning plane, but he died shortly afterwards from his injuries. Both men were awarded the AM but only Cannon lived to exchange his for the GC.
He died on 21 September 1975.

**Acting Flight Commander PAUL ROBERTSON** (Albert Medal)
*HORNSEA MERE, LINCOLNSHIRE, England*
28 February 1918
He was 26 years old and serving in the Royal Naval Air Service when his seaplane got out of control and spun to the ground. He jumped out just before it hit the ground and landed safely in the marshy ground. However, the pilot, Lieutenant H.C. Lemon, was trapped inside the aircraft, which had burst into flames. Despite the fact that the area around the seaplane quickly became a furnace of burning petrol, and that the bombs, ammunition and reserve petrol tank were all likely to explode, Robertson approached the wreckage and endeavoured to extricate the pilot, only giving up when he had been so severely burned on the face, hands and leg that his recovery was for some time in doubt. In fact he lost an eye. He displayed great gallantry, self-sacrifice and disregard for his own safety in his efforts to save the pilot.
Robertson served in both world wars. He died on 4 August 1975.

**Sub Lieutenant ARTHUR BAGOT** (Albert Medal)
*off the coast of DOVER, England*
12 April 1918
He was 29 years old and serving in the Royal Naval Volunteer Reserve when there was an explosion in the engine room of *ML356* and the forward tanks burst into flames. Some of the crew were blown overboard, and the remainder were driven aft by the flames and then taken off in a skiff. By this time flames were billowing from the aft cabin hatch and there was much burning petrol on the surface of the water. Seeing that the fire was now close to a depth charge, Bagot and another officer jumped into a dinghy, rowed to the wreck, got on board and removed the depth charge, thus preventing an explosion that might have caused serious loss of life among the crowds of English and French sailors on the quay.
Bagot never exchanged his AM for the GC. He was awarded the DSC for his actions in the Zeebrugge raid on 22/23 April 1918, where several VCs were

awarded. Bagot also served in the Second World War. He died on 21 November 1979. His cousin was Major Lanoe Hawker VC.

### Lieutenant RANDOLPH RIDLING (Albert Medal)
*BROCTON CAMP, STAFFORDSHIRE, England*
19 April 1918

He was 28 years old and serving in the New Zealand Rifle Brigade when a recruit under bombing instruction dropped a live Mills bomb in the throwing bay after pulling the pin out. Lacking the presence of mind to escape, Rifleman A.J. McCurdy kicked the bomb towards the entrance and retreated to the inner end of the bay. Ridling, the bombing officer, seeing the man's danger, went to him, seized him by the arms and started to carry him out of the bay, but the bomb exploded before he could get clear and Ridling was severely wounded in the groin. But for his coolness and bravery McCurdy would most likely have been killed; in fact he was only slightly wounded.

Ridling declined to exchange his AM for the GC. He died on 14 January 1975.

### Drawer JOHN McCABE (Edward Medal)
*STANRIGG COLLIERY, AIRDRIE, LANARKSHIRE, Scotland*
9 July 1918

He was 16 years old and working at the Stanrigg Colliery when there was an inrush of liquid moss. McCabe was with five other men at the bottom of shaft no. 3 when they were told that the moss had broken in. The other five men at once ascended the shaft and escaped, but McCabe, knowing there were men at the face a quarter of a mile away who might be cut off, returned to warn them. At this time he did not know where the break-in was, or whether the moss might not at any time fill the workings through which he returned, as in fact it did soon afterwards. He and the men he warned were ultimately collected and raised by another shift. He faced great and unknown danger, which could have been fatal, in order to enable others to escape. He is credited with saving fifty-eight lives.

He died on 29 January 1974.

### Lieutenant BERNARD ELLIS (Albert Medal)
*SHAHABAN, Mesopotamia (now Iraq)*
21 August 1918

He was 27 years old and serving in the 5th Battalion, The Buffs (Royal East Kent Regiment) when he was with a party of men under instruction in the firing of rifle grenades. A volley was fired, but one grenade, owing to a defective cartridge, did not leave the rifle, but fell back into the barrel with the fuse burning. The firer dropped the rifle and grenade in the trench, but Ellis, who was separated from him by four other men in the narrow trench, at once forced his way past them and seized the rifle. Unable to remove the grenade, he dropped the rifle and placed his steel helmet over the grenade, which exploded at once, severely injuring him. There is no doubt that his prompt action saved several men from certain death.

Ellis also served in the Home Guard during the Second World War. He died on 1 July 1979.

### Sub Lieutenant DAVID EVANS (Albert Medal)
*DOVER HARBOUR, England*
16 September 1918

He was 20 years old and serving in the Royal Naval Volunteer Reserve when there was an explosion amidships on HMS *Glatton*. The explosion and fire cut off the after part of the ship, killing or seriously injuring all the officers who were on board with one exception. The whole ship could have blown up at any moment.

Evans, Lieutenant George Belden, Petty Officer Albert Stoker and Able Seaman Edward Nunn were in boats that were rescuing men who had been blown overboard or jumped into the water. They proceeded on-board on their own initiative and entered the superstructure, which was full of dense smoke, and then went to the deck below. Behaving with the greatest gallantry and contempt of danger, they succeeded in rescuing seven or eight badly injured men from the mess deck, as well as fifteen men whom they rescued from the superstructure.

This work was carried out before the arrival of gas masks, and, although at one point they were driven out by the fire, they proceeded down again after hoses had been played on the flames. They continued until all chance of rescuing others had passed and the ship was abandoned; she was sunk by torpedo as the fire was spreading and it was impossible to flood the magazines. All four men were awarded the AM, but only Evans lived to exchange his for the GC.

He also served in the Second World War. Evans was Honorary Secretary of the Albert Medal Association (1966–1972) and a committee member of the VC&GC Association (1972–85). He died on 8 December 1985.

### Staff Nurse HARRIET FRASER (later BARRY) (Albert Medal)
*ROUSBRUGGE, Belgium*
1 October 1918

She was 29 years old and serving in the Territorial Force Nursing Service when a serious fire started in no. 36 Casualty Clearing Station. At the time some of the patients were undergoing operations. The first intimation of danger in the theatres was the lights going out, accompanied by volumes of smoke, and almost imme-diately the wooden walls burst into flames. Sisters Gertrude Carlin and Gladys White, along with Fraser, assisted in carrying the unconscious patients to safety, and then returned to the burning building to assist in retrieving the other patients. During this time the ether bottles and nitrous oxide cylinders were exploding, filling the air with fumes and flying fragments of steel.

She was named Harriet Elizabeth on her birth certificate, but Elizabeth Harriet on her death certificate. She died on 17 June 1980.

**Second Lieutenant GEOFFREY RACKHAM** (Albert Medal)

*LE CATEAU, France*

27 October 1918

He was 22 years old and serving in the Royal Army Service Corps, attached to 545th Siege Battery, Royal Garrison Artillery. Wakened by the fire alarm, Rackham hurried to the scene to find that flames 3–4ft high were issuing from the petrol tank of an ammunition truck loaded with shells. He put the cap on the tank, jumped into the driver's seat, started up the engine and drove the burning truck away from the rest of the convoy, while shells were exploding. Then he helped to put the fire out. By his prompt action he undoubtedly saved much loss of life.

He died on 10 January 1982.

**Acting Lieutenant HARRY 'WINGS' DAY** (Albert Medal)

*off CAPE TRAFALGAR*

9 November 1918

He was 20 years old and serving in the Royal Marine Light Infantry when his ship HMS *Britannia* was torpedoed by the German submarine *UB50*. There was a second, more violent, explosion as the ammunition went up and several fires were started, resulting in the spread of smoke and fumes throughout the ship. Shortly after the explosions Day went down to the wardroom to search for any wounded. He heard groaning forward of the wardroom, but found that the heavy wooden door had jammed and was immovable. He then burst open the trap hatch to the wardroom pantry and climbed through it. He discovered Engineer Lieutenant Stanley Weir and a steward alive and conscious, but unable to move. Fearing he would hurt them if he tried to drag them through the trap hatch single-handed, he climbed back into the wardroom aft and up on to the quarter-deck; finding two or three stokers, he returned with them and they eventually carried the dying officer and steward on to the deck and up to the forecastle. During his first visit to the wardroom Day was alone, in the dark, while the ship was already listing; also the fire was close to the 12-inch magazine. While carrying out this rescue, he inspected all scuttles and dead-lights in the wardroom and cabins before it, ascertaining that all were properly closed before leaving.

Day also served in the RAF during the Second World War, taking part in the 'Great Escape'. He died on 2 December 1977. His biography is called *Wings Day*, and his great-uncle was George Day VC.

**Fireman CHRISTOPHER FEETHAM** (Albert Medal)

*SUNDERLAND, England*

10 November 1918

He was 27 years old and serving in the Merchant Navy when a fire broke out in the messroom and adjoining saloon aboard SS *Hornsey*. Given the quantity of ammunition on board, there was a great risk of explosion. The whole ship's company helped to get the fire under control. The decisive factor, however, was

Feetham, who volunteered to be lowered down into the cabin. There, waist-deep in water, he was able to direct his hose on to that part of the fire that would have caused the ammunition to explode in a very short time. As it was, some of the ammunition cases were already scorched. It was at the greatest risk to his life that he went down alone to make this last effort, and he undoubtedly saved a very large number of lives, not just on the *Hornsey* but in the surrounding area.

Feetham was torpedoed twice during the First World War, and during the Second World War he was involved in building the Mulberry Harbours. He died on 2 October 1976.

# CHAPTER SIX

# George Crosses (Exchanges) Awarded between the World Wars

**Lieutenant EDMUND 'BILL' ABBOTT** (Albert Medal)
*INVERGORDON, Scotland*
5 August 1919
He was 24 years old and serving in the Royal Navy when there was an explosion below decks on the ex-German battlecruiser SMS *Baden*. Abbott immediately proceeded down the hatch to the main deck and saw that smoke was coming from the ladder-way tunnel leading to the shaft passage and after-room containing the cooling plant. His first efforts to get below proved futile, so he tried the starboard side tunnel; seeing it was clear, he collected a party of men and then descended again through the tunnel to the after-room. He made his way to the port side and found a dockyard workman lying unconscious. Assisted by the party, he got the man to the upper deck, but he was already dead.

Although greatly affected by fumes, Abbott called for volunteers and again went below to the rescue of another man whose groans had been heard, and succeeded in removing him out of danger. Throughout the proceedings this officer showed an utter disregard for his own safety.

Abbott served in both world wars. He died on 3 April 1974.

**Mr WALTER CLEALL** (Albert Medal)
*CARDIFF, Wales*
11 August 1919
He was 22 years old and on demobilisation leave from the Royal Army Service Corps when a fire broke out at the Royal Hotel. The fire had reached the sixth floor when a maid, Winnie Jones, was seen to come to a window on that floor. Cleall, who was in the assembled crowd below, at once entered the building and eventually succeeded in getting to the sixth floor and into a room from where he could see the maid. He climbed out of the window on to the narrow parapet, and reached the maid.

Above the ledge that afforded him a foothold was a stone balcony for a part of the intervening space, but a very dangerous corner had to be negotiated with a sheer 100ft drop to the street. However, he succeeded in carrying the maid back along the parapet and into the room from which he had come. A portion of the roof collapsed as the maid was assisted from the room. Cleall's action undoubtedly saved her life.

He died on 27 April 1983.

### Mate HENRY BUCKLE (Albert Medal)
*INVERGORDON, Scotland*
27 August 1919
He was 30 years old and serving in the Royal Navy. HMS *Tiger* was undergoing repairs when three men were overcome by noxious gas. Stoker Petty Officer Albert Bailey, accompanied by another man, made an unsuccessful attempt at rescue, both using respirators, but found them useless. The officer on watch, Henry Buckle, then arrived on the scene and, in spite of the risk to his own life, immediately went down and succeeded in passing a rope around one of the men. This man was rescued, but Buckle was considerably affected by the gas, and could do nothing further. Bailey, though still suffering from his previous attempt, repeated the operation, and succeeded in getting the other two men out, but both died. Buckle and Bailey were both awarded the AM, but Bailey died before he could exchange his.

Buckle declined to exchange his AM for the GC. He died on 22 January 1975.

### Fire Officer JOHN (incorrectly named as JAMES on his citation) BURKE (Empire Gallantry Medal)
*SALFORD/OPENSHAW, MANCHESTER, England*
26 November 1919 and 8 December 1925
He was 21 years old and serving as a fire officer for Armstrong Whitworth & Co. when at great personal risk he stopped a runaway horse which was towing an empty wagon in Salford. On 8 December 1925, now aged 26, he again at great personal risk stopped another runaway horse, this time pulling a float in Openshaw.

Burke also served in the First World War. He died on 29 June 1963.

### Park Keeper ALBERT WATERFIELD (Empire Gallantry Medal)
*RICHMOND, SURREY, England*
10 May 1921
He was 40 years old and working at Richmond Park when he saw two men carrying rifles. As he was walking towards them they started to run away and he gave chase. He followed them for about a mile until, as they crossed Beverley Brook near the Robin Hood Gate, they turned and called to him to stop or they would fire. Waterfield continued towards them; when he was only 40 or 50yds away, one of the men fired two shots at him but missed. The men, both members of the IRA, scaled a wall and ran into a lane; when captured some distance away, they were found to be carrying seventy-six rounds of ammunition with them.

They were trying to make an entry into White Lodge, the home of the Duke and Duchess of York, later King George VI and Queen Elizabeth. Waterfield showed great courage and it was due to his persistence in giving chase to two armed men that an attack on the royal family was prevented.

Waterfield also served in the First World War. He was the first recipient of the EGM (Civil Division). He died on 22 August 1968.

## Assistant Surgeon GEORGE RODRIGUES (sometime spelt RODRIQUES) (Empire Gallantry Medal)
*MALAPURAN, MALABAR, India*
24 September 1921

He was 29 years old and serving in the Indian Medical Department when, during the rebellions in Malabar, he saved the lives of several of his senior officers. Sadly no other information is known about him or this incident.

He died on 21 August 1962.

## Sergeant WILLIAM HAND (Empire Gallantry Medal)
*NILAMBUR, MALABAR, India*
24 September 1921

He was 24 years old and serving in the 2nd Battalion, Dorsetshire Regiment when, during the rebellions in Malabar, he was subject to an ambush. Hand, however, successfully bombed the enemy out of their positions. He and Private Miller subsequently showed great courage in clearing up the situation.

Hand had also served in the First World War, being awarded the MM. He died on 28 October 1961.

## Private FREDERICK CHANT (Empire Gallantry Medal)
*NILAMBUR, MALABAR, India*
24 September 1921

He was 21 years old and serving in the 2nd Battalion, Dorsetshire Regiment when he used his Lewis gun at close range against the enemy, who were occupying a house and firing at him. His gun jammed, but he calmly got up and fetched a rifle and maintained his fire on the rebels with coolness and deliberation. He, with Private Troake, subsequently showed great courage in clearing the rebels from the gardens and jungle around the house.

Chant died on 9 March 1968.

## Private THOMAS MILLER (Empire Gallantry Medal)
*NILAMBUR, MALABAR, India*
24 September 1921

He was 30 years old and serving in the 2nd Battalion, Dorsetshire Regiment when he displayed great gallantry by going forward towards a rebel ambush and firing on it at close range. He was instrumental in dislodging several snipers who were causing casualties among British soldiers. He, with Sergeant Hand, subsequently showed great courage in clearing up the situation.

Miller had also served in the First World War. He died on 13 December 1974.

### Private FREDERICK TROAKE (Empire Gallantry Medal)
*NILAMBUR, MALABAR, India*
24 September 1921
He was 25 years old and serving in the 2nd Battalion, Dorsetshire Regiment when, during the unrest in India, he showed conspicuous gallantry in advancing up to the fence around a house in which rebels had been located and in covering the rush of an officer and NCO who set fire to the roof, forcing the rebels out. He and Private Chant subsequently showed great courage in clearing the rebels from the gardens and jungle around the house.

Troake had also served in the First World War. He died on 27 April 1974.

### Special Constable SAMUEL ORR (Empire Gallantry Medal)
*BELFAST, Northern Ireland*
1922
He was 28 years old and serving in the Ulster Special Constabulary when he effected the capture of an armed criminal. Later the same year he tried to arrest two armed robbers, although he himself was unarmed. He succeeded in grappling with one, but was shot in the right arm by the other, subsequently losing the use of this arm.

Orr had also served in the First World War, during which he was awarded the MM. He died on 4 April 1958.

### Mr JOHN 'JACK' CHALMERS (Albert Medal)
*COOGEE BEACH, SYDNEY, Australia*
4 February 1922
He was 27 years old and a member of the North Bondi Life-saving Club when a swimmer named Milton Coughlan was attacked by a shark, which bit deeply into his left forearm. Chalmers, observing from the shore, immediately had a rope tied around his waist and, although he slipped and banged his head on a rock, he dived into the sea, swam out to Coughlan, who by now was floating helplessly in the water; he grabbed him round the body and held onto him while they were pulled back to shore. Coughlan, however, died from his injuries shortly after reaching hospital.

Chalmers had also served in the First World War, and had appeared in a film called *A Triumph of Love*. He died on 29 March 1982.

### Coxswain WILLIAM 'PINGO' or 'JUMBO' FLEMING (Empire Gallantry Medal)
*off the coast of GREAT YARMOUTH, England*
19–22 October 1922

He was 57 years old and serving in the RNLI. The SS *Hopelyn*'s steering failed and she was blown by a fierce storm onto Scroby Sands. The Caister lifeboat attempted to set out but without success, so at 11pm the Gorleston no. 1 pulling and sailing lifeboat *Kentwell* was towed out to sea by the tug *George Jewson*. By now the *Hopelyn* was breaking up, the ship was in darkness and the engine room was flooded, the crew taking shelter in the cabin. When Fleming's boat reached the ship there was no sign of life. While keeping a safe distance to prevent being smashed against the wreck, she remained nearby until 7am, returning to harbour assuming all the crew to be dead.

However, within three hours a flag was spotted on the *Hopelyn*, and at 10.15am Fleming and his crew set out again. Again the tug towed them out and when the tow-rope was cast off the crew hoisted the *Kentwell*'s sail. By now the tide had turned and the lack of draught forced the lifeboatmen to pump out the ballast. Fleming told his crew to row but huge waves picked them up and tossed them down first onto the sand, then against the *Hopelyn*, whereupon the lifeboat's mizzen outrigger was swept away and the broken plates of the *Hopelyn* tore into her hull.

It was a hopeless situation. As soon as they were able to refloat on the tide, the tug towed the *Kentwell* back in. Meanwhile the Eastern District Inspector of Lifeboats, Captain Carver, had called up the motor lifeboat *Agnes Cross* and it met up with Fleming, who changed boats and returned to the wreck, but again the heavy seas thwarted their attempts and the *Agnes Cross* was forced to return.

The next morning at 4.30am the *Agnes Cross* set to sea once again. By now the wreck was in a parlous state. But then the sea came to the rescue: a huge wave lifted the lifeboat up almost on to the after-deck and the twenty-four men aboard, realising this would be their only chance, scrambled into the lifeboat despite the massive waves breaking over them. By 7am they were back on dry land.

Fleming died on 30 September 1954.

## Mr THOMAS WHITEHEAD (Edward Medal)
*SUNDERLAND, England*
22 March 1922

He was 34 years old and working at Brotherton & Co. Ltd. One of the large cylinder stills was standing empty, and, as it was thought, disconnected from the adjoining stills. A worker named Dougherty descended into it by means of a rope ladder through a small manhole in the corner. When he reached the bottom he collapsed. One of his workmates, realising that gas must have accumulated in the still, immediately shouted for help and ran to get a rope. George Rogers, who was working nearby, immediately went down to help, but was also overcome and collapsed.

In the meantime other workmen had arrived. One of them, William King, at once entered the still with a handkerchief around his mouth and a rope attached to him. He too was overcome and had to be pulled out. Then Whitehead made two attempts to reach the men, first equipped with a respirator and then with a hood with oxygen pumped into it, but on both occasions he had to be pulled out. By now other workmen had removed the pitch-pipe from the bottom of the still and had begun forcing air into it. King then made another attempt wearing a respirator and a safety-belt around his body. He attached ropes to the two men and they were pulled out; artificial respiration was tried but they were found to be dead. The dangers were well known to the would-be rescuers, but they acted promptly and courageously, showing great coolness and intelligence in the measures used for the rescue attempt. Both King and Whitehead were awarded the EM, but King died before he could exchange his.

Whitehead declined to exchange his EM for the GC. He died on 27 August 1972.

### Miner BERT (born BERTIE) CRAIG (Edward Medal)
*MOUNTAIN ASH, GLAMORGAN, Wales*
14 November 1922

He was 23 years old and working at Nixon's Navigation Colliery when a worker named Jones was completely buried by a heavy fall of stones. Four other men were present at the time and made some attempts to get him out; although they could not see Jones, they could hear him moaning.

However, further falls were taking place, and the men considered the risk too great and retreated to cover. At this time Craig arrived on the scene. Hearing what had happened, he at once ran to where Jones was buried and began to remove the stones. In spite of his appeals for help, the other men hung back until the falls ceased. But then they came to his assistance, and Jones was extricated alive. Within two minutes of his release a large fall took place which would have killed them both.

Craig had also served in the First World War. He died on 14 December 1978.

### Mill Foreman ALFRED MORRIS (Edward Medal)
*OBUASI, Gold Coast (now Ghana)*
29 May 1923

He was 41 years old and working for the Ashanti Gold Mine. A cyanide solution was being prepared in a vat, when a native called Robert, who was working in the vat contrary to orders, was overcome by the fumes. Two other natives, Sikeyena and Guruba, attempted to rescue him but were themselves overcome. Mr Chardin, who was on the spot, realised the danger and without hesitation entered the vat by a ladder but he too was overcome by the fumes. Mr Morris and Mr Skinner then arrived and between them they managed to drag Chardin out. Skinner then collapsed but Morris tied a rope around himself, re-entered the vat and eventually succeeded in bringing out the three native men alive. Unfortunately Mr Chardin, Sikeyena and Robert all succumbed to the fumes. Both Morris and Chardin were awarded the EM.

Morris had also served in the Boer War, and in both world wars. He died on 24 November 1973.

**Constable FRANCIS MORTESHED** (Empire Gallantry Medal)
*BELFAST, Northern Ireland*
7 March 1924
He was 26 years old and serving in the Royal Ulster Constabulary when three masked men, armed with hand guns, attempted to rob the offices of Messrs Millards. Nelson Leech the book-keeper was shot and killed by Michael Pratley. Morteshed pursued the robbers and Pratley fired at him but the gun failed and he was duly arrested. Pratley was sentenced to death for murder.

Morteshed also served in the Second World War. He died on 14 April 1948.

**Miner HARRY WILSON** (Edward Medal)
*STAFFORDSHIRE, England*
10 March 1924
He was 21 years old and working at the Harriseahead Colliery when there was an inrush of water into the mine. Most of the workmen had already left, but it was discovered that Edwin Booth was missing. He had been working 130yds from the bottom of the shaft, and representations were made to Paling Baker, the manager, that it was impossible to rescue him. The bottom of the pit was three parts full of water and rising.

Baker, however, was resolute: he called for volunteers for a rescue party and Wilson was one of five men who responded and descended into the mine. They reached a ventilation door which they dared not open owing to the pressure of water behind it, and they therefore prepared to retire. Baker insisted that Booth could not be abandoned, but Wilson was the only man who volunteered to continue the rescue work.

Baker and Wilson managed to force open the ventilation door and allowed the water to escape gradually. They then waded to the place where Booth had been working, reaching him after great difficulty, and all three men were eventually drawn safely to the surface. Both Barker and Wilson ran a very great risk of being trapped under the low roof of the mine. They could not tell to what height the water would rise, and had it reached the roof, they would have lost their lives. Both men were awarded the EM, but Baker died before he could exchange his for the GC.

Wilson died on 26 March 1986.

**Chauffeur FREDERICK MARCH** (Empire Gallantry Medal)
*CAIRO, Egypt*
19 November 1924
He was 32 years old and working as chauffeur to the Governor-General of the Sudan, Sir Lee Stack, when seven Egyptians opened fire on the car in slow-moving traffic. Although wounded, March was able to manoeuvre the car through the chaos while his wounded passengers crouched in the back of the car. Sir Lee Stack died from his wounds two days later.

March also served in both world wars. He died on 30 October 1977.

**Mr KHALIFA MUHAMMAD** (Empire Gallantry Medal)

*WADI ADAROWFIE, Sudan*

27 November 1924

He was of unknown age and serving in the Berber Province Police when he showed conspicuous gallantry and skill. While in command of a three-man mounted police patrol, he arrested a murderer and three camel thieves in the face of armed opposition who were present in superior numbers.

He died on 29 July 1966.

**Nafar MUHAMMAD ABDULLA MUHAMMAD** (Empire Gallantry Medal)

*KHARTOUM, Sudan*

27/28 November 1924

He was of unknown age and serving in the Khartoum Police Force when two platoons of the 11th Sudanese Regiment ran amok. Three British officers and two Syrian medical officers were killed by the mutineers and nine other ranks were wounded. Muhammad was recommended for great gallantry displayed during the disturbances.

He died on 23 June 1978.

**Sol IBRAHIM NEGIB** (Empire Gallantry Medal)

*KHARTOUM, Sudan*

27/28 November 1924

He was of unknown age and serving in the Khartoum Police Force when two platoons of the 11th Sudanese Regiment ran amok. Three British officers and two Syrian medical officers were killed by the mutineers and nine other ranks were wounded. Negib was recommended for great gallantry displayed during the disturbances.

It is not known when he died.

**Shawish TAHA EL JAK EFFENDI** (Empire Gallantry Medal)

*KHARTOUM, Sudan*

27/28 November 1924

He was of unknown age and serving in the Khartoum Police Force when two platoons of the 11th Sudanese Regiment ran amok. Three British officers and two Syrian medical officers were killed by the mutineers and nine other ranks were wounded. Taha was recommended for great gallantry displayed during the disturbances.

It is not known when he died.

**Senior European Overseer JAMES JOHNSTON** (Edward Medal)

*CENTRAL PROVINCES, India*

7 January 1925

He was 33 years old and working at the Mohpani Colliery when a heavy roof fall took place, killing one miner and burying another named Nanoo Maora. When a report reached the Under-Manager, James Kipling, he immediately went to the scene accompanied by Johnston and Nani Khan, a timber drawer. They crawled through the fall and after fifteen minutes succeeded in extricating the trapped man. Within twenty minutes of the rescue some 20 tons of rock fell on the very spot where he had been buried. All three men were awarded the EM, but only Johnston lived to exchange his for the GC.

Johnston died on 7 September 1974.

## Petty Officer ROBERT CHALMERS (Empire Gallantry Medal)
*SHAMEEN, KWANTUNG PROVINCE, China*
23 June 1925

He was 31 years old and serving in the Royal Navy when during disturbances Chinese soldiers and students opened fire on the Victoria Hotel. The British retaliated, killing thirty-seven and wounding eighty. When the British ordered a cease fire, Chalmers ran along the front line under heavy fire, blowing the signal for 'cease fire' continuously, until, just as he was passing the Victoria Hotel, he was hit in both hands and fell into the hotel verandah.

Chalmers also served in both world wars. He died on 7 September 1974.

## Mr ROBERT PEARSON (Edward Medal)
*STOCKPORT, CHESHIRE, England*
11 July 1925

He was 29 years old and working at Henry Marsland Ltd, a textile company, when two boys, William Stothert and Arthur Bowden, were working in a vat. There was a sudden inrush of scalding liquid and steam owing to a mistake made in opening the pipe of another vat. The screams of the boys attracted the attention of other workers and attempts were made to get them out. Bowden was successfully drawn out but Stothert fell back in, owing to the burnt flesh of his hands giving way. Pearson, a labourer, then came upon the scene. He saw the terribly scalded Bowden and, on hearing that Stothert was still in the vat, he at once jumped into it, and after groping about found the boy and hoisted him up to enable those outside to drag him clear. Pearson's feet were severely scalded and he was almost unconscious on being dragged out. Both boys succumbed to their injuries but Pearson's effort to save Stothert's life was a very gallant one.

Pearson also served in the First World War. He died on 17 March 1973.

## Miner DONALD FLETCHER (Edward Medal)
*DERBYSHIRE, England*
10 September 1925

He was 23 years old and working at the Creswell Colliery when a heavy fall of rock completely buried a miner named Cooper. Some of the larger pieces of the roof became interlocked, affording him some protection from the full weight of the fall, and thus prevented his being crushed to death. Efforts were made to see where Cooper was lying, and it was found that his head was near the edge of the fall, so that it was possible to free it from debris. His shoulders were next freed but his body and legs were held fast. The only way to extricate him was for someone to crawl under the debris and gradually, stone by stone, release him from the debris. Fletcher at once volunteered for this task and was successful after two hours of continuous work. Great patience and skill were required, and in the course of the work Fletcher's body was completely under the fall with his head close to Cooper's feet. Throughout the operation Fletcher was exposed to the risk of being crushed to death either by a second fall or by a settling down of the first fall, but he performed his task skilfully and without regard for his own safety. His action was a very brave one involving great risk to his own life and, indeed, in the latter stages his position was as dangerous as Cooper's.

He died on 22 August 1986.

### Leading Hand GEORGE LOCK (often incorrectly spelt LOCKE) (Edward Medal)

*LONDON, England*
8 October 1925

He was 33 years old and working for Dorman Long & Co. Ltd when he was engaged in the erection of steel-work for the rebuilding of premises in Oxford Street. Lock and Frederick Dowser were standing on parallel girders on the fourth floor when Dowser tripped and fell, striking his head and ending up stunned on the girder. The girders were only 7in wide and 7ft apart. On seeing his comrade fall, Lock, with great presence of mind, immediately leapt across the intervening space and threw himself on Dowser's legs, pinning him to the girder until help arrived and they were dragged back to safety. But for Lock's prompt action, there is little doubt that Dowser would have fallen to his death.

He died on 10 June 1974, just a month before he was due to be invested with his exchange GC. It was presented to his family.

### Staff Sergeant REGINALD MALTBY (Empire Gallantry Medal)

*LAHORE, India*
5 June 1926

He was 44 years old and serving in the Royal Tank Corps when a little girl fell down a disused well and was drowning. Maltby climbed down the 40ft well and rescued her. He was originally recommended for the AM but this was 'down-graded' to the EGM.

He died on 17 December 1943.

### Mr ROBERT WILD (Empire Gallantry Medal)

*ROCHDALE, LANCASHIRE, England*
10 July 1926

He was 19 years old and working at Dunlop Cotton Mills when a fire broke out, caused by arcing at the switchboard in a sub-station. His work colleague Edward Matthews' clothes caught fire and Wild immediately set about extinguishing the flames with his bare hands.

Wild rarely told anyone about his GC. He died on 6 May 1976.

**Prison Officer CYRIL TUTTON** (Empire Gallantry Medal)

*ISLE OF WIGHT, England*

15 November 1926

He was 34 years old and working at Parkhurst Prison when a violent prisoner broke away from his party and climbed on to the roof of the Block Quarters. Without hesitation Tutton effected, single-handedly and at great personal risk, the arrest of the convict. The prisoner was armed with a slate in each hand, and the roof was some 60–70ft high.

Tutton had also served in the First World War. He died on 5 July 1967.

**Miner JOHN BEATTIE** (Empire Gallantry Medal)

*DURHAM, England*

19 November 1926

He was 33 years old and working at the Trimdon Grange Colliery when a tunnel collapsed, trapping miner Herbert Owens. Beattie, with Joseph Clark, worked for ten hours trying to dig the trapped man out, although they were in grave danger from falling debris, gas and spontaneously generated heat. Owens was found barely alive; he was badly burned and lost a leg. He died later from his injuries.

Beattie also served in the First World War. He died on 5 March 1952.

**Bricklayer JOSEPH CLARK** (Empire Gallantry Medal)

*DURHAM, England*

19 November 1926

He was 30 years old and working at the Trimdon Grange Colliery when a tunnel collapsed, trapping miner Herbert Owens. Clark, with John Beattie, worked for ten hours trying to dig the trapped man out, although they were in grave danger from falling debris, gas and spontaneously generated heat. Owens was found barely alive; he was badly burned and lost a leg. He died later from his injuries.

Clark had also served in the First World War. He died on 1 March 1965.

**Mr HERBERT HENDERSON** (Empire Gallantry Medal)

*LONDON, England*

6 December 1926

He was 24 years old and working at WA Henderson Film Treatment Works when a dangerous fire started. Henderson, although badly burned and in great danger, succeeded in carrying to safety a blazing cinematograph film, and in removing other films that were in danger of igniting, thereby preventing a major explosion.

He died on 12 May 1972.

**Mr STANLEY GIBBS** (Albert Medal)
*PORT HACKING, NEW SOUTH WALES, Australia*
3 January 1927

He was 18 years old and was returning to Port Hacking in a launch when he saw about eight children swimming. Mervyn Allum, Gibbs' girlfriend's brother, was suddenly attacked by a shark. At first it was thought he was drowning and Gibbs prepared to give assistance. Then the shark lifted him almost completely out of the water and Allum tried to push it off him with his hands.

Gibbs dived in and fought the shark with his hands, but it attacked Allum again and the water was red with blood. Eventually Gibbs succeeded in getting him away from the shark and, with help, onto the launch. The shark had taken all the flesh from the left leg to the hip clean off. He also had bite marks on his stomach and hands, and was pronounced dead on arrival at hospital.

This was on the day after his eighteenth birthday.

Gibbs also served in the Second World War. He died on 3 March 1991.

**Gunner JOHN FAIRCLOUGH** (Albert Medal)
*AMBALA, India*
27 April 1927

He was 26 years old and serving in 21 Medium Battery, Royal Field Artillery. Three Indian boys had gone to a godown in a lorry to get petrol, but they entered the building carrying a lantern. The naked light ignited the petrol vapour, and in a very short time the building was ablaze, trapping the boys. Fairclough, who happened to be passing, at once went to their aid. Despite the intense heat, he entered the building three times and rescued the boys. He was himself severely burned and unfortunately the boys died later.

Entering on three separate occasions a burning building containing highly flammable and explosive substances was an act of exceptional gallantry.

Fairclough declined to exchange his AM for the GC. He died on 24 October 1983.

**Lieutenant GEORGE BAIN-SMITH** (Albert Medal)
*MOUNT MUN, HIMALAYAS*
3 June 1927

He was 28 years old and serving in the Royal Regiment of Artillery, seconded to the Indian Army Ordnance Corps, when he was told of an accident 3,000ft up in the Himalayas in which Major Minchinton and two Gurkhas had been badly injured. One of the Gurkhas had been able to make his way down. Although he had no knowledge or experience of mountaineering, Bain-Smith set out at once to the rescue. He had no ice axe and was wearing smooth-soled boots and could only proceed by kicking footholds in the snow with his stockinged feet. When he reached the two injured men, he made a makeshift sledge from his coat; helped a little by the Gurkha, who was just able to move, he dragged the major some 500ft lower. He then had to get help from two shepherds and they managed to move down another 500ft but then progress again became impossible because of the roughness of the snow. Bain-Smith then sent one of the shepherds to get help, but he failed to return. So he set off again by himself and found four more shepherds. He was so exhausted by this time that he could only get along by crawling, but when he managed to get back to the injured men he sent the Gurkha down with two of the shepherds before making several unsuccessful attempts to continue the descent. At sunset the remaining shepherds deserted him, so, after staying for half an hour with the major, who was unconscious, if not already dead, and clad only in shirt, shorts and stockings, he made his way to a fire that he could see below the glacier; here he found the major's wife and a party of men. They could not tackle the mountain in the dark, but early next morning Bain-Smith escorted them to a point from where the major's body could be seen. He was by then on the verge of collapse and both his feet were frost-bitten.

He died on 22 January 1972.

### Petty Officer Stoker HERBERT MAHONEY (Empire Gallantry Medal)
*Mediterranean Sea*
July 1927
He was 30 years old and serving in the Royal Navy. HMS *Taurus*, a torpedo-boat destroyer, was steaming at high speed when the supports to the starboard fore turbo-fan fractured, causing the fan to drop; this in turn severed the main auxiliary exhaust steam pipe and several smaller pipes.

Mahoney ordered the boiler room cleared at once, but remained behind at great personal risk to close the stop valves and take other necessary action. The boiler room was filled with steam, and large pieces of metal were being hurled about by the still-running turbo-fan. By his prompt action and resolute behaviour, Mahoney averted what might have been a serious disaster.

Mahoney was killed in action on 1 June 1940, when his ship HMS *Basilisk* was dive-bombed off the coast of Dunkirk. His body was never recovered, but he is commemorated on the Plymouth Naval Memorial.

### Mr BERTRAM CROSBY (Edward Medal)
*REGENT'S PARK, LONDON, England*
9 September 1927
He was 17 years old and working at Film Waste Products Ltd when a fire broke out at the works in Redhill Street. A quantity of cinematograph film, which was being manipulated in a drying machine, ignited without warning, and the fire quickly spread to other film on adjacent benches. Crosby was passing through the drying room at the time, and at once ran to a door leading out into the yard, but on hearing a scream from near the drying machine he turned back and made his way towards the machine, the contents of which were burning fiercely. He was unable to see anyone and he returned to the yard.

Here he met the foreman and together, with Crosby leading, they re-entered the room. As they made their way in, Crosby saw a girl fall against one of the work tables; running to her, he half pulled and half dragged her towards the door. Outside they both fell. Crosby was stupefied by the heat and the fumes, and did not recover full consciousness until he found himself out in the yard with his clothes alight. He extinguished the flames and was subsequently taken to hospital. The girl subsequently died from her injuries.

As a result of his actions, Crosby was offered an apprenticeship with motor manufacturers Jowett. During the Second World War the company made Spitfire wings; this left him frustrated as he desperately wanted to fly but each time he applied he was turned down as it was considered that he was doing essential war work.

He died on 30 January 1972.

### Sub Foreman WILLIAM LLOYD (Edward Medal)
*NEWARK-ON-TRENT, England*
3 October 1927

He was 22 years old and working at Quibell Brothers Ltd when Mr Taylor was engaged in attending a grease-extracting plant used to remove grease from bones by means of petroleum benzene. Taylor noticed that benzene vapour was escaping from the extractor through the lid, which had been incorrectly left open, and with the help of another man he tried to close the lid. When Taylor realised the other man was affected by the fumes, he told him to leave the room, which he did. On recovering and finding that Taylor had not followed him out, the other man raised the alarm. Lloyd, who was not on duty but was passing the works on his way home, hearing what had happened, put a scarf around his mouth and ran to the upper floor of the building, where he found Taylor lying unconscious near the extractor. He succeeded in dragging him down the steps to a lower floor but was himself overcome and collapsed, and was later taken out of the building by other men.

Frank Boot, the works foreman, who was not on duty but had been summoned from his home, meanwhile arrived at the works, and, having put a handkerchief around his mouth, went into the building where he found Taylor. Boot dragged him to a point where other men could reach him, but himself became affected by the fumes. Both Lloyd and Boot displayed a very high degree of courage. At the time of the rescue the building was full of benzene fumes and a cloud of fumes was visible outside the building. Apart from the danger of suffocation, there was a serious risk of an explosion, and both men were well aware of this. Unfortunately Taylor did not recover. Both men were awarded the EM, but Boot did not live to exchange his for the GC.

Lloyd also served in the Second World War. He died on 16 June 1978.

### Lieutenant Colonel JAMES STEWART (Empire Gallantry Medal)
*between PEKING and TA T'UNG FU, China*
November 1927

He was 42 years old and serving in the Corps of Royal Engineers when Lieutenant T.S. Knowles went missing on Armistice Day. Although the North China winter was already closing in, Stewart immediately volunteered to organise a search into the mountains, and set off alone that same evening. At the time, hostilities between two rival war lords were in full swing and, as Knowles had fallen victim to one of the parties, considerable risk was attached to the rescue. Very little assistance was to be expected from local officials, who were only too anxious to conceal the truth, but Stewart tried no fewer than three avenues of approach, eventually being assured that Knowles had reached Tai Yuan Fu.

Stewart also served in both world wars. He died on 3 May 1946.

### Lieutenant REGINALD ARMYTAGE (Albert Medal)
*Malta*
23 May 1928
He was 25 years old and serving in the Royal Navy. During an examination of the bilge compartments on the port side of HMS *Warspite* the cover from the lower compartment was removed; it was found that the air was foul and poisonous. The chief stoker attempted to enter the compartment, although he was aware that it was in a dangerous condition. He was immediately overcome by gas, falling unconscious to the bottom of the compartment.

Lieutenant Armytage fetched his gas mask and, with a lifeline round him, entered the compartment, but when he reached the bottom he was overcome by gas. With great difficulty he was hauled up to the exit. He had stopped breathing and was removed to the Royal Naval Hospital in a precarious condition. He was well aware of the great risk he was taking.

Dick Oliver, who was in attendance with a shallow diving helmet, then volunteered to attempt a rescue, despite the fact that he had witnessed what had just happened. With considerable difficulty he was passed through the manholes of the upper and lower bilge compartments and eventually succeeded in reaching the chief stoker; he then passed a lifeline around him, allowing him to be hauled up. On emerging from the bilges, Oliver was a very bad colour and suffering from the effects of the gas.

Armytage declined to exchange his AM for the GC. He died on 9 November 1984.

### Leading Seaman DICK OLIVER (Albert Medal)
*Malta*
23 May 1928
He was 27 years old and serving in the Royal Navy. During an examination of the bilge compartments on the port side of HMS *Warspite* the cover from the lower compartment was removed; it was found that the air was foul and poisonous. The chief stoker attempted to enter the compartment, although he was aware that it was in a dangerous condition. He was immediately overcome by gas, falling unconscious to the bottom of the compartment.

Lieutenant Armytage fetched his gas mask and, with a lifeline round him, entered the compartment, but when he reached the bottom he was overcome by gas. With great difficulty he was hauled up to the exit. He had stopped breathing and was removed to the Royal Naval Hospital in a precarious condition. He was well aware of the great risk he was taking.

Dick Oliver, who was in attendance with a shallow diving helmet, then volunteered to attempt a rescue, despite the fact that he had witnessed what had just happened. With considerable difficulty he was passed through the manholes of the upper and lower bilge compartments and eventually succeeded in reaching the chief stoker; he then passed a lifeline around him, allowing him to be hauled up. On emerging from the bilges, Oliver was a very bad colour and suffering from the effects of the gas.

Oliver also served in both world wars and took part in the rescue of the crew from the submarine *Thetis* in 1939. Oliver declined to exchange his AM for the GC. He died on 5 February 1986.

### Principal Officer JOHN STOVES (Empire Gallantry Medal)
*between DONCASTER and SELBY, England*
12 June 1928

He was 54 years old and working as a prison officer. He was escorting a prisoner from London to Durham when the prisoner asked to be allowed to use the toilet. Permission was granted but, as he was being escorted along the corridor, some accomplices brushed against the accompanying officer, allowing the prisoner to get into the toilet and lock the door. Although handcuffed, he smashed a window and climbed out on to the footboard, hoping to make his escape when the train slowed down. Stoves climbed out of a door five compartments away (the nearer doors were all locked) and made his way along the footboard to the prisoner while the train was travelling at 60–70 miles an hour. He closed with the man, who was twenty years his junior, and for 18 miles they swayed precariously to and fro. Stoves held on to a door handle with one hand and the prisoner with the other. His adversary bit through his hand and later tried to drag him off the train, but he gallantly hung on until the train had almost stopped. He then allowed the prisoner to roll down an embankment, leapt after him and, after a short chase, caught him.

Stoves died on 3 September 1960.

### Leading Aircraftman WALTER ARNOLD (Empire Gallantry Medal)
*DIGBY, LINCOLNSHIRE, England*
20 June 1928

He was 21 years old and serving in the RAF when he was a passenger in an aircraft which crashed on landing and burst into flames. He managed to free himself from the wreckage, but, although fully aware of the grave risk he was taking, re-entered the burning wreck and succeeded in dragging the unconscious and injured pilot to safety. Arnold sustained burns to his face, neck and hands, but his prompt and courageous action undoubtedly saved the pilot's life.

Arnold also served in the Second World War. He died on 12 March 1988.

## Flying Officer WALTER ANDERSON (Empire Gallantry Medal)
*LEYSDOWN, SHEERNESS, KENT, England*
10 December 1928

He was 38 years old and serving in the RAF when Pilot Officer H.A. Constantine's aircraft crashed into the sea about 200yds from the shore. Anderson and Corporal Thomas McTeague immediately entered the sea from the shore and swam to his assistance. The weather was bitterly cold and an on-shore wind was blowing, making the sea rough. Constantine, fully clothed and suffering from injuries and shock, started to swim ashore, but was in a state of collapse when McTeague reached him. Although exhausted himself, McTeague supported him until Anderson arrived. The pilot was then brought to safety by their combined efforts, which involved swimming a distance of 100yds. The extremely prompt and timely action by these men, and the gallantry they displayed, undoubtedly saved Constantine's life.

Anderson had also served in the First World War. He died on 11 May 1959.

## Corporal THOMAS McTEAGUE (Empire Gallantry Medal)
*LEYSDOWN, SHEERNESS, KENT, England*
10 December 1928

He was 34 years old and serving in the RAF when Pilot Officer H.A. Constantine's aircraft crashed into the sea about 200yds from the shore. Flying Officer Walter Anderson and McTeague immediately entered the sea from the shore and swam to his assistance. The weather was bitterly cold and an on-shore wind was blowing, making the sea rough. Constantine, fully clothed and suffering from injuries and shock, started to swim ashore, but was in a state of collapse when McTeague reached him. Although exhausted himself, McTeague supported him until Anderson arrived. The pilot was then brought to safety by their combined efforts, which involved swimming a distance of 100yds. The extremely prompt and timely action by these men, and the gallantry they displayed, undoubtedly saved Constantine's life.

McTeague also served in the Second World War. He died on 12 April 1962.

## Sergeant REGINALD RIMMER (Empire Gallantry Medal)
*BOMBAY, India*
1929–1930

He was 27 years old and serving in the Bombay Police when, unarmed, he confronted a dangerous criminal brandishing a dagger. On approaching the man, he was stabbed through his right wrist. Bleeding profusely, he managed to hail a taxi and say 'hospital' before losing consciousness.

When he woke up he found himself in a maternity hospital, and it took some time for his colleagues to find him. His award was not for this act alone, but for numerous occasions on which he showed great courage and coolness.

Rimmer also served in the Second World War. He died on 21 February 1996.

### Mr ROBERT KAVANAUGH (Albert Medal)

*SYDNEY, Australia*
12 January 1929

He was 22 years old and swimming at Bondi Beach when 14-year-old Colin Stewart was attacked by a shark, suffering serious injuries to his right side and hip. Without hesitation, Kavanaugh swam to Stewart's assistance and had almost reached him when the shark made a second attack. Undeterred by the danger to himself, Kavanaugh secured hold of Stewart and struggled with him towards the shore. He had gone a considerable distance when he was met by two other men and together they carried the boy to the beach, where he was given medical attention. Sadly, Stewart died from his injuries the following day.

Kavanaugh also served in the Second World War. He died on 12 September 1976.

### Pit Lad JOHN (known as TOM) BAKER (Edward Medal)

*DURHAM, England*
17 May 1929

He was 17 years old and working at the South Garesfield Colliery when Deputy Richard Lowes was injured during blasting operations. Baker went down the pit with James Purvis and Overman Robert Glendenning; collecting a tram and stretcher, they went in search of the deputy. They were joined by Hewers John Kenny and Samuel Hughff. Meanwhile another party of five men had attempted a rescue, but four of them were overcome by gas while the fifth managed to crawl out just in time. The overman organised his party and through repeated efforts they succeeded in extricating the five men, three of whom were dead. The rescue party were all affected by the fumes and both Kenny and Hughff were overcome and had to be removed. For an hour, during which time the atmosphere was thick with smoke and gas, they knowingly and repeatedly risked their lives in determined efforts to save the lives of their colleagues. There is no doubt that but for their courageous act the death toll would have been much higher.

Baker served in the RAMC during the Second World War. He died on 7 December 2000.

### Pit Lad JAMES PURVIS (Edward Medal)

*DURHAM, England*
17 May 1929

He was 24 years old and working at the South Garesfield Colliery when Deputy Richard Lowes was injured during blasting operations. Purvis went down the pit with John Baker and Overman Robert Glendenning; collecting a tram and stretcher, they went in search of the deputy. They were joined by Hewers John Kenny and Samuel Hughff. Meanwhile another party of five men had attempted a rescue, but four of them were overcome by gas while the fifth managed to crawl out just in time. The overman organised his party and through repeated efforts they succeeded in extricating the five men, three of whom were dead. The rescue party were all affected by the fumes and both Kenny and Hughff were overcome and had to be removed. For an hour, during which time the atmosphere was thick with smoke and gas, they knowingly and repeatedly risked their lives in deter- mined efforts to save the lives of their colleagues. There is no doubt that but for their courageous act the death toll would have been much higher.

Purvis died on 12 February 1992.

### Flight Cadet WILLIAM McKECHNIE (Empire Gallantry Medal)
*CRANWELL AERODROME, England*
20 June 1929
He was 21 years old and serving in 106 Squadron, RAF when an aircraft piloted by Flight Cadet C.J. Giles crashed on landing and burst into flames. McKechnie, who had just landed himself, ran at full speed towards the scene, where petrol had spread over a wide area, with Giles lying in it, dazed. He was badly burned about the legs and face and his clothes were on fire. After dragging Giles clear of the flames, during which he was scorched and burned, McKechnie extinguished Giles's clothes. Had it not been for his action there is no doubt Giles would have burnt to death, as the burning petrol would have engulfed him.

McKechnie was killed in action on 30 August 1944 when his Lancaster bomber was shot down over Pokarber, Germany. His body was never recovered.

### Lieutenant Commander ALEXANDER MAXWELL-HYSLOP (Albert Medal)
*off the island of SKIATHOS, Mediterranean Sea*
26 July 1929
He was 34 years old and serving in the Royal Navy. HMS *Devonshire* was carrying out full calibre firing, but at the first salvo there was a heavy explosion in X turret, which blew off the turret roof. Marine Albert Streams was the only man in the gun turret who was not killed or fatally wounded. He instinctively climbed to the top of the turret but, on looking down and seeing the conditions, he climbed back into the smoke and flames, notwithstanding the grave risk of further explosions. He then helped to evacuate the dead and wounded; when all were removed, he collapsed.

Maxwell-Hyslop, who was in the fore control room when the explosion occurred, immediately went to the turret and climbed inside. He made a general examination of the turret, and descended the gun-well through the most dangerous conditions of fumes and smoke, necessitating the use of a lifeline, and he remained in the turret until the emergency was over, directing arrangements for the safety of the magazine, and supervising the evacuation of the wounded. He was fully aware of the danger from cordite fumes, and the grave risk of further explosions. Both men were awarded the AM, but Streams was killed in action in Sicily on 10 July 1943.

Maxwell-Hyslop also served in both world wars. He died on 28 August 1978.

### Midshipman ANTHONY COBHAM (Empire Gallantry Medal)
*off the island of SKIATHOS, Mediterranean Sea*
26 July 1929

He was 19 years old and serving in the Royal Navy. HMS *Devonshire* was carrying out full calibre firing when at the first salvo there was a heavy explosion in X turret, which blew off the turret roof. Marine Albert Streams was the only man in the gun turret who was not killed or fatally wounded. He instinctively climbed to the top of the turret but, on looking down and seeing the conditions, he climbed back into the smoke and flames, notwithstanding the grave risk of further explosions. He then helped to evacuate the dead and wounded; when all were removed, he collapsed.

Midshipman Cobham immediately took stretcher parties, including Able Seaman Niven, aft and ordered one crew to follow him and the other to rig hoses. On reaching the turret, they assisted the men who were on fire. Cobham and Niven did what they could for them and then went into the turret, where there was still a lot of cordite burning fiercely, Niven remarking: 'I'm not going to let him go down there alone.' They evacuated the wounded and brought out the dead bodies.

Cobham also served in the Second World War, and was on board HMS *Barham* when she was torpedoed and sunk with great loss of life. He died on 14 May 1993.

### Able Seaman GEORGE NIVEN (Empire Gallantry Medal)
*off the island of SKIATHOS, Mediterranean Sea*
26 July 1929

He was 32 years old and serving in the Royal Navy. HMS *Devonshire* was carrying out full calibre firing when at the first salvo there was a heavy explosion in X turret, which blew off the turret roof. Marine Albert Streams was the only man in the gun turret who was not killed or fatally wounded. He instinctively climbed to the top of the turret but, on looking down and seeing the conditions, he climbed back into the smoke and flames, notwithstanding the grave risk of further explosions. He then helped to evacuate the dead and wounded; when all were removed, he collapsed.

Midshipman Cobham immediately took stretcher parties, including Able Seaman Niven, aft and ordered one crew to follow him and the other to rig hoses. On reaching the turret, they assisted the men who were on fire. Cobham and Niven did what they could for them and then went into the turret, where there was still a lot of cordite burning fiercely, Niven remarking: 'I'm not going to let him go down there alone.' They evacuated the wounded and brought out the dead bodies.

Niven also served in both world wars. He died on 2 February 1947.

## Miner JOHN INGRAM GOUGH (Edward Medal)
*BURTON-ON-TRENT, England*
11 September 1929

He was 31 years old and working at the Bretby Colliery. The men were filling coal, but were warned to leave their work as a shot was about to be fired nearby. As they were leaving about 10 tons of roof fell and buried two men, Redfern and Hardwick. Deputy Samuel Crofts and others at once tried to release the trapped men, at great personal risk, as further falls were taking place. Crofts remained at work for twenty minutes trying to rescue Redfern, until a further large fall of about 100 tons occurred, killing Redfern. Croft was knocked down but he returned to work and only gave up when he crawled under the fall and found Redfern was dead.

While Crofts was trying to free Redfern, Gough and others were attempting to free Hardwick. At great personal risk, they removed the fallen coal from Hardwick's head and shoulders and placed over his body some covering timber, which undoubtedly saved his life when the second large fall occurred.

During these operations the rescuers were compelled to take cover from falling coal several times, and it was only after two hours' work of an exceedingly dangerous nature that they succeeded in rescuing Hardwick alive and recovering the body of Redfern.

Although all the rescue party showed great bravery and disregard for their own safety, Crofts and Gough were acknowledged by their comrades to have been the most prominent in risking their lives. Crofts was also awarded the EM but died before the exchange date.

Gough died on 23 March 1977.

## Mr JOHN SHEPHERD (Edward Medal)
*JARROW, CO. DURHAM, England*
16 October 1929

He was 30 years old and working at Palmers Shipbuilding & Iron Co. Ltd when he and Hugh Black were detailed to clean a steam boiler. Black entered the boiler and Shepherd was about to follow when he detected traces of gas. He called out to Black but received only a faint reply and immediately climbed inside to go to his aid. Shepherd found Black half-conscious some 25ft from the boiler manhole. He endeavoured to drag him to the opening but had to abandon the attempt as he was succumbing to the gas himself. He made his way out of the boiler, called for help and, though still seriously affected by the gas, returned with a rope which he tried to fasten round his comrade, who was by now unconscious.

Compressed air was used to clear the gas out of the boiler, and eventually a rescue party wearing respirators succeeded in extricating both men. Black unfortunately died a few hours later.

Shepherd died on 16 March 1983.

## Mr ALBERT TYLER (Edward Medal)
*WELWYN, HERTFORDSHIRE, England*
19 October 1929

He was 27 years old and working at a factory in Burnham Green cleaning and enlarging a cesspit with his brother Ernest and his father William, when Ernest became affected by gas. He had been lowered by a bucket attached to a rope, and was being brought back up at his own request when he fell out of the bucket while still 20ft from the top of the pit. William went down at once to rescue his son, but collapsed and became unconscious on reaching the bottom. Despite the collapse of his brother and father, which Albert had witnessed, he descended into the pit to rescue them. He was driven back four times by the gas but at the fifth attempt he succeeded in getting a rope around them. They were hauled to the surface but artificial respiration and oxygen failed to revive them.

Albert undoubtedly displayed great courage and determination in his attempts to save his father and brother. The rescue lasted over forty minutes and every time he entered the pit he must have been fully aware that he was endangering his own life.

He died on 28 December 1975.

## Pilot Officer SIDNEY WILTSHIRE (Empire Gallantry Medal)
*SLEAFORD, LINCOLNSHIRE, England*
21 October 1929

He was 19 years old and serving in the RAF when his aircraft crashed on landing at Temple Bruer Landing Ground and caught fire. Wiltshire extricated himself from the wreckage, then saw that his instructor, Flying Officer Power, was trapped. Although fully realising the risk he was taking, he re-entered the burning wreck and pulled out his instructor. Wiltshire suffered burns to his neck and face. Power's clothes were on fire and he would undoubtedly have lost his life but for the prompt action of his pupil. As it was, he was badly burnt and both officers were taken by air to Cranwell Hospital.

Wiltshire died on 29 September 2003.

## Mr GRANVILLE WASTIE (Edward Medal)
*NORTHLEIGH, OXFORDSHIRE, England*
25 November 1929

He was 26 years old and working as a farmer when his brother Hector, a bricklayer, descended a well some 30ft deep and 3ft wide; he was overcome by carbon dioxide gas about halfway down and fell unconscious into 30in of water. His brother Stanley went to his assistance but he too was overcome and collapsed, falling to the bottom of the well. Another workman, George Broughton, attempted to descend the well but when halfway down became faint and was pulled up by a rope which he had fastened around himself. By this time Granville had arrived. After tying a handkerchief over his face and a rope around himself, he descended the well and, tying a rope round Stanley, succeeded in bringing him alive to the surface. He then went down a second time and brought up Hector. But a doctor who was summoned found that he had drowned after falling unconscious. Granville almost certainly saved Stanley's life. He well understood the risk and exercised skill and foresight in effecting the rescue.

Granville also served in the Second World War. He did not even tell his son this story until over forty years later, when he exchanged his EM for the GC. He died on 24 March 1992.

### Sub Inspector GHULAM MOHI-ud-DIN (Empire Gallantry Medal)
*PUNJAB, India*
1930
He was of unknown age and serving in the Punjab Police Force when, from the beginning of the civil disobedience campaign, he had to deal with many very dangerous situations arising from the presence of large and hostile crowds. On several occasions, while behaving with commendable restraint, he took grave risks and was never deterred from such steps as were necessary to maintain law and order and the prestige of the government.

Ghulam died in 1972.

### Able Seaman GEORGE HARRISON (Empire Gallantry Medal)
*PORTSMOUTH HARBOUR, England*
15 February 1930
He was 35 years old and serving in the Royal Navy when dockyard workmen opened the starboard after-bilge compartments aboard HMS *Hood* for inspection. A shipwright named Langford entered through the manhole and was overcome by carbon monoxide and collapsed. A rescue party entered the bilge, but found great difficulty in locating him due to the very bad atmosphere and lack of lighting. The party had gas-masks but these were ineffective against carbon monoxide. Notwithstanding these difficulties, however, Harrison made his way through successive compartments and, at great personal risk, continued his search and, with assistance, eventually brought Langford out. At this point Harrison was in a state of collapse himself. Langford, although alive when brought out, died without regaining consciousness.

Harrison died on 4 June 1959.

### Sergeant ARNOLD BARRACLOUGH (Empire Gallantry Medal)
*CHITTAGONG, BENGAL, India*
18/19 April 1930
He was 30 years old and serving in the Assam–Bengal Railway Battalion, Indian Auxiliary Force when armed raiders attacked the police armoury and tele-

phone exchange, seizing all the available arms and ammunition, destroying communications and terrorising the population. Barraclough took a Lewis gun and, accompanied by the Superintendent of Police, brought the gun into action and engaged the raiders at close range. Although heavily fired upon, he went on firing until the raiders dispersed and fled into the jungle.

Barraclough also served in the Second World War. He died on 3 May 1974.

### Trooper CLIVE BAYLEY (Empire Gallantry Medal)
*JIJIRIABAHTALI, BENGAL, India*
22 April 1930

He was 22 years old and was serving in the Suma Valley Light Horse when raiders who had previously attacked the armouries and telephone exchange at Chittagong (see Arnold Barraclough entry, above) were located near Jijiriabahtali. As well as his unit, twenty men from the Eastern Frontier Rifles were sent to deal with them. The insurgents had occupied a wooded hill and engaged at once. Trooper Bayley, on the left of the attack, worked his way round through thick jungle and succeeded in killing three of the insurgents, including their leader, and wounding several others. His helmet was shot off but he was not injured.

He died on 30 June 1949.

### Pit Manager JOHN BELL (Empire Gallantry Medal)
*PRESTEA, Gold Coast (now Ghana)*
17 May 1930

He was 58 years old and working at the Ariston Gold Mine when several natives were involved in an accident. Bell went in search of these men, and was instrumental in saving them from being gassed. Two other men who went in search of Bell both died from the gas, as would Bell have done when he too fell unconscious, were it not for the fact that his mouth was next to a leak in a compressed air pipe.

He died in May 1950.

### Shri JOSEPH BAPTISTA d'SOUZA (Empire Gallantry Medal)
*BOMBAY, India*
27 May 1930

He was of unknown age and serving as an excise constable and orderly to the Excise Sub-Inspector when during a riot they were completely surrounded by the mob, being severely beaten and stoned. The Sub-Inspector ordered d'Souza to seek safety but he refused, staying at his post and protecting him. He stood by the now unconscious Sub-Inspector, continually blowing his whistle until police help arrived. His devotion to duty in the face of great danger undoubtedly saved the life of the Sub-Inspector.

He died on 26 December 1980.

**Leading Aircraftman ROBERT DOUGLAS** (Empire Gallantry Medal)
*KOHAT, NORTH-WEST FRONTIER, India (now Pakistan)*
13 June 1930

He was 24 years old and serving in 60 Squadron, RAF when an aircraft loaded with bombs crashed shortly after take-off, bursting into flames. Douglas was first on the scene and found the gunner lying near the wreckage with his clothes burning. Using an extinguisher, Douglas put out the fire and, after disentangling part of the gun equipment from the injured man, dragged him clear. With the assistance of another airman who had arrived on the scene, and after subduing a renewed burst of fire from the man's clothes, they got him into an ambulance. Then Douglas turned his attention to the pilot in the burning machine; he had approached to within 12yds of the wreckage when the first of the bombs exploded. Now realising that there was no hope of the pilot still being alive, he started to get clear and was 30yds away when a second bomb exploded.

Douglas also served in the Second World War. He died on 10 August 1959.

**Miner RICHARD KING** (Edward Medal)
*HEDLEY, CO. DURHAM, England*
29 September 1930

He was 25 years old and working at the South Moor Colliery when there was a heavy fall of roof, burying Frederick Beaumont. First on the scene was Victor King (Richard's father). He found that a small passage remained open by which Beaumont might be reached. With the assistance of Richard and John Tarn, he immediately built two chocks of timber to keep it open. The passage was 7yds long and 2ft square and the only method of rescue was for the three men to crawl along the passage way and lie at full length, two in the passage and one over Beaumont's body, and pass back, one at a time, the rocks that were pinning him down.

This work was carried on for nine hours by a team of men working in relays under the direction of the manager Walter Scott and the under-manager Robert Reed, until at last Beaumont was released. Four times he was almost out when another fall buried him.

In all nineteen men were awarded the EM for this rescue: John Akers, Thomas Buckley, Philip Cox, John Dart, Thomas Dixon, Charles Fox, Robert Johnston, James Kent, Richard King, Victor King, Joseph Lees, George Mason, George Nancollas, Robert Reed, Walter Scott, Walter Sheldrake, John Tarn, Thomas Uren and William Waugh, but only Richard King lived to exchange his EM for the GC.

He died on 23 November 1983.

**Lance Sergeant THOMAS ALDER** (Empire Gallantry Medal)
*YANGTSE–KIANG RIVER, China*
16/17 November 1930

He was 23 years old and serving in the 2nd Battalion, Green Howards

(Alexandra, Princess of Wales's Own Yorkshire Regiment) when he was in charge of three men employed on anti-piracy duties on board the SS *Wuhu*. While proceeding up-river, the ship was fired on by communists with guns and small arms on four occasions. Fire was returned and a number of casualties observed. At 4.30pm Alder and his party left the *Wuhu* in a sampan and proceeded two-and-a-half miles under constant fire from both banks to the assistance of the SS *Kiatung*, which had run aground and was under attack by communists. Upon reaching the *Kiatung* they boarded her, coming under fire from both banks until the 17th, when another vessel arrived to provide assistance. When they were relieved they only had forty-three rounds of ammunition left between them. Eventually, the *Kiatung* was towed off the sand bank, and during the return journey came under fire on a number of occasions.

Alder also served in the Second World War. He died on 5 March 1973.

### Constable EL IMAM YEHIA (Empire Gallantry Medal)
*KHARTOUM, Sudan*
1931
He was 19 years old and serving in the Khartoum Police Force when he saw a rabid dog attacking a man. He at once tried to kill it with his baton, but was unable to. He then strangled the dog with his bare hands, being severely bitten in the struggle. There is no doubt that by his prompt action and bravery he saved many from infection.

He died on 16 February 1987.

### Railway Flagman ARTHUR THOMAS (Edward Medal)
*KING'S CROSS STATION, LONDON, England*
14 January 1931
He was 35 years old and working for the Metropolitan Railway Company, now the London Underground, when Ernest Percival, who was engaged in dismantling a wooden staging fixed across the track, slipped and fell on to the track below. He was unconscious and lying face down across one running rail, with his head close to the negative rail. Thomas saw him fall and at the same time heard a train approaching the station from around the curve. Realising that a signal could not be seen by the driver in time for him to stop the train, Thomas immediately jumped down from the platform, ran across two positive and two negative rails carrying 600 volts, snatched Percival up from almost under the wheels of the train, and held him, still unconscious, in a small recess in the wall while the train passed within a few inches of them. Thomas was fully aware of the risk he faced and he displayed conspicuous gallantry in successfully rescuing Percival.

His actions are all the more incredible as he had injured his spine some time before this incident. He had also served in the First World War. Thomas declined to exchange his EM for the GC. He died on 1 November 1973.

**Sub Inspector BALDEV SINGH** (Empire Gallantry Medal)
*FEROZEPORE DISTRICT, PUNJAB, India*
June and July 1931
He was of unknown age and serving in the Punjab Police Force when he displayed great bravery in organising and leading an attack under fire on a dangerous gang of offenders in June. In July he narrowly escaped death in a successful raid on a house occupied by persons in unlawful possession of firearms.
He died in November 1983.

**Sub Inspector BHIM SINGH YADAVA** (Empire Gallantry Medal)
*PUNJAB, India*
June 1931
He was 30 years old and serving in the Punjab Police Force when he displayed great courage and a total disregard for danger in effecting the capture of a native who had shot dead two people and was attacking another.
He died on 17 November 1983.

**Assistant Store Keeper ALBERT MEADOWS** (Edward Medal)
*LONDON, England*
18 September 1931
He was 37 years old and working at the distillery of W.A. Gilbey Ltd in Camden Town. John Gale was cleaning out the residue in an empty cherry brandy vat when he was discovered unconscious by Frederick Wormald, having been gassed by the carbon dioxide generated by the fermentation of the residue. Wormald went into the vat but was unable to get Gale out. He then called Leonard Wright and went down a second time, but was himself affected by the gas and had to be helped out by Wright. Wright then tried but he too became unconscious at the bottom of the vat. In the meantime the manager had sent for assistance. Harold Hostler arrived on the scene and immediately entered the vat. He succeeded in dragging Wright to a sitting position near the foot of the ladder, but, feeling the effects of the gas, he had to come out of the vat. He made a second attempt with a wet cloth around his mouth and on his third attempt, with a rope around his waist, he succeeded in getting Gale to the foot of the ladder, but he was overcome when part way up the ladder and Gale slipped back into the vat. Hostler was drawn up by the rope.

Albert Meadows then volunteered to go into the vat, and at his second attempt, with a wet cloth around his mouth and a rope around his waist, he succeeded in rescuing Wright. Although partially affected by the gas, he made a third unsuccessful attempt to rescue Gale. He then asked for a length of rubber gas piping and placing it in his mouth to breathe through he went down a fourth time. He managed to put a rope around Gale and they were pulled up together. Both Gale and Wright recovered later.

Meadows also served in the Second World War. He died on 19 March 1988.

**Assistant Surveyor SAMUEL TEMPERLEY** (Edward Medal)
*BENTLEY, YORKSHIRE, England*
20 November 1931

He was 32 years old and working at the Bentley Colliery when there was a violent explosion of firedamp, followed by fires. Of forty-seven men and boys working at or near the coal face, all but two were either killed or died later. John Ward, the pony driver, who was near an adjacent part of the coal face, was blown off his feet and enveloped in a thick cloud of dust, but as soon as he recovered himself he went on his own initiative towards the face, guiding himself by rails and tubs, and assisted an injured man towards a place of safety. He repeatedly returned towards the face and helped to free injured men and bring them away, and continued working for three hours until completely exhausted.

Darker, Soulsby, Sykes and Yates also displayed great gallantry and perseverance in extricating the injured and taking them to safety. They had to work in an atmosphere that was hot and vitiated, with the risk of further explosions. In fact there were two more explosions in the mine.

Temperley, Ernest Allport, a member of the colliery rescue team, and Edgar Frazer were prominent in rescuing men from the area of the fires, which was explored somewhat later and where the danger was extreme. Temperley volunteered to lead a rescue bridge to the return airway, where some men were still alive, by way of the face, there being a fire on the direct route. Another explosion severely burned three members of the party and they went back, but Temperley, although not equipped with breathing gear, went on with one of the mine inspectors and rescued another injured man.

Allport played a prominent part in the rescue operations, displaying energy, initiative and bravery. He spent over three hours in breathing gear and during part of the night when his rescue apparatus required replenishing, he assisted in loading men on to stretchers. Subsequently, in answer to a call for volunteers after the second explosion, he seized some breathing gear and joined a rescue party which penetrated past a fire to rescue two men. Frazer explored more of the most dangerous area, displaying great gallantry in venturing among flames, smoke and afterdamp, although not equipped with breathing gear; on hearing moaning on the return airway he ran back to summon a rescue party, but returned to the airway without waiting for them. He then remained in the most dangerous area assisting to organise rescue operations and helped to take out past a fire two men recovered from the airway. Although exhausted, he continued his efforts until all the men who were reported to be in the area had been extricated, dead or alive.

All of the eight aforementioned men were awarded the Edward Medal, but John Ward and Edgar Frazer died before they could exchange their EMs for the GC. Temperley died on 15 December 1977.

**Miner RICHARD DARKER** (Edward Medal)
*BENTLEY, YORKSHIRE, England*
20 November 1931

William Fleming
(49) saved
twenty-four men
from drowning.
(Imperial War
Museum
Q80531)

Philip Yates
(116) rescued
trapped miners.
(*Tony Gledhill*)

John Rowlands (183) defused over 150 bombs. (*Tony Gledhill*)

Joan Pearson (204) pulled a pilot from his burning aircraft. (*Tony Gledhill*)

Bertram Archer (219) worked on over 200 bombs. (*Tony Gledhill*)

Richard Moore (226) took part in defusing seventeen parachute mines. (*Tony Gledhill*)

Harry Errington (228) rescued two colleagues from a basement fire. (*Tony Gledhill*)

Laurence Sinclair (239) pulled an injured man from a burning aircraft. (*Tony Gledhill*)

Lionel Matthews (274) defied the Japanese, although he was a prisoner of war. (*Australian War Memorial, Out of Copyright*)

John Gregson (278) saved an injured man from their sinking ship. (*Tony Gledhill*)

(*Right*) Charles Walker (279). The man in the middle is believed to be Stanley Gibbs (71). The man on the left is an as-yet-unidentified GC holder. (*Charles Walker*)

Charles Walker (279) aged 97 in 2010. (*Author's collection*)

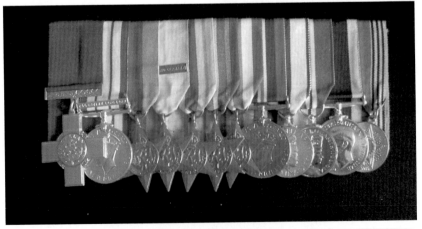

Charles Walker's medals. (*Author's collection*)

William Foster (280); at 61 years he is the oldest recipient of the GC. (*Imperial War Museum MH029020*)

Eynon Hawkins (288) swam though burning water to rescue two men. (*Imperial War Museum Q81175*)

Odette Sansom (later Hallowes) (295) was brutally tortured by the Gestapo. (*Tony Gledhill*)

John Bridge (303) cleared 207 depth-charges, both above and below the water.
(*Tony Gledhill*)

Geoffrey Riley (316) rescued a 76-year-old woman from a flood. (*Tony Gledhill*)

Henry Flintoff (319). At just 13 years old he grabbed hold of a bull's nose-ring and hung on to it to stop it attacking a farmer. (*Tony Gledhill*)

George Gosse (335) rendered three mines safe despite the detonators firing on all occasions. (*Australian War Memorial, Out of Copyright*)

Arthur Butson (351) helped rescue a man from a 106ft-deep crevasse. (*Tony Gledhill*)

Joseph Lynch (357) saved a colleague from drowning. (*Tony Gledhill*)

Alfred Lowe (360) left a place of safety to try to save a colleague from drowning. (*Alfred Lowe*)

Margaret Purves
(née Vaughan)
(361) saved a boy
from drowning.
(*M. Purves*)

Derek Kinne (369) made
repeated attempts to escape
from his Chinese captors.
(*Terry Hissey*)

Awang Anak
Rawang (371)
drove off several
bandit attacks
despite being
wounded. (*Tony
Gledhill*)

John Bamford (373). At 15 years and 7 months he is the youngest direct
recipient of the GC. (*Tony Gledhill*)

Frederick Fairfax (374) rescuing a comrade under fire. (*Tony Gledhill*)

Henry Stevens (378) was shot in the mouth by a gunman. (*Henry Stevens*)

Henry Stevens (378) aged 82 in 2010 old. (*Author's collection*)

Tony Gledhill (384) with his family on the day of his investiture. (*Tony Gledhill*)

Carl Walker (390) was shot by a gunman. (*Tony Gledhill*)

Stephen Styles (391) defused a 30lb terrorist bomb. (*Tony Gledhill*)

Jim Beaton (394) saved Princess Anne from a gunman. (*Tony Gledhill*)

Michael Pratt (397) took on an armed gang when off-duty and unarmed. (*Tony Gledhill*)

Barry Johnson (399). When told of the award, his wife said: 'That's nice. Have a cup of tea.' (*Barry Johnson*)

Christopher Finney (401) saved one of his tank crew when they came under 'friendly fire'. (*Tony Gledhill*)

Peter Norton (402) dealt with multiple IEDS over several months. (*Terry Hissey*)

Matthew Croucher (404) threw himself on to a grenade to save his comrades. (*Tony Gledhill*)

He was 20 years old and working at the Bentley Colliery when there was a violent explosion of firedamp, followed by fires. Of forty-seven men and boys working at or near the coal face, all but two were either killed or died later. John Ward, the pony driver, who was near an adjacent part of the coal face, was blown off his feet and enveloped in a thick cloud of dust, but as soon as he recovered himself he went on his own initiative towards the face, guiding himself by rails and tubs, and assisted an injured man towards a place of safety. He repeatedly returned towards the face and helped to free injured men and bring them away, and continued working for three hours until completely exhausted.

Darker, Soulsby, Sykes and Yates also displayed great gallantry and perseverance in extricating the injured and taking them to safety. They had to work in an atmosphere that was hot and vitiated, with the risk of further explosions. In fact there were two more explosions in the mine.

Temperley, Ernest Allport, a member of the colliery rescue team, and Edgar Frazer were prominent in rescuing men from the area of the fires, which was explored somewhat later and where the danger was extreme. Temperley volunteered to lead a rescue bridge to the return airway, where some men were still alive, by way of the face, there being a fire on the direct route. Another explosion severely burned three members of the party and they went back, but Temperley, although not equipped with breathing gear, went on with one of the mine inspectors and rescued another injured man.

All of the eight aforementioned men were awarded the Edward Medal, but John Ward and Edgar Frazer died before they could exchange their EMs for the GC. Darker died on 15 January 1988.

## Miner ERNEST ALLPORT (Edward Medal)
*BENTLEY, YORKSHIRE, England*
20 November 1931

He was 37 years old and working at the Bentley Colliery when there was a violent explosion of firedamp, followed by fires. Of forty-seven men and boys working at or near the coal face, all but two were either killed or died later. John Ward, the pony driver, who was near an adjacent part of the coal face, was blown off his feet and enveloped in a thick cloud of dust, but as soon as he recovered himself he went on his own initiative towards the face, guiding himself by rails and tubs, and assisted an injured man towards a place of safety. He repeatedly returned towards the face and helped to free injured men and bring them away, and continued working for three hours until completely exhausted.

Darker, Soulsby, Sykes and Yates also displayed great gallantry and perseverance in extricating the injured and taking them to safety. They had to work in an atmosphere that was hot and vitiated, with the risk of further explosions. In fact there were two more explosions in the mine.

Temperley, Ernest Allport, a member of the colliery rescue team, and Edgar Frazer were prominent in rescuing men from the area of the fires, which was explored somewhat later and where the danger was extreme. Temperley volunteered to lead a rescue bridge to the return airway, where some men were still alive, by way of the face, there being a fire on the direct route. Another explosion severely burned three members of the party and they went back, but Temperley, although not equipped with breathing gear, went on with one of the mine inspectors and rescued another injured man.

Allport played a prominent part in the rescue operations, displaying energy, initiative and bravery. He spent over three hours in breathing gear and during part of the night when his rescue apparatus required replenishing, he assisted in loading men on to stretchers. Subsequently, in answer to a call for volunteers after the second explosion, he seized some breathing gear and joined a rescue party which penetrated past a fire to rescue two men. Frazer explored more of the most dangerous area, displaying great gallantry in venturing among flames, smoke and afterdamp, although not equipped with breathing gear; on hearing moaning on the return airway he ran back to summon a rescue party, but returned to the airway without waiting for them. He then remained in the most dangerous area assisting to organise rescue operations and helped to take out past a fire two men recovered from the airway. Although exhausted, he continued his efforts until all the men who were reported to be in the area had been extricated, dead or alive.

All of the eight aforementioned men were awarded the Edward Medal, but John Ward and Edgar Frazer died before they could exchange their EMs for the GC. Allport died on 6 October 1987.

## Miner OLIVER SOULSBY (Edward Medal)
*BENTLEY, YORKSHIRE, England*
20 November 1931

He was 21 years old and working at the Bentley Colliery when there was a violent explosion of firedamp, followed by fires. Of forty-seven men and boys working at or near the coal face, all but two were either killed or died later. John Ward, the pony driver, who was near an adjacent part of the coal face, was blown off his feet and enveloped in a thick cloud of dust, but as soon as he recovered himself he went on his own initiative towards the face, guiding himself by rails and tubs, and assisted an injured man towards a place of safety. He repeatedly returned towards the face and helped to free injured men and bring them away, and continued working for three hours until completely exhausted.

Darker, Soulsby, Sykes and Yates also displayed great gallantry and perseverance in extricating the injured and taking them to safety. They had to work in an atmosphere that was hot and vitiated, with the risk of further explosions. In fact there were two more explosions in the mine.

Temperley, Ernest Allport, a member of the colliery rescue team, and Edgar Frazer were prominent in rescuing men from the area of the fires, which was explored somewhat later and where the danger was extreme. Temperley volunteered to lead a rescue bridge to the return airway, where some men were still alive, by way of the face, there being a fire on the direct route. Another explosion severely burned three members of the party and they went back, but Temperley, although not equipped with breathing gear, went on with one of the mine inspectors and rescued another injured man.

All of the eight aforementioned men were awarded the Edward Medal, but John Ward and Edgar Frazer died before they could exchange their EMs for the GC. Soulsby died on 5 January 1977.

### Miner FRANK SYKES (Edward Medal)
*BENTLEY, YORKSHIRE, England*
20 November 1931

He was 26 years old and working at the Bentley Colliery when there was a violent explosion of firedamp, followed by fires. Of forty-seven men and boys working at or near the coal face, all but two were either killed or died later. John Ward, the pony driver, who was near an adjacent part of the coal face, was blown off his feet and enveloped in a thick cloud of dust, but as soon as he recovered himself he went on his own initiative towards the face, guiding himself by rails and tubs, and assisted an injured man towards a place of safety. He repeatedly returned towards the face and helped to free injured men and bring them away, and continued working for three hours until completely exhausted.

Darker, Soulsby, Sykes and Yates also displayed great gallantry and perseverance in extricating the injured and taking them to safety. They had to work in an atmosphere that was hot and vitiated, with the risk of further explosions. In fact there were two more explosions in the mine.

Temperley, Ernest Allport, a member of the colliery rescue team, and Edgar Frazer were prominent in rescuing men from the area of the fires, which was explored somewhat later and where the danger was extreme. Temperley volunteered to lead a rescue bridge to the return airway, where some men were still alive, by way of the face, there being a fire on the direct route. Another explosion severely burned three members of the party and they went back, but Temperley, although not equipped with breathing gear, went on with one of the mine inspectors and rescued another injured man.

All of the eight aforementioned men were awarded the Edward Medal, but John Ward and Edgar Frazer died before they could exchange their EMs for the GC. Sykes died on 9 April 1982.

### Miner PHILIP YATES (Edward Medal)
*BENTLEY, YORKSHIRE, England*
20 November 1931

He was 18 years old and working at the Bentley Colliery when there was a violent explosion of firedamp, followed by fires. Of forty-seven men and boys working at or near the coal face, all but two were either killed or died later. John Ward, the pony driver, who was near an adjacent part of the coal face, was blown off his feet and enveloped in a thick cloud of dust, but as soon as he recovered himself he went on his own initiative towards the face, guiding himself by rails and tubs, and assisted an injured man towards a place of safety. He repeatedly returned towards the face and helped to free injured men and bring them away, and continued working for three hours until completely exhausted.

Darker, Soulsby, Sykes and Yates also displayed great gallantry and perseverance in extricating the injured and taking them to safety. They had to work in an atmosphere that was hot and vitiated, with the risk of further explosions. In fact there were two more explosions in the mine.

Temperley, Ernest Allport, a member of the colliery rescue team, and Edgar Frazer were prominent in rescuing men from the area of the fires, which was explored somewhat later and where the danger was extreme. Temperley volunteered to lead a rescue bridge to the return airway, where some men were still alive, by way of the face, there being a fire on the direct route. Another explosion severely burned three members of the party and they went back, but Temperley, although not equipped with breathing gear, went on with one of the mine inspectors and rescued another injured man.

Allport played a prominent part in the rescue operations, displaying energy, initiative and bravery. He spent over three hours in breathing gear and during part of the night when his rescue apparatus required replenishing, he assisted in loading men on to stretchers. Subsequently, in answer to a call for volunteers after the second explosion, he seized some breathing gear and joined a rescue party which penetrated past a fire to rescue two men. Frazer explored more of the most dangerous area, displaying great gallantry in venturing among flames, smoke and afterdamp, although not equipped with breathing gear; on hearing moaning on the return airway he ran back to summon a rescue party, but returned to the airway without waiting for them. He then remained in the most dangerous area assisting to organise rescue operations and helped to take out past a fire two men recovered from the airway. Although exhausted, he continued his efforts until all the men who were reported to be in the area had been extricated, dead or alive.

All of the eight aforementioned men were awarded the Edward Medal, but John Ward and Edgar Frazer died before they could exchange their EMs for the GC. Yates died on 14 February 1998.

**Miss EMMA TOWNSEND** (Empire Gallantry Medal)
*KINGSBRIDGE, SOUTH DEVON, England*
7 May 1932
She was 52 years old and visiting her sister in South Hams Cottage Hospital when a farmer, William Yeoman, attacked his 9-year-old son, also called William. First he fired a gun at him twice and then he hit him several times with it. Miss Townsend heard cries of 'Help' and went into the ward. She showed great courage in trying to prevent the attack, being hit about the head with the barrel of the gun, cutting her head open. William died from his wounds on 9 May.

Mr Yeoman had already killed his wife Olive, his daughter Kathleen and 15-month-old son Alfred at their farm. He was found guilty but insane and detained in a criminal lunatic asylum.

Townsend died on 8 March 1965.

**Flight Sergeant ERIC 'JOCK' BONAR** (Empire Gallantry Medal)
*RAF BARTON, MANCHESTER, England*
24 May 1932
He was 32 years old and serving in the RAF Volunteer Reserve when a training aircraft piloted by Flight Sergeant Jack Treadwell, with Leading Aircraftman William Lane as pupil, was seen to roll at low altitude, stall and then spin to earth out of control. It crashed and burst into flames. Bonar immediately rushed to the scene and, with an asbestos blanket covering him, plunged into the burning wreckage. Lane was in the front cockpit and it was impossible to get to him. However, he was able to reach Treadwell, releasing him from his harness and dragging him from the wreckage. He was rushed to hospital with very serious injuries from which he later died.

Bonar also served in both world wars. He died on 26 February 1991.

**Electrical Foreman OSMOND WILLIAMS** (Edward Medal)
*FREETOWN, Sierra Leone*
15 July 1932
He was 33 years old and working in the public works department when he received a phone call telling him that a live distribution wire had fallen into the street. He immediately went to investigate and on arrival saw a woman approaching the wire; he shouted to her to stop, but she continued on her way and became entangled in the wire. Mr Williams endeavoured to free the woman and, in spite of several severe shocks, succeeded in doing so. She was unconscious and not breathing; Williams used artificial respiration until her breathing appeared to be normal and then drove her to the hospital. He then returned and oversaw the repair of the broken wire. The woman subsequently died from the shocks she had received. Williams was an experienced electrician and was fully aware of the danger he was risking. At the time it was raining and he was wet through, which greatly increased the risk. There can be no doubt that he knowingly risked his life in going to the woman's rescue.

Williams had also served in the First World War. He died on 4 March 1981.

**Mr MIRGHANY AHMED MUHAMMAD** (Empire Gallantry Medal)
*KHARTOUM, Sudan*
18 September 1932
He was of unknown age. At the height of the Nile flood, at a point where the river is particularly dangerous, even for the strongest swimmer, he rescued three girls from certain death by drowning, the oldest of whom was just fifteen years old.

He died on 25 August 1951 or 1961.

**Shawish TAHA IDRIS** (Empire Gallantry Medal)

*Sudan*

September 1933

He was 33 years old and serving in the Blue Nile Province Police when a native NCO in charge of a police guard temporarily lost his self-control. After loading his rifle with nine rounds of ball ammunition, he ran amok. The guard, being unable to deal with the situation, sent for Idris, who immediately came to their assistance. He could not approach without being seen, and the armed man aimed at him from only a few paces away and pulled the trigger, but for some reason the cartridge did not fire, and Idris ran in and disarmed him.

He died on 31 May 1993.

**Mr ABDUS SAMID ABDUL WAHID GOLANDAZ** (Empire Gallantry Medal)

*SURAT, India*

16 September 1933

He was of unknown age and a landlord, property-owner and sand contractor. The river Tapti had swollen to such proportions that one of the sluices in the city wall had been damaged and water was pouring in through it, threatening to flood the city. Golandaz volunteered to dive into the flooded river and ascertain the nature and extent of the damage. He accomplished this brave feat successfully and then blocked the sluice with sandbags at considerable risk to his own life.

He owned a fleet of boats, which he often placed at the disposal of the authorities whenever Surat, Rander or the surrounding districts were threatened by floods. In 1930 he rescued the boys of the Government High School and the family of the excise inspector from flooding.

He died in 1949.

**Miner THOMAS THOMAS** (Edward Medal)

*BRYNAMMAN, GLAMORGAN, Wales*

21 September 1933

He was 21 years old and working at the Brynamman Colliery when there was an inrush of water at the pit. Thomas was working underground at the time. At great personal risk, he assisted a youth who had lost his lamp and was unable, in the darkness and water, to make his way to safety. They both reached a place where several others had gathered. The miners then divided into two groups, one group seeking a way out via an airway and the other via a roadway that was flooded and obstructed by a mass of timber and rails washed down by the water. Thomas took up the rear in the roadway group, which succeeded in reaching safety; he then returned, at considerable peril to himself, to find the other group, which then escaped by the same route, Thomas being the last to leave the pit.

He died on 19 July 1984.

**Babu RANGIT SINGH** (Empire Gallantry Medal)
*JHARVAN, SAHARANPUR DISTRICT, India*
1934

He was of unknown age and working as a revenue officer when he received information that a gang of twenty-five dacoits armed with shotguns and lathis were attacking the house of a wealthy Bania. He collected four men and proceeded at once to the house and attacked the dacoits, his only weapon being a pistol. Even when two of his men had been wounded and his pistol jammed, he continued to attack. Eventually, after wounding one of the gang, he succeeded in driving them off, and thus, by his prompt action and conspicuous bravery, was able to stop a very serious incident.

He died in October 1942.

**Major DOUGLAS BRETT** (Empire Gallantry Medal)
*CHITTAGONG, India*
7 January 1934

He was 37 years old and serving in the 9th Jat Regiment, Indian Army when four Hindu terrorists attacked a group of forty or fifty Europeans, including women and children, at the end of a cricket match. The terrorists were armed with a revolver and seven bombs. Two bombs were thrown but failed to explode. One of the terrorists then ran at the Europeans, firing his revolver rapidly as he went. Major Brett, who was unarmed, rushed at this man, grappled with him and forced him to the ground, holding his gun arm against the ground until help arrived. Captain Richard Deedes, seeing another terrorist running away, went in pursuit; he closed with the man and fell on him, holding him down until help arrived.

Brett died on 1 December 1963.

**Captain RICHARD DEEDES** (Empire Gallantry Medal)
*CHITTAGONG, India*
7 January 1934

He was 38 years old and serving in the King's Shropshire Light Infantry when four Hindu terrorists attacked a group of forty or fifty Europeans, including women and children, at the end of a cricket match. The terrorists were armed with a revolver and seven bombs. Two bombs were thrown but failed to explode. One of the terrorists then ran at the Europeans, firing his revolver rapidly as he went. Major Brett, who was unarmed, rushed at this man, grappled with him and forced him to the ground, holding his gun arm against the ground until help arrived. Captain Richard Deedes, seeing another terrorist running away, went in pursuit; he closed with the man and fell on him, holding him down until help arrived.

Deedes also served in both world wars. He died on 28 August 1975.

**Nursing Sister DOROTHY THOMAS** (Empire Gallantry Medal)

*MIDDLESEX, England*

26 January 1934

She was 28 years old and working as a nursing sister. A porter was changing the reducing valve on a large oxygen cylinder in the anaesthetic room of the main theatre at the Middlesex Hospital when there was an explosion, probably due to a piece of grit impinging on the valve and causing a spark. Following the explosion, the issuing oxygen caught fire and a stream of sparks and flames shot through the open door for a distance of 15ft. The theatre was immediately vacated as it was feared the cylinder would explode at any minute.

Sister Thomas waited behind until everyone was clear and then removed the ether from the anaesthetic room and shut the doors, minimising the effect of the expected explosion. After a moment's reflection, however, she decided that it was her duty to try to avert the wrecking of the theatre, so she re-entered the anaesthetic room, ran to the cylinder and turned it off by the tap below the valve.

Sister Thomas showed great bravery and coolness as she and all present believed that the cylinder might blow up at any moment. She died on 22 November 1989.

**Mr EDWARDO OMARA** (Empire Gallantry Medal)

*ADODOI, Uganda*

February and October 1934

He was 24 years old and a native game scout. Another game scout, who was anxious to punish a herd of marauding elephants, wounded two, but then one of them charged and pinned him to the ground. Omara pulled out the scout's rifle from between the elephant's feet, but was unable to reload it so he attacked the elephant with his spear. He drove it off and eventually killed it, and then carried the scout for three hours to Adilang, but the scout died from his injuries.

On another occasion, when an elephant which had been burnt in a bush fire and was consequently in a most dangerous temper, took possession of a village waterhole and terrorised the locals, Omara, at great personal risk and in the interests of his fellow villagers killed it with a heavy hunting spear.

He died in 1980.

**Shri BHUPENDRA NARAYAN SINGH** (Empire Gallantry Medal)

*DARJEELING, India*

8 May 1934

He was of unknown age and working for Garth Barwari, Bhagalpur District, Bihar and Orissa. The horses were being led in after the Governor's Cup race at Lebong racecourse when an attempt was made by two Bengali youths to assassinate the Governor, Sir John Anderson, who was standing in his box facing the racecourse. Mr Tandy-Green was on the judges' stand; hearing a gunshot, he looked around and saw a man pointing an automatic pistol at Anderson. He rushed at him immediately and brought him down. The two men rolled together

90

to the bottom of the steps, where Tandy-Green pinned the assailant to the ground until others came to his assistance, disarming and securing the youth.

Bhupendra Narayan Singh was in the race stand outside the Governor's box. On hearing the shot, and seeing that the other assailant was taking aim with his revolver resting on the rail separating the stand from the box, he immediately grappled with him, endeavouring to pull him back and at the same time to divert his aim. While the two were struggling, two shots were fired by the Governor's personal guard and the Superintendant of Police. These hit the assailant but failed to immobilise him. Both men fell to the ground and others came to assist, and the man was quickly overcome.

Bhupendra Narayan Singh died on 25 December 1961.

## Mr CHARLES TANDY-GREEN (Empire Gallantry Medal)
*DARJEELING, India*
8 May 1934
He was 36 years old and working at the Bengal Public Works Department. The horses were being led in after the Governor's Cup race at Lebong racecourse when an attempt was made by two Bengali youths to assassinate the Governor, Sir John Anderson, who was standing in his box facing the racecourse. Mr Tandy-Green was on the judges' stand; hearing a gunshot, he looked around and saw a man pointing an automatic pistol at Anderson. He rushed at him immediately and brought him down. The two men rolled together to the bottom of the steps, where Tandy-Green pinned the assailant to the ground until others came to his assistance, disarming and securing the youth.

Bhupendra Narayan Singh was in the race stand outside the Governor's box. On hearing the shot, and seeing that the other assailant was taking aim with his revolver resting on the rail separating the stand from the box, he immediately grappled with him, endeavouring to pull him back and at the same time to divert his aim. While the two were struggling, two shots were fired by the Governor's personal guard and the Superintendant of Police. These hit the assailant but failed to immobilise him. Both men fell to the ground and others came to assist, and the man was quickly overcome.

Tandy-Green also served in the Second World War. He died on 26 September 1978.

## Captain PATRICK TAYLOR (Empire Gallantry Medal)
*TASMAN SEA, Australia*
15 May 1935
He was 38 years old and working as a navigator and pilot. He was acting as navigator in the monoplane *Southern Cross*, piloted by Sir Charles Kingsford-Smith, when about 600 miles from Sydney the starboard engine failed and they had to turn back. The strain on the other two engines began to tell and soon the port engine began to use too much oil. Fuel and cargo were jettisoned but the aircraft lost height and at times was only a few feet above the water. Taylor climbed out

of the cockpit and carried oil by means of a vacuum flask to the overheating engine. In all, he had to do this six times. This incredible feat, and the skilful handling of the aircraft by the pilot, resulted in the plane arriving safely back at the airport after sixteen hours in the air.

Taylor also served in both world wars. He died on 15 December 1966.

### Lance Naik MATA DIN (Empire Gallantry Medal)
*QUETTA, India*
31 May 1935
He was 21 years old and serving in the 4th Battalion, Hyderabad Regiment, Indian Army when he showed conspicuous devotion to duty by excavating a man who was buried in a very dangerous place after an earthquake. Three rescue parties had already made attempts to free him, but had given up as there was very imminent danger of the working parties being buried alive.

Mata Din died on 29 May 1967.

### Private ROBERT SPOORS (Albert Medal)
*QUETTA, India*
31 May 1935
He was 24 years old and serving in the 1st Battalion, West Yorkshire Regiment (Prince of Wales's Own) when, after the earthquake, he entered Major O'Hanlon's house. It was in a very dangerous condition, but he cleared a path for Mrs O'Hanlon and was mainly responsible for saving her life. He then re-entered the house at great personal risk to save the nurse and baby, but was himself trapped in the debris and was later rescued by two men and brought out in an exhausted condition. He subsequently worked for long hours at the British Military Hospital.

Spoors also served in the Second World War, being awarded the MM. He died on 28 February 1984.

### Nurse FLORENCE ALLEN (Albert Medal)
*QUETTA, India*
31 May 1935
She was 28 years old and serving as a children's nurse to Christopher Turner when, during the Quetta earthquake, she was woken by the rumbling noise and falling masonry. She rushed over to Christopher's cot but was unable to lift him out because the mosquito net was in the way; as the house collapsed around her, she threw herself on top of the child. The boy escaped with just a small scratch but Allen was buried beneath the rubble for two days with both legs and an arm broken.

Speaking nearly fifty years later she recalled: 'Bones were broken in my arm and legs and they had a job to get me out. When you think that 35,000 people were killed by that earthquake it takes some thinking about. It's not something you forget. When I lay buried I remember calling out for water and saying "quickly".

A black hand appeared through the rubble with a cigarette case full of water. I never got to meet that man.'

In 1982 Florence Allen was attacked in her own flat. She was tipped from her wheelchair, punched and robbed. She commented later: 'If I hadn't been in a wheelchair, I would have had a go at him.' She died on 1 August 1985.

## Lieutenant JOHN COWLEY (Albert Medal)
*QUETTA, India*
31 May–1 June 1935
He was 29 years old and serving in the Corps of Royal Engineers. After the earthquake he and his party were the first to start relief work at the civil hospital, where the walls had collapsed, bringing down the roof on the inmates. At first the men were too few in number to lift off the roof, so they raised pieces up for short periods while Cowley crawled under them and dragged out survivors from their beds. The patients were already in the hospital before the earthquake and were mostly quite helpless. Cowley lifted many men in his arms regardless of the warnings that they were suffering from all manner of illnesses. Had it not been for his work and the excellent example shown by him to his men, very many more men would have died.

Cowley also served in the Second World War. He died on 7 January 1993.

## Havildar AHMED YAR (Empire Gallantry Medal)
*QUETTA, India*
31 May–1 June 1935
He was of unknown age and serving in the 24th Mountain Brigade, Royal Artillery, Indian Army. His unit was early on the scene of the earthquake. He worked down a hole 15ft below a very unsafe wall for five-and-a-half hours, extricating a man who was eventually found unharmed. During his time there were several aftershocks of great intensity, and in any of these there was the grave risk of being buried. This NCO was continuously on duty from the time of the earthquake until the battery returned to its lines on the evening of 3 June. He never failed to set the highest possible standards of leadership, discipline and personal work.

He died on 31 August 1986.

## Naik NANDLAL THAPA (Empire Gallantry Medal)
*QUETTA, India*
31 May–1 June 1935
He was 32 or 33 years old and serving in the 2nd Battalion, 8th Gurkha Rifles, Indian Army when his detachment was sent to help after the Quetta earthquake. On arrival there was no time to collect tools and they worked with their hands for three hours in one of the most severely damaged parts of the city. During this time minor shocks frequently occurred, causing further falls of masonry. This NCO showed conspicuous bravery in the manner in which he entered tottering

buildings in search of survivors and in the work and initiative he displayed in removing them. As a result of his disregard for his own safety, ten people were rescued alive. He fully realised the risks he ran, but was always ready to enter any building where there was any possibility of anybody remaining alive.

Thapa is the only Gurkha to be awarded the GC. He died on 27 June 1987.

### Lance Corporal GEORGE HENSHAW (Empire Gallantry Medal)
*QUETTA, India*
31 May–1 June 1935

He was 25 years old and serving in the 1st Battalion, Queen's Royal (West Surrey) Regiment. After the earthquake his unit was sent to the Quetta Grammar School. Henshaw showed an utter disregard for his own safety and was prominent in the rescue operations in what was an extremely dangerous building. Later he was employed in rescue work in St John's Road, where an Indian child was located below some wreckage, above which was a large amount of debris liable to fall at any moment. Henshaw dug under the wreckage and dragged the child out alive.

Henshaw also served in the Second World War. He died on 14 February 1973.

### Private ARTHUR BROOKS (Empire Gallantry Medal)
*QUETTA, India*
31 May–1 June 1935

He was 26 years old and serving in the 1st Battalion, Queen's Royal (West Surrey) Regiment. After the Quetta earthquake a party of military policemen located a man lying 18ft beneath debris and close to a wall in a very dangerous condition. They dug down to a point within 5ft of the man, but due to the imminent danger of the wall collapsing they were unable to get any further. Brooks then dug through the remainder of the wreckage with his bare hands, reached the man and removed him uninjured. Throughout he was in imminent danger of being buried alive. His action showed complete disregard for his personal safety. He had also been prominent in rescue work at the Quetta Grammar School.

He died in January 1957.

### Private ERNEST ELSTON (Empire Gallantry Medal)
*QUETTA, India*
31 May–1 June 1935

He was 26 years old and serving in the 1st Battalion, West Yorkshire Regiment (Prince of Wales's Own). After the earthquake he worked with untiring energy. He was personally responsible for saving the lives of several Indians buried under debris and worked at great risk for over four hours to rescue an Indian child entombed under a collapsed two-storey building. He had heard the child crying, and in order to reach it he had to tunnel his way beneath some very unsafe debris. In doing so he came across the dead bodies of several other family members, but found the child alive and brought it out safely.

Elston also served in the Second World War. He died on 8 August 1982.

**Lance Sergeant ALFRED 'JOE' LUNGLEY** (Empire Gallantry Medal)
*QUETTA, India*
2 June 1935
He was 29 years old and serving in the 24th Mountain Battery, Royal Artillery when an earthquake survivor was located in the wreckage of a house on the east side of Bruce Road. In order to extricate the man, it was necessary for Lungley to dig to the bottom of a deep hole surrounded and overhung by tottering masonry. This was liable to collapse during any minor shocks, several of which occurred during the rescue work. Lungley showed the greatest zeal and disregard for his own safety, although he was already suffering from a severe foot injury. The man was recovered alive.

Lungley also served in the Second World War. He died on 31 December 1989.

**Private RICHARD BLACKBURN** (Empire Gallantry Medal)
*KASAULI, India*
7 June 1935
He was 22 years old and serving in the 1st Battalion, Cheshire Regiment. During a forest fire, he was with a party of men threatened by the flames and obliged to retire. Captain Reed, who was in charge, became separated from his men and was unable to make his way to safety. Looking back, Blackburn saw Captain Reed stumbling about in a daze, his clothing alight. He immediately returned and extinguished the burning clothes with his hands and then took the captain to a place that offered some protection from the flames. But for Private Blackburn's action, it seems certain that Captain Reed would have perished in the fire. Unfortunately Captain Reed did not survive for very long.

Blackburn also served in the Second World War. He died on 31 January 1992.

**Colliery Agent NORMAN BASTER** (Edward Medal)
*SOUTH KIRKBY, YORKSHIRE, England*
22/23 August 1935
He was 43 years old and working at the South Kirkby Colliery when two explosions occurred in a district 1.5 miles from the shaft. It was thought that these were due to a gob fire, and it was decided to seal off part of the district by erecting stoppings. At 3pm on the 23rd this work was in progress; there were twenty-one men in the district, some near the face and others, including George Beaman, at distances up to 100yds away. A further explosion occurred, injuring a number of the men. Beaman and two others at once proceeded to look for and help the injured and with the assistance of others ten men were carried out of the district alive, although only one survived.

During repeated journeys to and from the face, some of the rescuers were affected by fumes and it was discovered that Mr Dale was missing. Although there was an increasing risk of further explosions, a search was started by Norman Baster; together with five other men he located Dale but he was dead. They proceeded to remove his body but another explosion caused burns to all six men.

This explosion also injured many of the men back at the shaft who were looking after the first men injured.

Baster got back and did what he could to reassure these men and then, with three others, including George Beaman, he went in and removed Dale's body and looked for another man called Ball, who was said to be missing. Baster had no breathing apparatus, and was so affected by the fumes that he had to retire, but Beaman and another man went on, only giving up when it was reported that Ball had reached the shaft.

After the rescue parties had left the mine, it was found that Ball was missing. James Pollitt led the rescue party that went back down the mine to find him, despite fears of another explosion. They succeeded in finding Ball and returned to the surface.

Baster also served in the Second World War. He died on 11 April 1987.

## Miner GEORGE BEAMAN (Edward Medal)
*SOUTH KIRKBY, YORKSHIRE, England*
22/23 August 1935

He was 31 years old and working at the South Kirkby Colliery when two explosions occurred in a district 1.5 miles from the shaft. It was thought that these were due to a gob fire, and it was decided to seal off part of the district by erecting stoppings. At 3pm on the 23rd this work was in progress; there were twenty-one men in the district, some near the face and others, including George Beaman, at distances up to 100yds away. A further explosion occurred, injuring a number of the men. Beaman and two others at once proceeded to look for and help the injured and with the assistance of others ten men were carried out of the district alive, although only one survived.

During repeated journeys to and from the face, some of the rescuers were affected by fumes and it was discovered that Mr Dale was missing. Although there was an increasing risk of further explosions, a search was started by Norman Baster; together with five other men he located Dale but he was dead. They proceeded to remove his body but another explosion caused burns to all six men. This explosion also injured many of the men back at the shaft who were looking after the first men injured.

Baster got back and did what he could to reassure these men and then, with three others, including George Beaman, he went in and removed Dale's body and looked for another man called Ball, who was said to be missing. Baster had no breathing apparatus, and was so affected by the fumes that he had to retire, but Beaman and another man went on, only giving up when it was reported that Ball had reached the shaft.

After the rescue parties had left the mine, it was found that Ball was missing. James Pollitt led the rescue party that went back down the mine to find him, despite fears of another explosion. They succeeded in finding Ball and returned to the surface.

Beaman also served in the Second World War. He died in June 1949.

**Under Manager JAMES POLLITT** (Edward Medal)
*SOUTH KIRKBY, YORKSHIRE, England*
22/23 August 1935

He was 38 years old and working at the South Kirkby Colliery when two explosions occurred in a district 1.5 miles from the shaft. It was thought that these were due to a gob fire, and it was decided to seal off part of the district by erecting stoppings. At 3pm on the 23rd this work was in progress; there were twenty-one men in the district, some near the face and others, including George Beaman, at distances up to 100yds away. A further explosion occurred, injuring a number of the men. Beaman and two others at once proceeded to look for and help the injured and with the assistance of others ten men were carried out of the district alive, although only one survived.

During repeated journeys to and from the face, some of the rescuers were affected by fumes and it was discovered that Mr Dale was missing. Although there was an increasing risk of further explosions, a search was started by Norman Baster; together with five other men he located Dale but he was dead. They proceeded to remove his body but another explosion caused burns to all six men. This explosion also injured many of the men back at the shaft who were looking after the first men injured.

Baster got back and did what he could to reassure these men and then, with three others, including George Beaman, he went in and removed Dale's body and looked for another man called Ball, who was said to be missing. Baster had no breathing apparatus, and was so affected by the fumes that he had to retire, but Beaman and another man went on, only giving up when it was reported that Ball had reached the shaft.

After the rescue parties had left the mine, it was found that Ball was missing. James Pollitt led the rescue party that went back down the mine to find him, despite fears of another explosion. They succeeded in finding Ball and returned to the surface.

Pollitt died on 8 September 1972.

**Yard Foreman EDWIN CROSSLEY** (Empire Gallantry Medal)
*CHATHAM, KENT, England*
October 1935

He was 51 years old and working as yard foreman at the Admiralty Dockyard when two workmen on board a ship descended into a compartment to recover tools and other items and were overcome by carbon monoxide gas. On hearing what had happened, Crossley seized a tackle and descended into the compartment with two skilled labourers. The rescuers were successful in securing one man and hoisting him through the hatchway above. They then secured the second man but, owing to the effects of the gas, could not help further and he was pulled up to safety by others on the deck above. The rescuers showed courage of the highest order and Crossley took the initiative to lead the party.

He died on 10 February 1976.

**Pit Manager GEORGE HESLOP** (Edward Medal)
*YORKSHIRE, England*
17 December 1935
He was 49 years old and working at the Loftus Ironstone Mine when a roof fall occurred. John Henry and Henry Murrell were buried in the debris. On arriving at the scene, although falls were still occurring, he at once crawled under the fall into a cavity of about 2ft until he reached Henry, but could not free him as his legs were trapped. He then instructed the men to pile a road through the fall to protect Henry from further falls. Then he again crawled under the fall and located Murrell, who was pinned by his foot. Heslop gave him a stimulant and then worked strenuously for four hours in a cavity so small that there was room for only one person, until he freed him. Falls were continually occurring and he was in danger of being buried himself, but despite calls from workmen and officials Heslop again crawled into the cavity to Henry and supervised his rescue, releasing him after being trapped for eight hours. Shortly afterwards there was a heavy fall and the whole piling which had been erected to assist in the rescue collapsed. Sadly both men died later from shock.

Heslop had also served in the First World War, in which he was awarded the MC. He declined to exchange his EM for the GC. He died on 29 March 1978.

**Yuzbashi El AMIN EFFENDI HEMEIDA** (sometimes spelt **HUMMEIDA**) (aka **AGABANI**) (Empire Gallantry Medal)
*OMDURMAN, Sudan*
4 January 1936
He was 36 years old and serving in the Sudan Defence Force. He was in charge of a party engaged in making explosive charges when a charge being assembled in another part of the room accidentally exploded, killing one NCO and injuring a Native Officer and eight NCOs. The building was extensively damaged and fire broke out in several places. Hemeida, although uninjured, was badly shaken and dazed. On recovering, and fully realising the likelihood of further explosions, he immediately went to the assistance of the injured, and then took active steps to extinguish the fires and remove the unharmed charges to a place of safety. His gallant action was instrumental in saving at least one life among the injured and undoubtedly prevented further explosions.

Hemeida also served in the Second World War. He died on 25 May 1973.

**European Shift Superintendent WILLIAM JAMIESON** (Empire Gallantry Medal)
*PRESTEA, Gold Coast (now Ghana)*
7 January 1936
He was 37 years old and working at the Ariston Gold Mine. When he was being lowered underground he found a native workman lying unconscious on the shaft station. As the man appeared to have been gassed, Jamieson, with a companion, decided to investigate the cause. On passing through the ventilation door at the

back of the shaft station they found three more boys lying about 50ft from the door. It was evident that they had also been gassed; they were removed to the shaft station. After another 900ft they found another boy lying across the track; Mr Jamieson sent him back with two boys and continued alone to the working face. There he found six more boys lying in a very serious condition and he at once proceeded to drag them back out of the fumes. He eventually had to be helped out of the mine himself as he was unable to walk without assistance. His prompt and gallant action, carried out at great personal risk, undoubtedly saved many lives.

He died on 28 September 1965.

### Lance Corporal WILLIAM BARNETT (Empire Gallantry Medal)
*Palestine*
15 April–14 September 1936
He was 23 years old and serving in the 1st Battalion, Royal Scots Fusiliers at a time when the Arabs were discontented with the continued British presence and increasing Jewish immigration. The initial disturbances lasted from April to October. There were many incidents, and in one week alone 168 Arabs and Jews were killed. Barnett distinguished himself during these emergency operations.

Barnett also served in the Second World War. He died on 10 September 1972.

### Inspector GEORGE ADAMSON (Empire Gallantry Medal)
*CALCUTTA, India*
6 May 1936
He was 40 years old and serving in the River Traffic Police when he, with Assistant River Surveyor Cecil Kelly acting as pilot, was in charge of two Port Police launches escorting a cargo of defective dynamite being taken for destruction up the River Hooghly in a barge. The barge proved to be quite unseaworthy, and after travelling 15 miles up the river was in danger of sinking. Adamson and his men's only responsibility was for escorting the cargo, but despite this they tried, at great personal risk to themselves, to keep the barge afloat by bailing water from 7pm to midnight, when it was found necessary to beach the barge. In spite of the dynamite exuding nitroglycerine, Adamson worked with two sergeants indefatigably in the water and the dark to guide the barge ashore by hand. This took five-and-a-half hours. The barge was then partially unloaded, but the last 2 tons could not be moved because of its dangerous condition, and the barge was refloated, towed into deep water and sunk. Adamson rendered great assistance during the whole operation, and stood by in a police launch in spite of the danger. Kelly supervised the handling of the barge throughout and without his skilled assistance the feat could not have been accomplished. Although it was not his duty as pilot, he remained in the barge while it was towed off the beach and, until it was safely sunk, supervised its handling in the current with the aid of two launches. The dynamite could have exploded at any time in its condition. Both men were awarded the EGM.

Adamson also served in both world wars. He died on 14 March 1976.

**Assistant River Surveyor CECIL KELLY** (Empire Gallantry Medal)

*CALCUTTA, India*

6 May 1936

He was 36 years old and serving in the Port Commissioners when he was acting as pilot of two Port Police launches, with Inspector George Adamson, escorting a cargo of defective dynamite being taken for destruction up the River Hooghly in a barge. The barge proved to be quite unseaworthy, and after travelling 15 miles up the river was in danger of sinking. Adamson and his men's only responsibility was for escorting the cargo, but despite this they tried, at great personal risk to themselves, to keep the barge afloat by bailing water from 7pm to midnight, when it was found necessary to beach the barge. In spite of the dynamite exuding nitro-glycerine, Adamson worked with two sergeants indefatigably in the water and the dark to guide the barge ashore by hand. This took five-and-a-half hours. The barge was then partially unloaded, but the last 2 tons could not be moved because of its dangerous condition, and the barge was refloated, towed into deep water and sunk. Adamson rendered great assistance during the whole operation, and stood by in a police launch in spite of the danger. Kelly supervised the handling of the barge throughout and without his skilled assistance the feat could not have been accomplished. Although it was not his duty as pilot, he remained in the barge while it was towed off the beach and, until it was safely sunk, supervised its handling in the current with the aid of two launches. The dynamite could have exploded at any time in its condition. Both men were awarded the EGM.

Kelly died on 23 November 1948.

**Begum ASHRA-un-NISA** (often incorrectly spelt **ASHRAF**) (Empire Gallantry Medal)

*HYDERABAD, India*

14 June 1936

She was of unknown age when a fire broke out in the Moti Mahal cinema. She was sitting in the purdah balcony with many women and children. The fire cut off both exits, so she stripped herself of her sari, tied it to the balcony railing and lowered five women to the lower floor, from where they escaped. Her own escape she left so long that she was unable to descend by the sari and had to jump, injuring herself in so doing and actually losing consciousness. Fourteen people burnt to death in the blaze.

Ashra-un-Nisa died in 1947.

**Private FRANK NAUGHTON** (Empire Gallantry Medal)

*RIVER INDRAYANI, India*

5 August 1936

He was 21 years old and serving in the Royal Tank Corps when he was engaged in recovering an armoured car which had broken down on an 'Irish Bridge' (probably a ford). When Lance Corporal S. Temple lost his footing and was in imminent danger of being swept away by the current, Private Robert Campbell

100

released his grip on the lifeline and held on to Temple, but both men were swept into the river, where there were very swift and dangerous currents.

Private Naughton, who was fully clothed, immediately dived off the bridge to render assistance. He was drawn under the water several times, and it was only with the utmost difficulty that he was able to overcome the strong currents. He regained shallow water and was almost exhausted. Despite this, when he saw a body appear on the surface, 40yds away, he again entered the water, and swimming with difficulty succeeded in bringing Temple, who was by this time unconscious, into shallow water, from where both men were assisted ashore. By his courageous action and absolute disregard for his personal safety, he saved the life of Private Temple. But sadly Private Campbell drowned.

Naughton also served in the Second World War. He died on 18 June 2004, the last survivor of the 1940 EGM exchanges.

### Senior Shipwright Diver CHARLES 'POP' or 'FISTICUFFS' DUFFIN (Empire Gallantry Medal)
*PORTSMOUTH, England*
19/20 August 1936
He was 50 years old and was working at HM Dockyard when a diver, Charles Gustar, was engaged under water examining the launching gear below HMS *Aurora*. Signals of distress were received, so the stand-by diver, George Brown, went down and found Gustar jammed between the top of a dagger plank connecting launching poppets and the bottom of the hull. Duffin was sent for, as an additional diver to co-operate in the rescue work. Gustar was found to be securely wedged, with his head, arms and weights hanging over the inboard side of the inside dagger planks and his trunk and legs between the inner and outer planks. Duffin then squeezed himself up between the two adjacent planks and with a handsaw cut through the plank on one side, while Brown released the two 10-inch screws joining the plank to the next plank.

By this means the portion of the plank imprisoning Gustar was removed. Duffin seized Gustar and forced him down between his own body and the poppets, towards Brown, who dragged him down and took him to the surface. The risks were great as at any time Duffin could have been trapped in the same way as Gustar. Duffin said of the rescue, 'It was nothing at all really – just an incident in a day's work.'

He died on 5 January 1959.

### Dr ROBERT SAUNDERS (Edward Medal)
*SALISBURY, Rhodesia*
4/5 January 1937
He was 32 years old and working as a doctor in Salisbury when there was an accident in the Tebekwe Mine. Howard Sheasby was trapped underground by a fall of rock and was completely buried. Dr Saunders arrived on the scene at 3.30pm, by which time a rescue party had succeeded in recovering most of the

spillage from around Sheasby's body. It was found, however, that his left hand was firmly held between two timbers. He remained in this dangerous position until 12.30pm the following day.

During the whole of this time (with the exception of short breaks for food) Dr Saunders remained underground rendering every medical assistance under extremely difficult and dangerous conditions. Sheasby's situation was such that, in order to attend his patient at all, the doctor had to lie on top of him with his back in close proximity to a dangerously shaky roof, any disturbance of which would have resulted in a fall of rock sufficient to crush them both.

After sixteen hours, and when all efforts to free him had failed, it was decided to amputate his arm. The conditions only allowed left-handed work and the operation was carried out by a left-handed volunteer, Mr J.M. Barry, under the personal supervision of Dr Saunders. Sheasby was then transported to the surface, where he made a full recovery.

Saunders died on 14 September 1981.

### Pilot Officer GERALD CLOSE (Empire Gallantry Medal)
*WAZIRISTAN, India*
13 April 1937
He was 23 years old and serving in 59 Squadron, RAF when a Westland Wapiti laden with bombs crashed on take-off and burst into flames at Miranshah aerodrome. Close hastened to the scene of the accident and, in spite of the explosion of bombs and small arms ammunition, made persistent attempts to extinguish the flames and to rescue the crew until ordered to withdraw by a senior officer.

Close was killed in action while bombing Boulogne docks on 9 May 1941.

### Naik BARKAT SINGH (Empire Gallantry Medal)
*MEERUT, India*
2 May 1937
He was 32 years old and serving in the 10th Battalion, 2nd Punjab Regiment when Sepoy Kanshi Ram, of the same unit, ran amok. He shot dead the guard commander and mortally wounded another sepoy of the guard, then went off with his rifle loaded and bayonet fixed, with additional rounds in his pouches and shouting, 'If any Hindu comes near me I will shoot him.' He pursued Subadar Gopi Ram with the intention of killing him. On temporarily losing sight of Ram, he stood undecided for a second, looking around for him, with his rifle at the high port, ready to shoot. While in this position he was grappled by Naik Barkat Singh, who was unarmed, and who showed great promptitude and courage in seizing the sepoy and pinioning his arms until others came to overpower him.

He died on 18 December 1991.

**Lieutenant PATRICK HUMPHREYS** (Empire Gallantry Medal)

*off the coast of ALMERIA, Spain*

13 May 1937

He was 24 years old and serving in the Royal Navy during the Spanish Civil War. When HMS *Hunter* was hit by a mine, Humphreys led a rescue party to the stoker petty officers' and torpedomen's mess decks. To reach the men on this deck, his party had to jump down 8ft, the ladder having being blown away, into 3ft of fuel oil and on to a deck that might not have been intact. During this time they remained in imminent risk of falling through the shattered deck into the oil and water below. Moreover, they were under the impression that the ship was about to founder. Their exertions to save life consisted in dragging living and dead men from under wreckage and out of the fuel oil and passing them up on deck. This operation lasted five to ten minutes. The rescued men were in very severe danger from swallowing fuel oil and had they been left they would undoubtedly have died.

As well as Humphreys, Petty Officer James Smail and Able Seamen James Collings, Ernest Thomas and Herbert Abrahams were also awarded the EGM. Stoker Petty Officer Peter Perring and Acting Leading Seaman Sidney Bevington were awarded the EGM for their part in helping to keep the ship afloat for as long as possible. Only Humphreys lived to exchange his medal for the GC.

Humphreys also served in the Second World War. He was killed in an aircraft crash on 26 November 1943.

**Miner DAVID BOOKER** (Edward Medal)

*SOUTH STAFFORDSHIRE, England*

14 May 1937

He was 26 years old and working at the Littleton Colliery when he, with his brother Samuel, was part of a rescue party trying to locate three missing men during a firedamp. Some of the party also collapsed, thereby adding to the task of the rescue workers. The brothers forced their way on four or five times, and were jointly responsible for extricating four rescuers who had succumbed to gas. All of these survived except Mr Richard Walmsley, the Under-Manager; the three missing men also died, bringing the total deaths to four. Both brothers were awarded the EM.

David died on 30 March 1982. They are the only brothers to be awarded the GC.

**Miner SAMUEL BOOKER** (Edward Medal)

*SOUTH STAFFORDSHIRE, England*

14 May 1937

He was 26 years old and working at the Littleton Colliery when he, with his brother David, was part of a rescue party trying to locate three missing men during a firedamp. Some of the party also collapsed, thereby adding to the task of the rescue workers. The brothers forced their way on four or five times, and were jointly responsible for extricating four rescuers who had succumbed to gas. All of these survived except Mr Richard Walmsley, the Under-Manager; the three missing men also died, bringing the total deaths to four. Both brothers were awarded the EM.

Samuel died in December 1979. They are the only brothers to be awarded the GC.

### Overman (Rescue Brigade Captain) AZARIAH (known as EZRA) CLARKE (Edward Medal)

*CHESTERTON, STAFFORDSHIRE, England*

2 July 1937

He was 46 years old and working at the Holditch Colliery when a fire started in the Four Feet Seam. It spread rapidly, but of the fifty-five men working in the affected area at the time all except two got away from the danger zone. As soon as it was realised that two men were missing, an unsuccessful search was made. At 6.50am there was an explosion and one of the search party was afterwards found to be missing. A call had been put out for the Colliery Rescue Brigade and by 7.30am Clarke had assembled three others at the pithead and proceeded to lead them below ground. The party met the managing director in the area of the fire, and he instructed them to search for the man who had been lost after the explosion.

They started their search in the hot, dusty atmosphere, foul with gas and smoke. On reaching a fall which blocked the way, they retraced their steps, but continued looking for the missing man, without success. The Rescue Brigade, now numbering five, next went in search of the two men lost at the time of the original fire. A severe explosion then occurred, resulting in the deaths of twenty-seven men, most of whom had been sent down to erect stoppings to seal off the fire.

During the two hours they had been underground the Rescue Brigade had survived two more explosions and had been working under the greatest difficulty. They then returned to the surface to renew their oxygen. Clarke again led his men into the danger zone, moving through falls of ground and derailed tubs, and passing other debris produced by the explosions; putting out a fire on the way, they came upon a number of badly injured men and dead bodies. They helped as much as they could and arranged for stretchers to be sent down for them. Clarke then went on, with assistance, to make a further examination of the workings with a view to ensuring that no living person had been left behind. By 3.35pm, satisfied that there was no one left and knowing that further explosions were likely, Clarke withdrew his men from the mine.

Later, some doubts arose as to whether there might still be some injured men alive in the pit; Clarke once again led his men down the mine. Despite an exhaustive search, they found no one and returned to the surface at 8pm.

Clarke had also served in the First World War. He died on 17 February 1975.

**Aircraftman WILLIAM McALONEY** (Albert Medal)
*HAMILTON, VICTORIA, Australia*
31 August 1937
He was 27 years old and serving in 1 Squadron, Royal Australian Air Force when a Hawker Demon fighter crashed on take-off. Despite the fact that the aircraft was burning from nose to tail, McAloney dashed into the flames and continued his efforts to rescue the crew until he was pulled away in an unconscious condition, having received severe burns that necessitated his removal to hospital. The crew, Flying Officer K. McKenzie, and Sergeant N. Torrens-Witherow, died in the inferno.

McAloney also served in the Second World War. He died on 31 August 1995.

**Private JOSEPH MOTT** (Empire Gallantry Medal)
*HAIFA, Palestine*
25 December 1937
He was 23 years old and serving in the 1st Battalion, Essex Regiment when a bomb was thrown into the Jordania Café, which was crowded with soldiers and civilians at the time. It landed at the feet of Private Mott; with the utmost coolness, he picked it up and hurled it through the window into the empty street, where it exploded with great force. This highly courageous act undoubtedly saved the lives of many people in the café.

Mott also served in the Second World War. He died on 12 January 1983.

**Rais RASHID ABDUL FATTAH** (Empire Gallantry Medal)
*Jordan*
1 and 4 March 1938
He was 37 years old and serving in the Trans-Jordan Frontier Force when he led a dismounted charge with his troop on a village strongly held by armed bandits. The attack involved house-to-house fighting under heavy fire, and, through his exceptional qualities of leadership and coolness, succeeded in capturing the village. On 4 July he again advanced to attack another village. He was heavily fired on, but by exceptional resource and bold leadership, he was able to seize a hill close to the village.

Fattah served in both world wars. He died on 21 August 1975.

**Quarryman BENJAMIN JONES** (Edward Medal)
*ABERGELE, Wales*
21 May 1938
He was 19 years old and working at the Llysfaen Quarry when he was about to carry out blasting with William Williams and a man called Roberts. Williams lit one fuse, Jones two and Roberts three, but then Roberts stood on a stone which tipped up and trapped his foot so that he could not move. The shots were timed to go off in eighty seconds. Williams and Jones tried to release Roberts, but failed. Then Williams shouted to the others to pull out the fuses and promptly pulled

out four himself. Jones pulled out one and Roberts the other. In doing so they ran the considerable risk of the detonators exploding. The prompt action of Williams and Jones undoubtedly saved Roberts' life at great risk to themselves. Both men were awarded the EM, but only Jones lived to exchange his for the GC.

Jones also served in the Second World War. He died on 5 August 1975.

### Qaid YOUSEF HUSSEIN ALI BEY (Arabic spelling YOSEF BEY ALI) (Empire Gallantry Medal)
*KHIRBET, SAMRA, Jordan*
5 July 1938
He was 38 years old and serving in the Trans-Jordan Frontier Force when he displayed exceptional leadership and initiative. By his example, when his men were nearly exhausted by heat and under heavy fire, he was an inspiration to further efforts which resulted in the defeat of an enemy gang, capturing prisoners and weapons. In spite of his life being threatened, he continued to produce valuable intelligence.

Ali Bey also served in the Second World War; in the words of his son, 'He worked with Winston Churchill and Charles de Gaulle during the Second World War.' He died on 18 October 1985.

### Chief Engine Room Artificer FREDERICK ANDERSON (Empire Gallantry Medal)
*SHANGHAI, China*
25 July 1938
He was 35 years old and serving in the Royal Navy when a Chinese gunman fired on an inspector of the Salt Revenue Office, wounding him. Anderson and Detective Sergeant Hillhouse gave chase. The would-be assassin then fired on a Chinese police officer, who, falling to the ground, fired one shot at the assailant, with effect. Anderson and Hillhouse closed in on the gunman. Anderson was slightly in front, which meant Hillhouse was unable to fire. Anderson then jumped on to the back of the assailant and began grappling with him; he, however, managed to fire another round, grazing Hillhouse's leg. When HIllhouse was able to manoeuvre into position, he fired two shots at the assailant, who then dropped his pistol and was arrested.

Anderson also served in the Second World War. He died on 31 July 1986.

### Pit Deputy FRED HALLER (born HAWLER) (Edward Medal)
*DONCASTER, YORKSHIRE, England*
8 October 1938
He was 46 years old and working at Rossington Main Colliery when a driver named Dakin, who was engaged in enlarging the road, went missing. Planks from a fence that shut off a heading due to dangerous amounts of gas had been pushed aside and a light could be seen some distance up the heading. Godfrey and his son, who had been working with Dakin, concluded he must have entered the

heading for some reason, so Godfrey's son went for help while Godfrey turned on a compressed air hose but it did not reach the fence. When Haller arrived he sent for more hosepipe and, taking a singlet that was saturated with water, he went up the heading to rescue Dakin, whom he could see some 40yds away. Advancing cautiously so as not to exhaust himself, he reached the unconscious man and, with considerable effort, dragged him back to the fence, where he arrived in an exhausted condition. There is no doubt that Dakin would have died were it not for Haller's action.

Haller had also served in the First World War. He died on 17 September 1983.

## Mr ERNEST KENT (Edward Medal)
*LONDON, England*
25/26 October 1938

He was 24 years old and working at Hackney Wick Stadium when a gang of workmen were engaged in piling work. Metal cylinders about 15in in diameter were being sunk into the ground, the earth inside then being removed. At about 2.30am they encountered an obstruction. Herbert Baker, a small man, volunteered to be lowered down into the cylinder, presumably so he could clear the obstruction with his feet. About 12ft down he called for help, and the men began to pull him up, but before he reached the top he lost his grip and fell to the bottom of the cylinder.

Kent, who was also a small man, volunteered to be lowered down head first in an attempt to pull Baker out. However, he gave signs of being distressed and was hauled up in a state of semi-collapse and bleeding from the mouth. Another man, Frank Davlin, then volunteered to be lowered but his shoulders got stuck and he had to be pulled back up. In the meantime Kent had recovered somewhat and insisted on being lowered down again. This time he succeeded in grasping hold of Baker; as they were pulled up, Kent had just sufficient strength to retain his grip until helpers grabbed Baker. Then Kent collapsed. Both men were rushed to hospital, where Baker was found to be dead.

Kent also served in the Second World War. He died on 23 August 1973.

## Fitter ROBERT LITTLE (Edward Medal)
*BLACKLEY, MANCHESTER, England*
11 January 1939

He was 41 years old and working at British Dyestuffs Corporation Ltd when Mr Martin, a fitter engaged on repairs in a chemical reaction pan, fell into the pan. Little, who was in charge of the shift, was called and, while rescue apparatus was being brought over, descended into the pan at great personal risk and found Martin to be unconscious. Due to the deadly gas, Little had to leave the pan but he re-entered it and started to carry his unconscious colleague up the ladder. Unfortunately, however, another man, Mr Wynne, who had started to go down the ladder, collapsed and fell on top of Little and the almost-rescued Martin, knocking them both to the bottom, where all three remained unconscious. The rescue party then arrived and brought them all to the surface. Little was the only one still alive.

Little had also served in the First World War. He died on 31 May 1976.

## Assistant Civil Engineer HAROLD CHARRINGTON (Empire Gallantry Medal)

*between JERUSALEM and HAIFA, Palestine*
3 February 1939

He was 28 years old and working for the Air Ministry Works Department when the aircraft he was travelling in went into an uncontrollable spin in poor weather, whereupon the pilot ordered everyone to bale out. Another passenger, Mr B. Timbers, also of the Air Ministry Works Department, attempted to climb over the side of the cockpit, but the air pressure held him down. He then managed to assume a position across the cockpit in an attempt to get out backwards and head first. He was still unable to get away so Charrington stayed to help him get clear, instead of going over the side himself.

Once Timbers had jumped, Charrington, with great difficulty, left the aircraft himself. By the time he made his escape he was so close to the ground that a few more seconds' delay would have been fatal. He hit the ground almost immediately after his parachute opened.

He died on 7 July 1976.

## Mr JOHN (known as JACK) DIXON (Edward Medal)

*LINCOLN, England*
16 February 1939

He was 25 years old and working at Robey & Co. Ltd when there was an accident which resulted in two large overhead electric cranes and the foundry roof being set on fire. Dixon, an electrician, who was on the crane gantry to watch the electrical equipment, was able to escape from immediate danger. One of the crane drivers, Whittaker, managed to climb out of the cabin but collapsed on top of the crane with his clothes ablaze. Seeing this, Dixon promptly went back to rescue him and managed to extinguish the flames, although the fire was at its height. Then he carried Whittaker to the crane in the next bay, out on to the roof and 31ft down a ladder to the ground. Dixon then collapsed; he was badly burned about the arms and upper body, and was absent from work for ten weeks. His action undoubtedly saved Whittaker's life.

He died on 13 April 1984.

## Mulazim THEODORE 'BOG' BOGDANOVITCH (sometimes spelt BOGDANOVICH) (Empire Gallantry Medal)

*ZEMAL, Jordan*
11 March 1939

He was 39 years old and serving in the Trans-Jordan Frontier Force when he was in charge of a mechanised troop dispatched to locate a reported band of armed raiders. He succeeded in finding them and pinned them down in a wadi until reinforcements arrived. He then, though under heavy fire, displayed outstanding leadership in advancing to the attack under cover of light machine-gun fire. When his superior officer, Lieutenant Macadam, was killed, he took charge of the situation, and gallantly led his men into the wadi, inflicting heavy casualties on them and driving the remainder on to the reinforcing men.

Bogdanovitch also served in the Second World War. He was assassinated by EOKA terrorists in Cyprus on 20 April 1956.

### Corporal THOMAS ATKINSON (Empire Gallantry Medal)
*JINSAFUT CAMP, Palestine*
15 March 1939
He was 23 years old and serving in the 1st Battalion, Green Howards (Alexandra, Princess of Wales's Own Yorkshire Regiment) when a truck caught fire. With Private Thomas McAvoy, Atkinson organised the removal of the remainder of the transport to a point clear of the burning truck.

Without this initiative and energy in rallying the drivers, and assisting them to move their trucks out of danger, the rest of the transport would have caught fire. Atkinson was subsequently indefatigable in his efforts to subdue the fire right up to the time that he was severely burnt while endeavouring to save the life of a comrade.

To avoid another explosion, McAvoy carried out the approved but dangerous task of piercing the petrol tank of the burning truck with a pickaxe. He too was badly burned, but together they succeeded in preventing a far worse disaster.

For the same incident Acting Company Sergeant Major John Brindle and Private Thomas Fowler were awarded the BEM for Meritorious Service.

Atkinson also served in the Second World War. He died on 26 March 1997.

### Private THOMAS McAVOY (Empire Gallantry Medal)
*JINSAFUT CAMP, Palestine*
15 March 1939
He was 29 years old and serving in the 1st Battalion, Green Howards (Alexandra, Princess of Wales's Own Yorkshire Regiment) when a truck caught fire. With Private Thomas McAvoy, Atkinson organised the removal of the remainder of the transport to a point clear of the burning truck.

Without this initiative and energy in rallying the drivers, and assisting them to move their trucks out of danger, the rest of the transport would have caught fire. Atkinson was subsequently indefatigable in his efforts to subdue the fire right up to the time that he was severely burnt while endeavouring to save the life of a comrade.

To avoid another explosion, McAvoy carried out the approved but dangerous task of piercing the petrol tank of the burning truck with a pickaxe. He too was badly burned, but together they succeeded in preventing a far worse disaster.

For the same incident Acting Company Sergeant Major John Brindle and Private Thomas Fowler were awarded the BEM for Meritorious Service.

McAvoy also served in the Second World War. He died on 20 May 1977.

## Mr FREDERICK CHILD (Empire Gallantry Medal)
*LONDON, England*
29 March 1939

He was 42 years old and walking across Hammersmith Bridge when he noticed a small leather suitcase on the structure of the bridge. Upon examination, he saw that it was smoking, so he climbed through the structure onto the side of the bridge and threw the case into the river. The explosion which followed sent up a 60ft column of water; this was followed by a second explosion on the bridge, but no one was hurt owing to Child's courage and presence of mind.

Child also served in both world wars. He died on 20 November 1975.

## Jib Crane Driver BERNARD FISHER (Edward Medal)
*SHEFFIELD, England*
26 April 1939

He was 27 years old and working for Steel, Peech & Tozer Ltd when a fire broke out in the cabin of an electrically driven gantry crane running at a height of 55ft. Its driver, William Hird, shouted for help before losing consciousness. Fisher, who was driving a travelling jib crane, heard the shouting and saw the fire. He promptly climbed from his own cab and ascended the ladder to the crane track. He crossed the 80ft span and descended the vertical ladder into the now blazing cabin. He then carried Hird through a trapdoor and up a vertical ladder 12ft to safety. Fisher's action, which was carried out at great personal risk, almost certainly saved Hird's life. He told a reporter: 'It was one of those things you do for a workmate without thinking of the danger.'

He died on 12 April 1992.

# CHAPTER SEVEN

# George Crosses Awarded during the Second World War

**Radio Officer JAMES TURNER** (Empire Gallantry Medal)
*off CAPE VINCENT, Portugal*
6 September 1939
He was 32 years old and serving in the Merchant Navy when his ship SS *Manaar* was torpedoed by the *U-38*. The torpedo exploded amidships, and the submarine then surfaced and commenced firing on the stricken vessel. After about twenty minutes the captain gave the order to abandon ship, and the boats were lowered. Turner insisted on staying behind to help two wounded Lascars. He tried to lower a lifeboat, which crashed into the sea, and then he carried a severely wounded Lascar to another boat, which was blown to pieces by shellfire with him in it. Turner then swam out to the crashed boat and pulled it alongside. The other Lascar climbed down a rope into the boat, which Turner cut adrift, and they joined the Master's boat. All of this was under shellfire.

Turner died in the Hither Green rail crash in Kent on 5 November 1967.

**Flying Officer REGINALD GRAVELEY** (Empire Gallantry Medal)
*France*
20 September 1939
He was 24 years old and serving in 88 Squadron, RAF when his Fairey Battle bomber was shot down in flames. Although badly burned, he pulled the observer, Sergeant Everett, from the wreckage and then returned for the air gunner, Aircraftman John. However, he found him dead and was unable to lift him from the cockpit. Although shot down near Aachen in Germany, the Battle crashed in France.

Graveley died on 16 September 1961.

**Commander RICHARD JOLLY** (Empire Gallantry Medal)
*off the east coast of Scotland*
16 October 1939
He was 43 years old and serving in the Royal Navy when his ship HMS *Mohawk*

was attacked by enemy aircraft and suffered many casualties. Jolly was severely wounded in the stomach but refused to leave the bridge or allow himself to be attended to; he continued to direct the *Mohawk* for the 35-mile passage home, which took 1 hour 20 minutes. He was too weak for his orders to be heard, but they were repeated by his wounded navigating officer. He was repeatedly invited to go down to receive medical attention but refused, saying 'Leave me – go and look after the others.' Having brought his ship safely back to port, Commander Jolly rang off the main engines and immediately collapsed. He died some five hours after being landed.

He had also served in the First World War.

### Research Officer CHARLES 'JACK' HOWARD (Earl of Suffolk and Berkshire)
*LONDON, England*
1939–12 May 1941
He was 34 years old and serving as Chief Field Research and Experimental Officer. His primary work was to investigate and make trials of the methods required for dealing with new types of unexploded bombs. With a specially equipped van he would go straight to the location of an unexploded bomb, and set about dismantling and examining the weapon. He would then work out ways to defeat the booby traps and other devices incorporated in them. His team was known as 'The Holy Trinity'.

One of the most formidable types of booby trap with which he had to deal was the so-called ZUS 40, a device that gripped the inside end of the bomb fuse and fired the main charge when the fuse was removed. To counter it he cut a hole through the casing of the bomb itself and was then able to remove the whole core containing the ZUS 40 in one complete unit. The next step was to remove the main charge by means of inserting a high-pressure steam jet. This was a tremendously important and life-saving development; although a slow and tedious process, it meant that every type of bomb and mine (except acoustic mines) could be handled with much increased safety. On 12 May 1941 Howard and his two assistants took an old and rusted bomb that had been collected from a bomb dump the previous day, and went to examine it. The bomb exploded unexpectedly, killing all three men. Howard's assistants were awarded the King's Commendation for Brave Conduct.

### Acting Wing Commander JOHN ROWLANDS
*England*
1940–1943
He was 25 years old and serving in the RAF Volunteer Reserve. He was involved in bomb disposal, and in all he worked on 150 bombs and 11 mines, including the following:

15 May 1942, Cowes: tried out the new Stevens' Stopper for German long-delay clockwork fuses in pouring rain at the bottom of a 30ft hole;

1 July 1942, Cambridge: dismantled a previously unknown explosive incendiary bomb;

August 1942, Wolverhampton: dismantled a new incendiary bomb, cleared the town of another 300 bombs and did trials on them, after which information was forwarded to the authorities;

14 October 1942, Benbecula: dealt with bombs and depth-charges on a crashed B-17 Flying Fortress;

6 March 1943: removed a British long-delay fuse with anti-withdrawal device from a high explosive bomb;

10 March 1943, Chedburgh: dealt with two high explosive bombs in a crashed Stirling bomber. Both bombs were fitted with an anti-withdrawal device. Again all procedures to render them safe were new;

30 March 1943, Mildenhall: dealt with a 1,000lb bomb jettisoned by Allied aircraft which was 4ft deep in soft earth. In all it took nearly thirty hours to render it safe as the equipment failed after the first eighty minutes;

31 March 1943: rendered safe a 500lb bomb.

In 1943 the bomb dump at RAF Snaith accidently detonated, setting off a chain reaction. As the blazing fires threatened to detonate yet more bombs and ammunition, Rowlands and his team cleared the area and made safe what they could. This work went on for ten days.

In 1961 he was appointed Special Attaché at the British Embassy in Washington. He died on 4 June 2006.

## Miner CHARLES SMITH (Edward Medal)
*ASKERN, YORKSHIRE, England*
3 January 1940

Smith was 31 years old and working at the Askern Main Colliery when there was a roof fall and Charles Liversidge was buried. Smith and Matthew Thompson were on hand and at once started rescue work. The colliery agent, Mr Gwyn Morgan, arrived a few minutes after and took charge of the operation. They played a prominent part in the dangerous work of clearing away the debris. With great difficulty a way was cleared under the fall, and it was found that Liversidge was completely buried except for his head and shoulders. His arms were pinned by rocks and a steel bar. Morgan succeeded in removing a stone that was pinning one arm. Later, when Thompson had failed to free Liversidge due to another rock fall, Morgan succeeded in getting through to him, and after thirty minutes' work in the most cramped conditions was able to free him and pass him through to the other rescuers.

Throughout both men displayed outstanding courage, working in difficult and dangerous conditions. A further heavy fall later in the day completely closed the passage through which the rescue had been made. All three men were awarded the EM, but Morgan died before the exchange date.

Smith also served in the Royal Artillery. He died on 25 October 1987.

**Miner MATTHEW THOMPSON** (Edward Medal)

*ASKERN, YORKSHIRE, England*

3 January 1940

He was 41 years old and working at the Askern Main Colliery when there was a roof fall and Charles Liversidge was buried. Smith and Matthew Thompson were on hand and at once started rescue work. The colliery agent, Mr Gwyn Morgan, arrived a few minutes after and took charge of the operation. They played a prominent part in the dangerous work of clearing away the debris. With great difficulty a way was cleared under the fall, and it was found that Liversidge was completely buried except for his head and shoulders. His arms were pinned by rocks and a steel bar. Morgan succeeded in removing a stone that was pinning one arm. Later, when Thompson had failed to free Liversidge due to another rock fall, Morgan succeeded in getting through to him, and after thirty minutes' work in the most cramped conditions was able to free him and pass him through to the other rescuers.

Throughout both men displayed outstanding courage, working in difficult and dangerous conditions. A further heavy fall later in the day completely closed the passage through which the rescue had been made. All three men were awarded the EM, but Morgan died before the exchange date.

Thompson declined to exchange his EM for the GC. He died on 19 April 1981.

**Corporal JOHN McCLYMONT** (Empire Gallantry Medal)

*BISHOPBRIGGS, GLASGOW, Scotland*

18 January 1940

He was 36 years old and serving in the Auxiliary Air Force when a Walrus amphibian, catapulted from HMS *Norfolk*, crashed at 18 Balloon Centre and burst into flames. McClymont was one of a group who ran to the burning aircraft and helped to extricate one of the airmen. As the flames were increasing in intensity, and ammunition and Very lights were continually exploding, everyone was ordered to stand away from the aircraft. McClymont heard the order but considered it did not prevent a single-handed rescue attempt being made and remained behind for this purpose.

An officer returned shortly to help him and together they succeeded in extricating the other airman just before the petrol tank exploded. McClymont's hands were badly burned. Sadly, however, the other crew members had been killed instantaneously on impact.

McClymont died on 10 June 1996.

**Explosive Worker LEO O'HAGEN** (sometimes spelt **O'HAGAN**) (Empire Gallantry Medal)

*WALTHAM ABBEY, ESSEX, England*

18 January 1940

He was 25 years old and working at the Royal Gunpowder Factory when an explosion ripped through the no. 5 mixing house, killing the three men working there as well as two men working in no. 20 stove nearby. O'Hagen, Sewell and Sylvester were working in no. 2 washing house only 150yds from the explosion, which damaged the hot water and air services. Over 1,000lb of unstable nitroglycerine was being processed. The three men stood by their post for some two hours until the services were restored and then continued with their work until the whole charge had been brought to a state of stability. During this time there were further explosions. Had they fled for safety, it is highly probable that the whole charge of nitroglycerine under their care would have exploded, killing many more people.

O'Hagen also served in the Royal Navy later in the war. He died in May 1968.

## Explosive Worker STANLEY SEWELL (Edward Medal)
*WALTHAM ABBEY, ESSEX, England*
18 January 1940
He was 33 years old and working at the Royal Gunpowder Factory when an explosion ripped through the no. 5 mixing house, killing the three men working there as well as two men working in no. 20 stove nearby. O'Hagen, Sewell and Sylvester were working in no. 2 washing house only 150yds from the explosion, which damaged the hot water and air services. Over 1,000lb of unstable nitroglycerine was being processed. The three men stood by their post for some two hours until the services were restored and then continued with their work until the whole charge had been brought to a state of stability. During this time there were further explosions. Had they fled for safety, it is highly probable that the whole charge of nitroglycerine under their care would have exploded, killing many more people.

Sewell died on 26 May 1969.

## Explosive Worker WILLIAM SYLVESTER (Empire Gallantry Medal)
*WALTHAM ABBEY, ESSEX, England*
18 January 1940
He was 25 years old and working at the Royal Gunpowder Factory when an explosion ripped through the no. 5 mixing house, killing the three men working there as well as two men working in no. 20 stove nearby. O'Hagen, Sewell and Sylvester were working in no. 2 washing house only 150yds from the explosion, which damaged the hot water and air services. Over 1,000lb of unstable nitroglycerine was being processed. The three men stood by their post for some two hours until the services were restored and then continued with their work until the whole charge had been brought to a state of stability. During this time there were further explosions. Had they fled for safety, it is highly probable that the whole charge of nitroglycerine under their care would have exploded, killing many more people.

Sylvester died on 21 February 1996.

**Jemadar Badragga (Escort) PIR KHAN** (Empire Gallantry Medal)
*BANNU, India*
3 February 1940
He was 43 years old and serving in the Corps of Royal Engineers, Indian Army when his convoy was ambushed by some thirty hostile tribesmen on the Tochi Road. After the first volley, Colonel Hasted, Major Cator and Pir Khan managed to obtain cover behind a low irrigation culvert wall at the side of the road. Pir Khan took up a firing position round the edge of the wall and immediately opened fire on the tribesmen, who were less than 40yds away, thereby forcing most of them to take cover. He continued to fire and frustrated any attempt to outflank the officers along the road in spite of a hail of bullets being aimed in his direction. When the tribesmen finally started to withdraw, Pir Khan had only three rounds left out of the fifty he had started with. During the enemy withdrawal he helped to give assistance under fire to the wounded and dying. His actions undoubtedly saved the lives of Hasted and Cator. He also prevented the looting of the cars and the mutilation of the dead and dying.

Pir Khan had also served in the First World War. He died in 1957.

**Flight Lieutenant JOHN DOWLAND** (born **DOWLAND-RYAN**)
*IMMINGHAM DOCK, LINCOLNSHIRE, England*
11 February 1940
He was 25 years old and serving in 69 Squadron, RAF when the SS *Kildare* was hit by two bombs. One exploded in the grain cargo, which shifted, causing the ship to list heavily; the other lodged in the after deck cabin but did not explode. The ship limped into Immingham Dock. Dowland, with Armament Instructor Leonard Harrison, fitted a voltmeter to drain the electric charge. The locking rings were removed and the defused bomb was lowered into a truck for further examination. This was done to all defused bombs in order to keep up with new developments.

Dowland was killed in action near Malta on 13 January 1942.

**Civilian Armament Instructor LEONARD HARRISON**
*IMMINGHAM DOCK, LINCOLNSHIRE, England*
11 February 1940
He was 33 years old and serving in the Air Ministry when the SS *Kildare* was hit by two bombs. One exploded in the grain cargo, which shifted, causing the ship to list heavily; the other lodged in the after deck cabin but did not explode. The ship limped into Immingham Dock. Harrison, with Flight Lieutenant John Dowland, fitted a voltmeter to drain the electric charge. The locking rings were removed and the defused bomb was lowered into a truck for further examination. This was done to all defused bombs in order to keep up with new developments.

Harrison was honorary treasurer of the VC&GC Association from 1968 to 1976. He died on 15 July 1989.

**Mine Agent THOMAS JAMESON** (Edward Medal)
*ST HELENS, England*
14/15 February 1940
He was 42 years old and working at the Bold Colliery when there was a serious roof fall in the main loading level, completely trapping five men. Rescue operations started immediately and within 1¼ hours the first man, Heyes, was freed. He walked out of the pit unaided and was able to tell the pit agent, Thomas Jameson, who had arrived and taken charge, the approximate location of the other four men. Jameson, assisted by Carl Schofield, whose father was one of the buried men, removed stones and earth, working only with their hands, there being no room to use a shovel. The rescue operation continued, with William Jones, Perry Broughton, Joe Hughes, Richard Mayor and Mr Howitt taking turns, and after a prolonged effort Cunningham was freed by 2am next morning. During this time there was another fall from the side which pinned Jones by the leg but he was freed uninjured. At about 3am Tulley was also rescued. The last two men, including Schofield's father, could be seen but were dead. Their bodies were recovered. Had it not been for the Jameson's skilful directions, assisted by Schofield, the number of deaths would almost certainly have been higher.

All this occurred on Jameson's birthday. He died on 29 March 1980.

**Overman CARL SCHOFIELD** (Edward Medal)
*ST HELENS, England*
14/15 February 1940
He was 38 years old and working at the Bold Colliery when there was a serious roof fall in the main loading level, completely trapping five men. Rescue operations started immediately and within 1¼ hours the first man, Heyes, was freed. He walked out of the pit unaided and was able to tell the pit agent, Thomas Jameson, who had arrived and taken charge, the approximate location of the other four men. Jameson, assisted by Carl Schofield, whose father was one of the buried men, removed stones and earth, working only with their hands, there being no room to use a shovel. The rescue operation continued, with William Jones, Perry Broughton, Joe Hughes, Richard Mayor and Mr Howitt taking turns, and after a prolonged effort Cunningham was freed by 2am next morning. During this time there was another fall from the side which pinned Jones by the leg but he was freed uninjured. At about 3am Tulley was also rescued. The last two men, including Schofield's father, could be seen but were dead. Their bodies were recovered. Had it not been for the Jameson's skilful directions, assisted by Schofield, the number of deaths would almost certainly have been higher.

Schofield died on 7 January 1978.

**Flying Officer ANTHONY TOLLEMACHE** (Empire Gallantry Medal)
*MANSTON, KENT, England*
11 March 1940
He was 26 years old and serving in 600 Squadron, Auxiliary Air Force when

the aircraft he was flying hit a tree and crashed into a field, bursting into flames. Tollemache was thrown clear, and his gunner LAC Smith was able to escape. However, realising that his passenger, Second Lieutenant Philip Sperling, was still in the wreck, Tollemache, with complete disregard for the exploding ammunition, endeavoured to break into the forward hatch and rescue him. He persisted in this gallant attempt until driven off with his clothes blazing. His efforts, although in vain, resulted in injuries so serious that it nearly cost him his life.

Tollemache died on 20 February 1977 as a result of a traffic accident. He was posthumously awarded the Efficiency Award Bar in 2006.

### Leading Aircraftman MICHAEL 'MICK' CAMPION (Empire Gallantry Medal)
*UPWOOD, HUNTINGDONSHIRE, England*
12 March 1940
He was 23 years old and serving in 90 Squadron, RAF when two Blenheim bombers taking off from RAF Upwood collided, bursting into flames. Campion and Aircraftman Ernest Frost were among the first to arrive at the scene, where the crew of one aircraft had escaped unaided. Not knowing that the pilot was the sole occupant of the other bomber, Frost entered the rear cockpit, which was full of smoke and fumes, searching for the wireless operator. Satisfying himself that no one was there, he climbed out and, nearly exhausted, ran to the front cockpit, where Campion was trying to rescue the pilot, Sergeant Alphonse Hermmels. Working heroically, and at great risk to themselves, they extricated the pilot from the burning wreckage. Shortly afterwards the petrol tanks exploded and the whole aircraft was rapidly burned out. Unfortunately Hermmels died from his injuries.

Campion died on 4 December 1943, when his B17 bomber crashed into the sea while taking off. His body was not recovered.

### Aircraftman ERNEST 'CHRIS' FROST (Empire Gallantry Medal)
*UPWOOD, HUNTINGDONSHIRE, England*
12 March 1940
He was 22 years old and serving in 90 Squadron, RAF when two Blenheim bombers taking off from RAF Upwood collided, bursting into flames. Frost and Leading Aircraftman Michael Campion were among the first to arrive at the scene, where the crew of one aircraft had escaped unaided. Not knowing that the pilot was the sole occupant of the other bomber, Frost entered the rear cockpit, which was full of smoke and fumes, searching for the wireless operator. Satisfying himself that no one was there, he climbed out and, nearly exhausted, ran to the front cockpit, where Campion was trying to rescue the pilot, Sergeant Alphonse Hermmels. Working heroically, and at great risk to themselves, they extricated the pilot from the burning wreckage. Shortly afterwards the petrol tanks exploded and the whole aircraft was rapidly burned out. Unfortunately Hermmels died from his injuries.

Frost went on to fly jet fighters in the 1950s. He died on 28 July 1969.

**Sub Lieutenant ALEXANDER 'SANDY' HODGE** (Empire Gallantry Medal)
*Indian Ocean*
14 March 1940
He was 24 years old and serving in the Royal Naval Volunteer Reserve when a 250lb bomb detonated while being fused in the bomb-room of HMS *Eagle*, killing thirteen and wounding five. Hodge went into the bomb-room and was able to rescue several badly injured men. He found one man crushed under two heavy bombs, which could not be moved single-handedly. Obtaining help, he dragged the man clear, and sent him up on deck. He did not leave until he had satisfied himself that no one was left alive. He showed outstanding courage, without any thought for himself and not knowing if further explosions might occur.
He died on 4 January 1997.

**Mr GERALD WINTER** (Empire Gallantry Medal)
*PORTSLADE, SUSSEX, England*
21 March 1940
He was 39 years old and working in a field when a Mk I Blenheim crashed nearby, bursting into flames. Winter ran to the scene, where he met Corporal Lapwood, who informed him that three men were still inside the aircraft. Winter immediately extricated Leading Aircraftman Oultram, and then climbed into the gun turret in an effort to locate the remaining crew. He saw two figures at the front of the aircraft, but they were beyond his reach. Climbing down from the turret, he tried with great gallantry to approach the nose of the aircraft but was unable to do so owing to the exploding ammunition and the intense heat of the flames, not only from the wreckage but from the gorse bushes around it. Pilot Officer Henry Hulton and Sergeant Oliver Dumbreck both died in the flames.
Winter died on 8 January 1971.

**Assistant Foreman JOHN McCABE** (Empire Gallantry Medal)
*IRVINE, Scotland*
2 April 1940
He was 43 years old and working at the Royal Ordnance Factory when there was an explosion, followed by a fire. McCabe attempted to empty the contents of the vessel to a drowning pit, but by this time the fire had spread to other vessels; after warning their men to escape, McCabe, Thomas Asquith and Hugh McLelland tried to use the appliance that worked from outside the building to empty all the vessels inside. McCabe himself worked the same appliance from within the building. In doing so, he was killed by an explosion. Asquith was awarded the MBE and McLelland the BEM.

**Lieutenant JOHN LOW** (Empire Gallantry Medal)
*North Sea*
29 April 1940
He was 29 years old and serving in the Royal Navy when HM Submarine *Unity*

was struck by the Norwegian freighter *Atle Jarl* at night. At the time, Low and Able Seaman Henry Miller were on duty in the submarine control room. When the order to abandon ship was given by the submarine's commander, they were instrumental in helping every crew member to escape. The captain asked for the main motors to be stopped and Miller volunteered to do this. The submarine sank in a few minutes, with only Miller and Low still on board. All the rest of the crew were picked up, except for Leading Seaman James Hare and Stoker 1st Class Cecil Shelton, who drowned during the night. Both Miller and Low were awarded the EGM.

### Able Seaman HENRY 'DUSTY' MILLER (Empire Gallantry Medal)
*North Sea*
29 April 1940
He was 39 years old and serving in the Royal Navy when HM Submarine *Unity* was struck by the Norwegian freighter *Atle Jarl* at night. At the time, Miller and Lieutenant John Low were on duty in the submarine control room. When the order to abandon ship was given by the submarine's commander, they were instrumental in helping every crew member to escape. The captain asked for the main motors to be stopped and Miller volunteered to do this. The submarine sank in a few minutes, with only Miller and Low still on board. All the rest of the crew were picked up, except for Leading Seaman James Hare and Stoker 1st Class Cecil Shelton, who drowned during the night. Both Miller and Low were awarded the EGM.

Miller had also served in the First World War.

### Captain JENKIN (aka J.R.O.) THOMPSON
*DUNKIRK, France; SICILY, SALERNO and ANZIO, Italy*
May 1940–23/24 January 1944
He was 28 years old and serving in the Royal Army Medical Corps. During the Dunkirk evacuation Thompson was a doctor on board HMHS *Paris;* when his ship came under attack from enemy aircraft, he displayed unfailing care for his patients combined with a total disregard for his own safety. (It is worth noting that all hospital ships carried a Red Cross and lights to identify themselves.)

On board HMHS *St David*, between 10 and 14 July 1943 at Sicily and 10 and 15 September 1943 at Salerno, he again showed a complete disregard for his own safety while under enemy bomb attack.

On 23/24 January 1944 at Anzio HMHS *St David* was hit by bombs and started to sink. Thompson organised parties to carry the seriously wounded to safety in the boats and by his efforts the lives of all the patients except one were saved. When the ship was about to founder and all were ordered to save themselves, he did nothing of the sort, but returned alone in an endeavour to save the one remaining patient who was still lying trapped below decks. He could not save this man, so he remained with him and they went down with the ship together.

120

**Corporal JOAN PEARSON** (Empire Gallantry Medal)
*RAF DETLING, KENT, England*
31 May 1940
She was 29 years old and serving in the WAAF. When an Anson bomber crashed and burst into flames at around 1am near to her quarters, she immediately got up and went to the scene. She found the navigator dead and Pilot Officer David Bond stunned; rousing him, she released his parachute harness and helped him to get clear. When they were about 30yds away, a 120lb bomb exploded and Pearson threw herself on top of the pilot to protect him from the blast. She remained with him until a stretcher party arrived. She then returned to the burning aircraft to look for the three other crew members. One was dead but the other two got out alive. She preferred not to talk about her heroism, seeing her part in saving the pilot's life as nothing more than doing her duty.

She died on 25 July 2000.

**Captain ROBERT JEPHSON-JONES**
*Malta*
June–November 1940
He was 35 years old and serving in the Royal Army Ordnance Corps. At the time there were no expert Royal Engineer bomb disposal units on the island. With incredible courage Jephson-Jones and Lieutenant William Eastman dealt with 275 unexploded bombs.

Jephson-Jones died on 27 October 1985.

**Lieutenant WILLIAM EASTMAN**
*Malta*
June–November 1940
He was 28 years old and serving in the Royal Army Ordnance Corps. At the time there were no expert Royal Engineer bomb disposal units on the island. With incredible courage Eastman and Captain Robert Jephson-Jones dealt with 275 unexploded bombs.

Eastman died on 8 April 1980 after a number of strokes.

**The Island of MALTA**
June 1940–October 1942
From June 1940 to October 1942 Malta was subjected to 3,215 air-raid warnings – an average of one every seven hours for two-and-a-half years. Some 14,000 tons of bombs were dropped on the island, killing 1,468 civilians, destroying or damaging 24,000 buildings and 1,129 aircraft.

The battle began on 10 June 1940, the defence of Malta resting on three Gloster Gladiator biplanes known as Faith, Hope and Charity. For three weeks they took on the full weight of the Italian Air Force. However, at the end of June four Hurricanes arrived to bolster the defences, to face nearly 200 enemy aircraft.

On 2 August 1940 HMS *Argus* came within 200 miles of Malta and flew off twelve Hurricanes and two Blackburn Skuas to the island. By this time the Germans had joined in the battle and were now concentrating on the docks and airfields.

On 17 November HMS *Argus* arrived with fourteen more aircraft, but the Italian fleet forced the carrier to turn away and she had to release her aircraft at extreme range. Only four Hurricanes and one Skua reached the island, the rest ditching in the sea.

When HMS *Illustrious* steamed into Malta's Grand Harbour in January 1941 with a convoy, she was listing and down by the stern. During the next few hours the sirens sounded for enemy aircraft several times. The plan to defend *Illustrious* was to put up a curtain of anti-aircraft fire which the enemy dive-bombers would have to fly through. For 1 hour and 45 minutes over seventy aircraft came in. Some 200 buildings were destroyed and 500 damaged during this one raid alone. Two days later eighty-five dive-bombers attacked the airfields at Luqa and Hal in an attempt to destroy some of the fighters protecting *Illustrious*. Luqa was out of action for a time. The next day, 19 January, the Germans again attacked the harbour, losing nineteen aircraft, and *Illustrious* escaped to Alexandria.

In February the second assault from the air began, and the enemy made large -scale mine-laying raids on the harbours. During this time the harbour came under attack eleven nights in succession, but remained open. The heavy raids went on until June 1941, when most of the Luftwaffe left for the invasion of Russia.

Six months later, at the beginning of 1942, the Luftwaffe returned to finish the job. In March the onslaught was at its height, but by now HMS *Eagle* had brought in fifteen Spitfires to add to the island's defences. During April alone 6,728 tons of bombs fell on Malta; as well as damaging the docks and all three airfields, 300 civilians were killed. On average 170 bombers came over every day, three raids a day being typical.

On 15 April 1942 the island of Malta was awarded the George Cross, the King making the announcement thus: 'To honour her brave people I award the George Cross to the Island Fortress of Malta to bear witness to a heroism and devotion that will long be famous in history. George R.I.'

On 20 April fifty-four Spitfires flew in from the USS *Wasp*, forty-seven of them reaching the island. The enemy then sent in over 300 bombers in one day to destroy them. Within three days of landing, they were all grounded. Then the enemy made a fatal mistake by easing up for a few days at the end of April and sixty-four more Spitfires from USS *Wasp* and HMS *Eagle* got through to the island.

On 9 May the Germans made nine raids, but the increasing numbers of British fighters were beginning to have an effect. The next day was destined to be the climax of the battle. The mine-laying cruiser HMS *Welshman* was due to berth in Grand Harbour soon after dawn. At 5.45am the Luftwaffe came in force. But the Germans were in for three shocks: a smokescreen, a blistering anti-aircraft barrage and squadrons of Spitfires and Hurricanes. The attackers lost twenty-three aircraft during several raids. After this the Germans made fewer daylight raids, switching to night attacks instead, but their losses were still substantial. The battle still raged, but now in the Allies' favour. Malta was still besieged and short of supplies. The last raid on Malta GC was carried out on 11 October 1942.

**Pilot Officer EDWARD PARKER** (Empire Gallantry Medal)
*SCAMPTON, LINCOLNSHIRE, England*
8 June 1940
He was 30 years old and serving in 49 Squadron, RAF Volunteer Reserve when his Bristol Beaufighter's port engine failed just after take-off. Displaying great coolness, he tried to fly straight on, but found he could gain neither height nor speed with his heavily loaded aircraft. He reduced speed to 80mph, switched off his engines and tried to land in a field in complete darkness. However, the bomber crashed and burst into flames. Parker got clear of the wreck, only to find that the wireless operator was still lying near the burning aircraft. With complete disregard for his own safety, and well aware there were four 500lb bombs in the wreckage, he returned and carried him to safety. During his action one of the bombs exploded and Parker saved the airman further injury by throwing him to the ground.

Parker was also awarded the DFC. He was killed in action on the night of 16/17 January 1943 when his Lancaster bomber was shot down over Berlin.

**Foundryman JOHN FARR** (Empire Gallantry Medal)
*SLOUGH, England*
12 June 1940
He was 27 years old and working at the High Duty Alloys factory, part of Hawker-Siddeley, when there was an explosion. In spite of the grave danger due to molten metal and the risk of electrocution from loose high-tension cables, Farr removed a colleague from the danger zone. He then returned to the foundry with his brother Douglas and between them they cleared two large furnaces, each containing 1,000lbs of molten aluminium, working in complete darkness. The brothers volunteered for that duty in spite of falling debris and the dangerous condition of the building's structure and roof. Douglas was awarded the BEM.

John died on 24 January 1973.

**Aircraftman 1st Class VIVIAN 'BOB' HOLLOWDAY**
*CRANFIELD, BEDFORDSHIRE, England*
2 July and August 1940
He was 23 years old and serving in the RAF when, returning to camp, he witnessed an aircraft crash and burst into flames. He rushed to the site and made his way through the wreckage; finding the pilot's clothes were on fire, he put out the flames with his bare hands. Had the pilot, Sergeant Noel Davies not been killed instantly in the impact, Hollowday's action would in all probability have saved his life.

In August 1940, when once again he was returning to camp, an aircraft spun to the ground and exploded. Hollowday immediately went to the crash site. There was a second explosion and ammunition was bursting around all the time, but despite this he borrowed a gas mask, wrapped two sacks over himself and spent some time in the flames, making four attempts before releasing the first occupant. He then re-entered the burning wreckage and successfully removed the second. All three crew, however, were already dead. Hollowday displayed amazing courage on both occasions.

Hollowday was a member of the VC&GC Association Committee from 1958 to 1977. He died on 15 April 1977.

### Lieutenant EDWARD REYNOLDS (Empire Gallantry Medal)
*CONGRESBURY/BRISTOL, England*
17 August and 3 September 1940
He was 23 years old and serving in the Corps of Royal Engineers when a 250kg bomb landed in a garden, but did not explode. On digging down 17ft, he found that it had a new type of fuse, about which no instructions had been received. However, he removed the fuse and found that it had a clockwork delayed action. This was of great merit due to the lack of any exact knowledge of this type of fuse.

On 1 September a large bomb fell in Temple Street, wrecking the front of some business premises. However, on 3 September an unexploded 250kg bomb was found in the debris. Reynolds, summoned to the scene, found it had a clockwork fuse that was still ticking; according to orders, he applied for instructions, suggesting that the sooner it was dealt with the better. Permission was given to attempt to disarm the bomb due to the effect on public morale. Lieutenant Reynolds removed the fuse and rendered the bomb inoperative. The risk in doing so was very considerable.

He died on 14 December 1955.

### Lance Sergeant WILLIAM BUTTON (Empire Gallantry Medal)
*LONDON, England*
18 August 1940
He was 38 years old and serving in the Corps of Royal Engineers when he was ordered to continue excavating an unexploded bomb with his section. Although he well knew that, owing to the time already spent on excavation, the bomb could explode at any moment, he continued the work with his men with great coolness. Eventually the bomb exploded, killing five sappers of his section and throwing Button a considerable distance. Although considerably shaken, he collected the rest of his men at a safe distance, ascertained that none of them was injured, notified the First Aid Detachment and reported to his section officer.

He died on 10 March 1969.

**Second Lieutenant ELLIS TALBOT** (Empire Gallantry Medal)
*LOUGHOR, Wales*
24/25 August 1940

He was 20 years old and serving in the Corps of Royal Engineers when he had to deal with an unexploded bomb, which was so deep it took twelve-and-a-half hours to dig down to it. When the bomb was brought to the surface, he diagnosed it as a delayed-action type and ordered his men to a safe distance while he examined it. As the bomb appeared to be a new type, he decided to remove it to a place where it could do little damage if it exploded. Keeping his men under cover, he carried the bomb on his shoulder for 200yds and placed it in a safe spot. From the start there was a risk the bomb could explode and he set a fine example of courage and devotion to duty.

He was killed in a flying accident on 9 October 1941.

**Second Lieutenant WALLACE ANDREWS** (Empire Gallantry Medal)
*CROYDON, SURREY, England*
26 August 1940

He was 31 years old and serving in the Corps of Royal Engineers when he was called to deal with an unexploded bomb that had fallen on Croham Hurst golf course, near an airfield. When the fuse was withdrawn about an inch and a half, it would drop back into position, actuated by what appeared to be magnetism or a spring. Andrews made several attempts to remove the fuse but without success. He then placed his section under cover and, after tying a piece of cord to the ring of the fuse discharger, pulled it hard, with the result that the bomb exploded. He was blown a considerable distance and two of his men received splinter wounds.

Andrews died from heart failure on 30 July 1944, brought on by the stress he experienced while carrying out his duties.

**Acting Squadron Leader ERIC MOXEY**
*KENT, England*
27 August 1940

He was 46 years old and serving in the RAF Volunteer Reserve when two unexploded bombs were reported at Biggin Hill Aerodrome. Moxey, a technical intelligence officer, immediately volunteered to proceed to the site and remove them. He was fully aware of the risk involved, having already dealt with many unexploded bombs. One of the bombs exploded, killing him instantly. His CO recommended him for the GC saying: 'In my opinion Moxey was the bravest man I ever met.' Moxey invented a device for extracting fuses, which he called a 'Freddie'. He had also served in the First World War.

## Acting Major HERBERT BAREFOOT
*England*
September–October 1940
He was 42 years old and serving in the Corps of Royal Engineers. A pioneer in bomb disposal, Barefoot dealt with some of the first unexploded bombs to fall on Britain. He worked on the first suspended parachute magnetic mine, as a result of which he was able to put invaluable information at the disposal of the authorities. His bravery and devotion to duty were an inspiration to the men under him.
He died on 23 December 1958.

## Temporary Lieutenant ROBERT (known as SELBY) ARMITAGE
*England*
September–October 1940
He was 35 years old and serving in the Royal Naval Reserve when over a period of time he did a great deal of dangerous work in disabling mines, accepting the risks in the course of his duty. On one occasion he dealt with a mine hanging from a tree in Orpington, Kent. It could only be reached from a ladder, which offered no chance of escape if the fuse had been activated. On another occasion he heard the clock ticking and was only 30yds away when the bomb exploded. In spite of this, he returned with undaunted bravery to carry on with the same work the next day. He was the first direct naval GC. Armitage was also awarded the GM.
Armitage had also taken part in the evacuation of the BEF from Dunkirk. He killed himself on 26 May 1982 following a stroke.

## Acting Flight Lieutenant WILSON 'BOMBS' CHARLTON
*England*
September–October 1940
He was 30 years old and serving in the RAF. At the height of the Blitz he dealt with over 200 bombs. He worked by night and day rendering safe all types of unexploded bombs. Later in the war he was a prisoner of the Japanese; he escaped but was recaptured.
Charlton died on 12 May 1953.

## Acting Lieutenant BERTRAM 'ARCHIE' ARCHER
*LLANDARCY, SWANSEA, Wales*
2 September 1940
He was 25 years old and serving in the Corps of Royal Engineers when he was called out with his section to deal with a whole stick of unexploded bombs that had fallen on the Anglo-Iranian Oil Company's refinery. Several tanks were on fire, which added greatly to the danger and difficulty of the work. While they were working on the more dangerous bombs, two others exploded and it was obvious that the one they were working on might do likewise at any moment. They

continued working on it, however, for several hours until Archer had removed the fuse and rendered it harmless. In all he worked on over 200 bombs.

Later, during the war he crashed his lorry and broke his leg; his wife is reputed to have remarked, 'Thank God for that.' He was the Chairman of the VC&GC Association from 1994 to 2006. At the time of going to press, he is one of twenty living recipients of the award.

## Hospital Porter ALBERT DOLPHIN
*NEW CROSS, LONDON, England*
7 September 1940

He was 44 years old and working at South Eastern Hospital when a high-explosive bomb fell on the kitchens of Ward Block I, killing four nurses and injuring the night sister and patients in the adjoining ward. Nurse Sole, who was in the ward kitchen, was thrown through the collapsing floor into the passage below. Together with other helpers, Dolphin rushed to the site and found her pinned by a block of masonry across her legs. While they were working to free her, the wall was heard to crack and it subsequently collapsed. The workers had plenty of time to jump clear but Dolphin remained and he was subsequently found lying face down across the nurse with his head towards the wall which had collapsed on top of him. When found he was dead, but Nurse Sole was extricated alive, although badly injured. There is no doubt that Dolphin deliberately remained where he was and threw himself across her body to protect her.

Dolphin had also served in the First World War.

## Doctor ARTHUR MERRIMAN
*LONDON, England*
11 September 1940

He was 47 years old and serving as a part-time experimental officer in the Directorate of Scientific Research when he was called to a bomb that had landed in Regents Street. Together with Dr H.J. Gough and Captain Kennedy, he used a new device to steam out the explosive from the bomb. The bomb was ticking and it was decided that all they could do was get as much explosive out as possible before it exploded. Their timing was perfect; they went on working to the last possible minute. The bomb exploded four hours later, but the explosion only caused some broken windows. This story is all the more amazing as Merriman was supposed to be a part-time officer with mainly office duties; however, he often went out to deal with bombs in person.

Merriman had also served in the First World War. He was the author of many books. He died on 4 November 1972.

## Temporary Lieutenant ROBERT 'JOCK' DAVIES
*LONDON, England*
12 September 1940

He was 39 years old and serving in the Corps of Royal Engineers when he was with a party of sappers including Sapper George Wyllie. They were sent to recover a bomb that had fallen near St Paul's Cathedral. It had been a night of heavy raids on London and it was not at first realised exactly where the bomb was. Wyllie eventually discovered the bomb deep down under the pavement. However, a gas main had been fractured and the gas caught fire, so the mains had to be switched off before work could start. The bomb was a 17 Series long-delay fuse type, which were usually blown up where they lay, but as it was very near to St Paul's Underground station Davies decided to remove it. Wyllie was instrumental in removing the bomb. Twice the cable broke and twice he went back down the hole to reattach it. Once the bomb was recovered, Lieutenant Davies drove it away for disposal. This bomb could have exploded at any time during the recovery or while being driven away, as they were known to be booby-trapped. Both men were awarded the GC. In the same incident Sergeant James Wilson and Lance Corporal Herbert Leigh were awarded the BEM.

Davies had also served in the First World War. He died on 27 September 1975.

### Sapper GEORGE WYLLIE (sometimes misspelt WYLIE)
*LONDON, England*
12 September 1940

He was 31 years old and serving in the Corps of Royal Engineers when he was with a party of sappers and Temporary Lieutenant Robert Davies. They were sent to recover a bomb that had fallen near St Paul's Cathedral. It had been a night of heavy raids on London and it was not at first realised exactly where the bomb was. Wyllie eventually discovered the bomb deep down under the pavement. However, a gas main had been fractured and the gas caught fire, so the mains had to be switched off before work could start. The bomb was a 17 Series long-delay fuse type, which were usually blown up where they lay, but as it was very near to St Paul's Underground station Davies decided to remove it. Wyllie was instrumental in removing the bomb. Twice the cable broke and twice he went back down the hole to reattach it. Once the bomb was recovered, Lieutenant Davies drove it away for disposal. This bomb could have exploded at any time during the recovery or while being driven away, as they were known to be booby-trapped. Both men were awarded the GC. In the same incident Sergeant James Wilson and Lance Corporal Herbert Leigh were awarded the BEM.

Wyllie died on 1 February 1987.

### Detachment Leader THOMAS ALDERSON
*BRIDLINGTON, YORKSHIRE, England*
15–20 September 1940

He was 37 years old and serving in the ARP. During five days of bombing, a pair of semi-detached houses were totally demolished, trapping Miss Machon alive in the debris. Alderson tunnelled under the wreckage and rescued the woman without further injury to her. What a way to spend your 37th birthday!

A few days later two five-storey buildings were destroyed and debris penetrated into the cellar where people were trapped. Six people were buried under the debris in one cellar, which had completely given way. Alderson partly effected a way into it by tunnelling 13–14ft under the wreckage and, for three-and-a-half hours he worked unceasingly in exceedingly cramped conditions. Although bruised, he succeeded in freeing all six people without further injury.

When another building was bombed, trapping five people in the cellar, Alderson again led the rescue work, tunnelling from the pavement through the foundations to the cellar. He also personally tunnelled under the wreckage and rescued two people, one of whom subsequently died, from under a refrigerator, which was in danger of collapse as debris was removed.

A wall, three storeys high and swaying in the wind, was directly above the position where the rescue party was working. Nevertheless Alderson worked almost continuously under the wreckage for five hours, during which time enemy bombers were heard overhead.

He died on 28 October 1965 after a long illness.

## Lieutenant Commander RICHARD RYAN
*CLACTON, ESSEX, England*
16–21 September 1940
He was 37 years old and serving in the Royal Navy when he was one of two officers who dealt with a Type C magnetic mine that fell at Clacton. When the first magnetic mines fell on London, Ryan, with Chief Petty Officer Reginald Ellingworth, came forward without hesitation for the perilous work of making them safe, although with their unrivalled knowledge they were well aware of the dangers. The clock of the bomb fuse was normally timed to explode twenty-two seconds after impact. If it failed to do so, it might be restarted by the slightest movement. Together they dealt with six of these mines, one of them in a canal where they worked waist-deep in mud and water, making any escape impossible. The fuse could only be found and removed by groping for it under water. At Hornchurch they made safe a very hazardous mine which threatened the aero-drome and an explosives factory, and then they went to Dagenham to tackle a mine hanging by a parachute in a warehouse. Tragically, it exploded, killing them both. It is perhaps ironic that they were killed by a mine in the air, given that they were both naval officers who specialised in mines that had fallen in water. Both men were awarded the GC.

## Temporary Sub Lieutenant RICHARD MOORE
*CLACTON, ESSEX, England*
16–21 September 1940
He was 24 years old and serving in the Royal Naval Volunteer Reserve when the Luftwaffe dropped twenty-five parachute mines over London, where they caused widespread damage. Moore, with Lieutenant Commander Richard Ryan, volunteered to render safe the seventeen that did not explode. On 21 September

Moore, Ryan and Chief Petty Officer Reginald Ellingworth went to Dagenham to deal with several unexploded mines. Moore carefully examined one and found that the fuse ring had become distorted; resorting to the method prac-tised by many disposal men of simply using whatever tool was to hand, he borrowed a drill from the factory outside which the mine was lying. He drilled two holes on opposite sides of the ring so that it broke, enabling him to remove the fuse, aware that at any time the mine could explode. As he was in the process of removing the trigger, Ryan arrived from neutralising another mine. They had a short conversation and Ryan moved off to deal with the last of the mines with Ellingworth. This was hanging from a parachute in a warehouse 200yds away. Without warning it exploded, killing them both. All three men were awarded the GC.

Moore died on 25 April 2003.

### Chief Petty Officer REGINALD ELLINGWORTH
*CLACTON, ESSEX, England*
16–21 September 1940
He was 42 years old and serving in the Royal Navy when he was one of two officers who dealt with a Type C magnetic mine that fell at Clacton. When the first magnetic mines fell on London, Ryan, with Chief Petty Officer Reginald Ellingworth, came forward without hesitation for the perilous work of making them safe, although with their unrivalled knowledge they were well aware of the dangers. The clock of the bomb fuse was normally timed to explode twenty-two seconds after impact. If it failed to do so, it might be restarted by the slightest movement. Together they dealt with six of these mines, one of them in a canal where they worked waist-deep in mud and water, making any escape impossible. The fuse could only be found and removed by groping for it under water. At Hornchurch they made safe a very hazardous mine which threatened the aero-drome and an explosives factory, and then they went to Dagenham to tackle a mine hanging by a parachute in a warehouse. Tragically, it exploded, killing them both. It is perhaps ironic that they were killed by a mine in the air, given that they were both naval officers who specialised in mines that had fallen in water. Both men were awarded the GC.

Ellingworth had also served in the First World War.

### Auxiliary Fireman HARRY ERRINGTON
*LONDON, England*
17 September 1940
He was 30 years old and serving in the Auxiliary Fire Service. He was resting with two other firemen in the basement of Jackson's Garage, which they were using as a makeshift shelter, when the building was hit by a high-explosive bomb. The blast blew Errington across the basement. Although dazed and injured, he made his way back to the other two auxiliaries, whom he found pinned down, flat on their backs, by debris. A fierce fire had broken out and the trapped firemen

were in imminent danger of being burnt to death. The heat of the fire was so intense that Errington had to protect himself with a blanket. After working with his bare hands, he managed to release the injured firemen, John Hollingshead and John Terry, and dragged them from under the wreckage and away from the fire.

All the while, burning debris was falling into the basement and there was considerable danger of a further collapse. Errington then carried John Hollingshead up a narrow stone staircase that was partially blocked with debris into the courtyard, and then made his way through an adjoining building and into the street. Despite the appalling conditions he then returned and brought out John Terry. Both the rescued men survived.

Errington was Treasurer of the VC&GC Association from 1981 to 2004. He had a great love of basketball and in 2004 the Annual England Basketball Administrator's Award was renamed the Harry Errington Award in his honour. He died on 15 December 2004.

### Chief Combustion Officer ROY HARRIS
*THORNTON HEATH, SURREY, England*
18 September 1940
He was 37 years old and serving in the ARP Engineers Service when an un-exploded bomb fell into a house on Langdale Road. Massive air raids had begun a few days earlier and the problem of dealing with so many bombs at one time was a new one. Harris dismantled it, this being one of eighty-five such acts carried out by him. It should be noted here that Harris was not trained for bomb disposal.

In 1942 he volunteered for the Royal Engineers. During an inspection, the GC ribbon was not recognized by a high-ranking officer, who promptly told him, 'We don't allow civil decorations to be worn in the Army.' However, when told of the ribbon's significance, the officer subsequently apologised.

Harris had also served in the Home Guard. He died on 11 August 1973 (not the 18th, as is often stated).

### Acting Captain MICHAEL 'MAX' BLANEY
*ESSEX, England*
18 September, 20 October and 13 December 1940
He was 30 years old and serving in the Corps of Royal Engineers when a bomb fell in Manor Way, a few yards from the junction with the East Ham and Barking bypass, and failed to explode. Captain Blaney was called to the scene and removed the bomb. On 20 October an unexploded bomb was reported in Park Avenue, East Ham. Unusually it had two very dangerous time fuses, and constituted a very real danger to the public and the Bomb Disposal Section. Blaney personally defused this bomb; it was his usual practice to work alone on these occasions.

On 13 December he was called to remove the fuse from an unexploded bomb that had fallen in premises abutting Romford Road, Manor Park, several days previously. He had planned to fit a 'Q' coil around the bomb but, due to its cumbersomeness, he abandoned the idea and instead attempted to steady the bomb as it was pulled clear. Unfortunately the bomb exploded, killing Blaney and nine others.

In 1931 Blaney had also saved the life of a young boy named Carroll from drowning at Sandycove, Co. Down.

## Lieutenant JOHN PATTON
*WEYBRIDGE, SURREY, England*
21 September 1940

He was 25 years old and serving in the 1st Battalion, Corps of Royal Canadian Engineers when, despite having no training in delayed action bombs, he volunteered to move to a safe distance an unexploded bomb that had been found in the Hawker Aircraft Factory. Having analysed the situation and studied the bomb, he sent for a truck and a length of cable, and then called for more volunteers. Four members of the Home Guard, Sergeant Tillyard-Burrows, W.J. Avery, E.A. Maslyn and C. Chaplain, came forward to help Patton roll the bomb on to a piece of corrugated iron, secure it with cable and attach it to the truck. With Patton sitting on the back of the truck taking care of the bomb, Captain Cunnington drove the truck to a bomb crater, where it exploded a few hours later. The Home Guard men were each awarded the BEM and Cunnington was awarded the George Medal.

Patton died on 13 May 1996.

## Sub Lieutenant GEOFFREY TURNER
*LIVERPOOL and SEAFORTH, England*
21 December 1940

He was 36 years old and serving in the Royal Naval Volunteer Reserve when a bomb fell in Great Howard Street, Liverpool. It was partly suspended by its parachute, with its nose on the ground floor and the fuse hidden. Great care had to be taken in handling this mine, which weighed nearly a ton. Turner was successful in removing the fuse before it could explode. Then he had to deal with another bomb that fell in Cambridge Street, Seaforth. The bomb itself was badly damaged, and it was essential that it should be cleared as soon as possible as the Liverpool–Southport railway line ran nearby. Turner rigged a wire and moved the bomb so as to expose the fuse and fit a safety gag, but the fuse was damaged and only the top half came away, leaving the clockwork and operating mechanism in the bomb. He then tried to pick out the remains of the fuse with his fingers. He had nearly managed this when the clock started ticking and he retired hurriedly. There was no explosion, so he waited five minutes and then returned to finish the work, not knowing, of course, how many more seconds the fuse had still to run. As soon as he touched the fuse the clock started again and almost at once the bomb exploded. Turner was wounded and very severely shocked, but by some miracle he survived. In 1943 he was awarded the George Medal for further mine disposals.

He died on 9 February 1959.

## ARP Warden LEONARD MILES
*ILFORD, ESSEX, England*
21/22 September 1940

He was 36 years old and serving in the ARP. He was on duty when he was warned of the imminent danger of an explosion nearby. He could have taken to the public shelter only a few yards away, but instead his sense of duty forced him to run towards the scene to warn members of the public he knew to be in their houses. He had succeeded in warning some of the residents when the explosion occurred, inflicting serious injuries that proved fatal.

While lying awaiting the ambulance to remove him to hospital, he was conscious and obviously suffering; this did not reduce his sense of duty and when a fellow warden approached him to render what aid he could, Miles instructed him to attend first to the fire which had been caused by a fractured gas main.

## Temporary Sub Lieutenant JOHN MILLER (later DUPPA-MILLER)
*RODING RIVER, LOUGHTON, ESSEX, England*
23 September 1940

He was 37 years old and serving in the Royal Naval Volunteer Reserve when he and Able Seaman Stephen Tuckwell had to deal with a mine that was buried in the mud. They got a canoe and went looking for the mine and found it nose down in the mud. Tuckwell was ordered to stay at a safe distance but he refused, arguing that as Duppa-Miller would be working under at least a foot of water he would need Tucker to hand down the tools. They managed to get one fuse out, but could not reach the other; if the clock had started, there would have been no chance of escape. Then they appealed to some crane-drivers who had come to see what was happening, and they at once volunteered to help. Ropes were placed around the mine and, with the assistance of the crane-drivers, it was dragged slowly out of the creek and on to the wharf. The removal of the final fuse was carried out in comparative comfort.

Duppa-Miller was recommended for a Bar to his GC by the First Lord of the Admiralty, which would have made him the first, and indeed only, GC and Bar, but it was not approved. He died on 15 December 1994.

## Able Seaman STEPHEN TUCKWELL
*RODING RIVER, LOUGHTON, ESSEX, England*
23 September 1940

He was 43 years old and serving in the Royal Naval Volunteer Reserve when he and Temporary Sub Lieutenant John Duppa-Miller had to deal with a mine that was buried in the mud. They got a canoe and went looking for the mine and found it nose down in the mud. Tuckwell was ordered to stay at a safe distance but he refused, arguing that as Duppa-Miller would be working under at least a foot of water he would need Tucker to hand down the tools. They managed to get one fuse out, but could not reach the other; if the clock had started, there would have been no chance of escape. Then they appealed to some crane-drivers who had come to see what was happening, and they at once volunteered to help. Ropes were placed around the mine and, with the assistance of the crane-drivers, it was dragged slowly out of the creek and on to the wharf. The removal of the final fuse was carried out in comparative comfort.

Tuckwell died on 2 October 1966.

### Shunter NORMAN TUNNA
*BIRKENHEAD, MERSEYSIDE, England*
26 September 1940
He was 32 years old and working for the Great Western Railway when a large number of incendiary bombs fell on and around the goods station and sidings at Morpeth Dock. Among the wagons was a train-load of ammunition, petrol, bombs and fuses. Most of the incendiaries were extinguished by the prompt action of the staff on duty before much damage could be done, but a serious fire broke out.

Tunna climbed on top of a covered wagon containing 250lb bombs and discovered two incendiary bombs burning there. With complete disregard for his personal safety, he removed the cover, extinguished the fire and then removed the bombs from the truck. Fireman Frank Newns brought him buckets of water while Ivor Davies helped with the pump. Tunna's action displayed courage of a very high degree and eliminated the risk of further explosions. Newns and Davies were awarded the George Medal.

He died on 4 December 1970.

### Temporary Sub Lieutenant WILLIAM TAYLOR
*England*
26 September–17 October 1940
He was 31 years old and serving in the Royal Naval Volunteer Reserve when, during September and October 1940, he disarmed a total of fourteen mines. His first mine was a 'monster' at 9ft long and weighing 4,000lbs. This mine's fuse would detonate in seventeen seconds if triggered. On another occasion he dealt with a mine that had landed at the RAF Depot Uxbridge, which he described as 'easy'. In Kirby Road, Portsmouth he tackled a C Type parachute mine in the back garden of a terraced house. It was buried so deeply that he attached a microphone to it to listen for the fuse mechanism if it began to tick.

In another incident Taylor remembers that 'a bomb went off on me as I was working [on it] and blew me right through two houses. I came down four streets away. I knew exactly what had gone wrong, all I wanted to do was to tell my boss what had happened for the sake of the rest of the crew.' He telephoned his CO before going to hospital.

He died on 16 January 1999.

## Acting Second Hand JOHN MITCHELL (Albert Medal)
*Iceland*
27 September 1940

He was 23 years old and serving in the Royal Naval Volunteer Reserve when Chief Engineman Wedderburn fell into the harbour between two trawlers. He could not swim, and was soon unconscious. A seaman who jumped in to save him was soon in difficulties himself. Mitchell, hearing shouting, clambered over a vessel to the quay, ran 100yds, climbed across two ships and jumped into the water. He seized Wedderburn by his hair, and held up the other man until a rope was passed down. This he secured with a bowline around the now helpless seaman, using one hand, while he supported both men and himself by gripping the rope with his teeth. The seaman was then hauled out of the water by the men in a trawler. Mitchell, although fully clad and wearing sea boots, supported Wedderburn by treading water until a pilot ladder could be lowered. He made the rope fast around Wedderburn, and steadied him as he was hauled out. Mitchell had been in the very cold water for thirty-five minutes, and was unconscious when rescued.

Mitchell was also awarded the BEM while serving in the Metropolitan Police. He died on 12 April 1972.

## Wing Commander LAURENCE 'LAURIE' SINCLAIR
*WATTISHAM, England*
30 September 1940

He was 38 years old and serving in 110 Squadron, RAF. A Blenheim bomber was taking off from RAF Wattisham when one engine cut out and the bomber crashed in flames. Sinclair immediately went to the scene to help, but two 250lb bombs exploded before he reached it. Undeterred, and knowing full well that there were two more 250lb bombs on board, he pressed on and dashed into the burning wreck. Of the three crew he was able to drag out the air gunner, Sergeant Walters, and take him to an ambulance. Unfortunately he died from his injuries. The pilot, Sergeant J. Merrett, was killed. The navigator, Sergeant Byron, survived but Sinclair did not discover this for fifty years.

Sinclair was later ADC to King George VI. He was treasurer of the VC&GC Association from 1957 to 1959 and then a committee member until his death. Sinclair was the author of *Strike to Defend*. He died on 14 May 2002.

## Temporary Sub Lieutenant JOHN BABINGTON
*CHATHAM DOCKYARD, KENT, England*
Autumn 1940

He was 29 years old and serving in the Royal Naval Volunteer Reserve when he volunteered to deal with a very dangerous bomb that was believed to be fitted with an anti-withdrawal device. (An RAF officer had recently been killed dealing with his type of bomb.) Babington was lowered into a 16ft pit where he tied a line to the head of the fuse; under tension, however, the line broke. He again went down into the pit. In all he had to make three attempts to remove the fuse before finally directing the lifting of the bomb, which was then taken away. As a result of his action much new information was learnt about this type of bomb.

He died on 24 March 1992.

### Section Commander GEORGE INWOOD
*BIRMINGHAM, England*
15/16 October 1940

He was 34 years old and serving in the Home Guard. After a heavy air raid, Inwood and six other men, with the aid of the police, discovered a number of people trapped in a cellar in Bishop Street. Inwood was lowered into the cellar by rope and managed to bring two men out alive. The rescue was particularly difficult as not only was he working in a gas-filled space but those he was trying to save were already unconscious. Although suffering the effects of gas, he insisted on going down again, but collapsed and died.

### Second Lieutenant ALEXANDER 'SANDY' CAMPBELL
*COVENTRY, England*
17 October 1940

He was 42 years old and serving in the Corps of Royal Engineers when he and Sergeant Michael Gibson were called to deal with an unexploded bomb which had fallen on the Triumph Engineering Company's works. War production in two factories had stopped because of it, and a large number of people living nearby had been evacuated. Campbell found the bomb was fitted with a delayed action fuse which it was impossible to remove, so he decided to transport it to a safe place. This was done by lorry. He lay alongside the bomb so that he could hear if it started ticking and could warn Gibson, the driver, to stop and run for cover. Next the two men carried it a mile from Priory Street to Whitley Common, where they successfully made the bomb safe.

Campbell and Gibson were killed on 18 October 1940 while working on another unexploded bomb. Both men were awarded the GC. Campbell had also served in the First World War.

### Temporary Sub Lieutenant JACK EASTON
*LONDON, England*
17 October 1940

He was 34 years old and serving in the Royal Naval Volunteer Reserve when a mine fell in Hoxton, East London, but failed to explode. A large area had to be evacuated. Easton, together with Able Seaman Bennett Southwell, set off down the empty street to deal with it. The mine had crashed through a roof and was hanging by its parachute only 6in from the floor, swaying about. The room was very dark and the door could not be opened more than a foot for fear of disturbing the bomb. Easton decided to dismantle the bomb where it was, and told Southwell to stay in the passage outside and hand him the necessary tools. They started work but had only been at it for about a minute when the bomb slipped and there was the sound of falling brickwork as the chimney pot overhead collapsed. Easton heard the whirr of the mechanism and knew that he had exactly twelve seconds in which to get clear. He shouted to Southwell to run and ran himself, reaching a surface air-raid shelter just as the bomb exploded. When Easton recovered consciousness he was buried deep beneath the debris, his back broken. Southwell, who had run further down the street to where he thought it was safe, was killed by the explosion, which destroyed six streets. It was six weeks before Southwell's body was recovered from the debris. Easton was in plaster for a year, but recovered and continued his service in command of a minesweeper. Both men were awarded the GC.

Easton died on 29 November 1994.

### Sergeant MICHAEL GIBSON
*COVENTRY, England*
17 October 1940

He was 34 years old and serving in the Corps of Royal Engineers when he and Second Lieutenant Alexander Campbell were called to deal with an unexploded bomb which had fallen on the Triumph Engineering Company's works. War production in two factories had stopped because of it, and a large number of people living nearby had been evacuated. Campbell found the bomb was fitted with a delayed action fuse which it was impossible to remove, so he decided to transport it to a safe place. This was done by lorry. Campbell lay alongside the bomb so that he could hear if it started ticking and could warn Gibson, the driver, to stop and run for cover. Next the two men carried it a mile from Priory Street to Whitley Common, where they successfully made the bomb safe.

Campbell and Gibson were killed on 18 October 1940 while working on another unexploded bomb. Both men were awarded the GC.

### Able Seaman BENNETT SOUTHWELL
*LONDON, England*
17 October 1940

He was 27 years old and serving in the Royal Navy when a mine fell in Hoxton, East London, but failed to explode. A large area had to be evacuated. Easton, together with Able Seaman Bennett Southwell, set off down the empty street to deal with it. The mine had crashed through a roof and was hanging by its parachute only 6in from the floor, swaying about. The room was very dark and the door could not be opened more than a foot for fear of disturbing the bomb. Easton decided to dismantle the bomb where it was, and told Southwell to stay in the passage outside and hand him the necessary tools. They started work but had only been at it for about a minute when the bomb slipped and there was the sound of falling brickwork as the chimney pot overhead collapsed. Easton heard the whirr of the mechanism and knew that he had exactly twelve seconds in which to get clear. He shouted to Southwell to run and ran himself, reaching a surface air-raid shelter just as the bomb exploded. When Easton recovered consciousness he was buried deep beneath the debris, his back broken. Southwell, who had run further down the street to where he thought it was safe, was killed by the explosion, which destroyed six streets. It was six weeks before Southwell's body was recovered from the debris. Easton was in plaster for a year, but recovered and continued his service in command of a minesweeper. Both men were awarded the GC.

### Special Constable BRANDON MOSS
*COVENTRY, England*
20/21 October 1940
He was 31 years old and serving in the Coventry Special Constabulary when a house was completely demolished by a bomb, burying the three occupants. He led a rescue party in clearing an entry to the trapped victims under extremely dangerous conditions owing to the debris and leaking gas. When conditions became critically dangerous, he alone worked his way through a space he cleared and was responsible for saving their lives.

Other people were buried in the adjoining buildings and Moss at once led the rescue. The workers became exhausted after many hours of work, but he laboured unceasingly and inspiringly throughout the night, again with debris falling around him, and as a result of his efforts one person was rescued alive and four bodies recovered. During this whole time bombs were still falling and it was known that there was a delayed action bomb only 200yds away. Some books state 14/15 November for this action, but this is incorrect.

Moss was the first policeman to be awarded the GC, having initially been recommended for the George Medal, which was then upgraded to the GC. He died on 9 August 1999.

### Sub Lieutenant PETER DANCKWERTS
*LONDON, England*
late 1940
He was 24 years old and serving in the Royal Naval Volunteer Reserve. After less than six weeks in the service, he set out to deal with mines in his area, without orders and with incomplete equipment. He had only ever touched a mine under instruction, but he worked almost without rest for 48 hours and successfully dealt with 16 enemy mines.

On one occasion he and Chief Petty Officer J. Beadle found two mines hanging from a parachute with their noses touching the floor. Their footsteps started the clock in one of them, but when they retreated the clock stopped. So they went back, undaunted, and dealt with the mine, knowing full well that its clock was highly sensitive and would only have a few seconds left to run. However, Danckwerts managed to withdraw the fuse and then he dealt with the other mine.

Danckwerts also took part in the invasion of Sicily. He died on 25 October 1984.

### Sergeant RAYMOND LEWIN

*TAL-HANDAQ, Malta*

3 November 1940

He was 25 years old and serving in 148 Squadron, RAF Volunteer Reserve when the Wellington bomber he was flying crashed shortly after take-off and burst into flames. Lewin extricated himself from the wreckage and saw three of his crew climbing out. He ordered them to get clear, then ran around the blazing wing in which the petrol tanks were burning and crawled under it to rescue his injured co-pilot. Despite his own injuries – a cracked kneecap and severe contusions on the face and legs – he half-dragged and half-carried the wounded man some 40yds from the aircraft to a hole, where he lay on top of him just as the bombs exploded. This superbly gallant deed was performed in the certain knowledge that the bombs would explode. The co-pilot later died of his injuries.

Lewin died on 21 November 1941, when the bomber he was in crashed on landing at Oakington, England.

### Temporary Lieutenant HAROLD NEWGASS

*LIVERPOOL, England*

28 November 1940

He was 40 years old and serving in the Royal Naval Volunteer Reserve when a bomb fell on the Garston Gas Works, paralysing industry over a large area. The bomb had fallen through the top of a large gasometer and the parachute had become entangled in the roof. The bomb itself was resting nose down but in an almost upright position on the floor, in 7ft of foul, oily water, and leaning against one of the brick pillars that supported the roof. The bomb's fuse was against the pillar and it had to be turned in order to access it. Lieutenant Newgass tackled the bomb on his own, in one of the most dangerous assignments ever undertaken. He could only breathe using oxygen supplied in cylinders, six of which he used during the operation. On the first cylinder he did his inspection and made his plan. On the second he took down his tools and a ladder. On the third he put sandbags around the nose and lashed the top of the bomb to the iron roof support. On the fourth he turned the bomb, removed the fuse and unit primer and detonator. On the fifth he turned the bomb again and undid the clock keep ring and on the last he withdrew the clock, and the bomb was safe. At the time it was regarded by some as the most hazardous bomb disposal ever carried out.

Newgass died on 17 November 1984.

### Sub Lieutenant FRANCIS BROOKE-SMITH

*MANCHESTER SHIP CANAL, England*

December 1940

He was 28 years old and serving in the Royal Naval Reserve when an unexploded bomb fell on the Fire-Float *Firefly*. Brooke-Smith found the bomb was firmly wedged, but by using a rope he was able to pull it slightly clear of the engine room casing; then, lying head downwards on the sloping casing, he managed to place a safety gag in the bomb-fuse. The clock then started to tick, but he stayed where he was and finally managed to stop it before the explosion occurred. This was the first time he had dealt with a bomb using a gag on the bomb-fuse and he had to do so in most difficult circumstances, using a torch and unable to see the bomb-fuse itself.

On 18 October 1941 his ship was torpedoed off the coast of Ireland. Brooke-Smith died in a traffic accident on 3 December 1952, while riding his bike.

### Able Seaman ALFRED MILES (Albert Medal)

*FIFE, Scotland*

I December 1940

He was 41 years old and serving in the Royal Navy. HMS *Saltash* was passing from one dock basin to another, and a wire had been run out from the starboard bow to the weather corner of a gate so as to hold the bow up to the wind. The wire was taken to the windlass, but this was too slow, and so men were picking up the slack by hand, leaving some loose turns of wire on the deck. As the ship drew level the order was passed to turn up. The wire was taken from the windlass to the bollards. Able Seaman Thompson was standing in a bight of wire; Miles called out to him to get clear, but Thompson failed to do so and the wire drew taut around his ankles. Miles knew that Thompson could be hauled through the bull-ring, and that if he himself were caught in the wire he would be in the same position, yet he tried to force the bight open with his hands. His right hand was jammed between the wire and Thompson's ankle. He said nothing and still tried to free his shipmate as Thompson was dragged along the deck towards the bull-ring. They were saved, and Thompson was taken off the ship in time to save his life. However, Miles lost his hand.

Miles had also served in the First World War. He died on 27 May 1989.

### Station & Rescue Officer WILLIAM MOSEDALE

*BIRMINGHAM, England*

12 December 1940

He was 46 years old and serving in the Birmingham Fire Brigade when an auxiliary fire station was completely demolished by a very large bomb. A number of firemen were trapped in the station and civilians were buried in an adjoining house which had also been demolished.

Mosedale immediately began tunnelling and propping-up operations. Tons of debris covered the site and he fully realised that at any moment he might be buried by a further collapse. When the first tunnel was completed and the control room reached, he found that there were still men whom he could not extricate. So he carried out another tunnelling operation from a different direction, and again entered the control room. Five men were found, one dead, the others all injured. Mosedale administered oxygen to the injured men and they were taken out.

The entrance to the cellar of the adjoining house was full of debris. Mosedale directed operations for its removal, only to find that the cellar itself had collapsed.

He nevertheless persisted and, after a time, reached seven trapped people. Three had been killed outright when the roof collapsed. He gave oxygen to the remaining four and succeeded in extricating them.

It was then necessary to begin tunnelling again to reach four other victims trapped in the cellar of the fire station. Mosedale completed his tunnel and entered the cellar. Four men who were still alive were given oxygen and removed. He is credited with saving 12 lives.

In an interview in 1968 Mosedale said, 'Don't for God's sake write about me as a hero. I wasn't. Just a fireman doing his duty. Dammit, I was in the rescue department, wasn't I.' He died on 27 March 1971.

### Pit Manager THOMAS HULME (Edward Medal)
*LEIGH, LANCASHIRE, England*
23 January 1941

He was 37 years old and working at the Personage Colliery when there was a fall of roof above the coal face. Two hewers were trapped; one was quickly released but the other, Thomas Wignall, could not get away, and as the fall was continuing he was in an extremely dangerous position. The only access to him was along the conveyor belt, over which the roof had squeezed down to 2ft. Hulme crawled along the belt, a distance of about 6 to 8ft, and although he had to lie prone on the belt and there was the possibility of a total collapse, he stayed there for about one-and-a-half hours. He succeeded in building three hard wood chocks around Wignall to prevent the roof closing down on him, and afterwards helped Wignall to get clear of the debris so that he could roll over onto the conveyor belt and crawl out, practically unhurt. In his rescue he showed outstanding courage and saved Wignall's life at the risk of his own.

Hulme died on 22 October 1988.

### Cadet DAVID HAY (Albert Medal)
*off the coast of Sierra Leone*
29 January 1941

He was 19 years old and serving in the Merchant Navy when the German surface raider *Kormoran* opened fire on his ship SS *Eurylochus*. Despite returning fire, the *Eurylochus* was hit, her upper works being wrecked. As the ship stopped, two boats and two rafts were got away but the rest were shot to pieces. Hay reached a raft, but, although sharks were swimming all around him, he dived in again and rescued the radio officer.

A German boarding party examined the cargo holds and found 16 heavy bombers. The German captain, Theodore Detmets, gave the order to sink the ship with a torpedo, but as it was fired a searchlight spotted a lifeboat crew trying to re-board the *Eurylochus*. Detmets tried to warn them with a 'torpedo fired' message but it went unheeded. As the torpedo struck the lifeboat, its occupants disappeared. In all, 38 crew were lost but the remaining 42 were taken aboard the *Kormoran*.

Hay declined to exchange his AM for the GC. He died on 23 January 1979.

## Corporal JAMES SCULLY
*BIRKENHEAD, MERSEYSIDE, England*
8 March 1941

He was 31 years old and serving in the Pioneer Corps when he was in a party led by Lieutenant Chittenden. They went to the scene of some demolished houses and started searching for trapped people; Scully located a man and a woman. With great difficulty, he managed to penetrate the debris and get to where they were buried. Lieutenant Chittenden followed him and they used wood to shore up the debris, but had no means of cutting it into proper lengths.

A rescue party then arrived with tools and all available help was mustered. The two men worked tremendously hard in their efforts to clear away the wreckage. Scully remained with the trapped people and prevented any more debris falling on them. A long plank was inserted to take most of the weight but as the result of further falls the props began to sway out of position. There was then a very real danger of the mass of debris falling in and burying the injured. Realising this, Scully placed his back under the plank to try to prevent the props from giving way completely. He steadied them for a time but gradually the weight increased until the props slipped. This left Scully holding up one end of the plank and Chittenden the other. Scully could have got away at this point but he knew that if he did so the debris would fall and probably kill the trapped people, so he stayed under the plank. As the weight increased it forced him down until he lay across the trapped man. Chittenden, who was still holding the other end of the plank, reached over and supported Scully's head to prevent him being suffocated by having his head pressed into the debris. He managed to keep his head clear but was becoming exhausted. Despite this, he kept up his spirits and continued to talk encouragingly to the woman. Scully stayed in this position for more than seven hours, until the rescue party were able to free him and the casualties. Lieutenant Chittenden was awarded the GM.

Scully died on 28 December 1974. His nephew is Brendan Foster, Olympian and TV presenter.

## Temporary Lieutenant ERNEST 'MICK' GIDDEN
*LONDON, England*
17 April 1941

He was 31 years old and serving in the Royal Naval Volunteer Reserve when he was called to a mine that had fallen on Hungerford Bridge. He found that the mine lay across a live electric wire, with the bomb fuse primer release mechanism facing downwards. He had to turn the bomb over before he could remove the fuse. The metal casing of the bomb had melted due to the heat and in order to fit the gag to prevent detonation he first had to remove the casing with a hammer and chisel, a process which took six hours. All the time the sleepers along the track were burning, so they were not only hot but making loud noises, so that it was much harder to listen for the ticking of the clock. Gidden then unhurriedly moved the bomb away in a wheelbarrow.

Gidden was also awarded the GM for bomb disposal. He died on 20 December 1961.

### Ordinary Seaman ALBERT HOWARTH (Albert Medal)
*Mediterranean Sea*
9 May 1941
He was one day short of his 24th birthday and serving in the Royal Navy aboard HMS *Foresight* when the SS *Empire Song* hit two mines, setting her on fire. The captain ordered her abandoned. Howarth was part of a boat's crew sent to board the burning ship but as they drew near her, she blew up, throwing the boat's crew into the water. Howarth could see near him a stoker who was badly shaken, so he held him up for ten minutes until a lifebelt was thrown to him. This he put around the stoker. Before being hauled on board his ship himself, he made sure that his shipmate was safe. When he himself reached the deck, after nearly thirty minutes in the water, it was seen that his right foot had been blown off.

He died on 13 June 1976.

### Mr PERCY WELLER (Edward Medal)
*PARKGATE, NEWDIGATE, SURREY, England*
16 May 1941
He was 42 years old and working at the Schermuly factory when an explosion occurred in a building where explosives were being broken down. Fire broke out. Clark, a workman, was badly burned; Mr Weller entered the burning building and succeeded in rescuing Clark, but he subsequently died from his injuries. In effecting this rescue Weller ran great personal risks, not only from the fire but also from the danger of further explosions, which in fact did occur shortly afterwards, demolishing the building.

Another man, 17-year-old D.J.T. Card, was also recommended for his part in fighting the fire, but for some reason he did not receive any award.

Weller also served in both world wars. He died from myocardial infarction on 22 April 1979.

### Lieutenant HUGH 'HUGHIE' SYME
*England*
19 May 1941–25 December 1942
He was 38 years old and serving in the Royal Australian Naval Reserve, and spent twenty-one months working in bomb disposal all over the country. He dealt with nineteen mine recovery or disposal operations, including five acoustic, eight magnetic and two acoustic-magnetic mines. He was also responsible for the recovery of the only Type T sinker mine. Much importance was attached to his work on this mine when he located it and recovered it intact, together with its sinker, in November 1942. On this occasion, after removing the mine from the drifter *Noontide*, he had to operate up to his knees in mud and, at a vital stage, was hanging head down in a hole, in the mud. He would have

had no chance of escape if the bomb had exploded. The information gained from this mine was invaluable.

Syme was also awarded the GM and Bar. He died on 7 November 1965.

## Squadron Leader the Reverend HERBERT PUGH
*Atlantic Ocean*
5 July 1941

He was 42 years old and serving in the RAF Volunteer Reserve when the SS *Anselm* was torpedoed. Pugh was everywhere, helping the injured into the boats. It soon became obvious that the ship was sinking, but on hearing that a number of injured men were still trapped in the hold, he insisted on being lowered into it. He simply explained that he must be where his men were, and he knelt with them in prayer as the ship went down. Pugh had every opportunity of saving his own life but he gave up his life to bring comfort to others.

He had also served in the First World War.

## Mr WILLIAM BAXTER (Edward Medal)
*COVENTRY, England*
8 July 1941

He was 33 years old and working at the Standard Motor Company when there was an accident in the Service Department. Mr Ross was trapped by the arms between the rope and pulley at the end of a 130ft-long latticework crane jib, so that he was in imminent danger of either bleeding to death or falling from a great height. Mr Baxter obtained a rope and some first aid dressings and climbed to the top of the jib; having lashed Mr Ross more securely, he applied the dressings and a tourniquet. He then stayed with him for an hour until a rescue was effected by the fire brigade. There is little doubt that, but for Baxter's action, Mr Ross would have died either through loss of blood or by falling from the jib.

Baxter died on 4 April 1995.

## Corporal JAMES 'SCOTTY' HENDRY
*LOCH LAGGAN, Scotland*
13 June 1941

He was 29 years old and serving in the Corps of Canadian Engineers when his company was tasked with constructing a tunnel. Hendry came out of the tunnel to find the powder house on fire. Shouting a warning, he then ran to warn the compressor man and the steel sharpeners in the workshop nearby. Although he could have got himself clear, he then went to the powder house to try to put out the fire. Others were also in danger, and, if the magazine blew up, the resulting damage would have stopped work for some time. There was an explosion in which Hendry was killed, but his warning helped to save the lives of many.

**Bombardier HENRY (known as HERBERT) REED**
*North Sea*
20/21 June 1941
He was 30 years old and serving in no. 2 Battery, 1st Marine Anti-Aircraft Regiment, Royal Artillery. His ship, SS *Cormount*, was attacked by bombers and E-boats; despite sustaining a direct bomb hit amidships, *Cormount* replied at once with defensive fire, and the gunners went on firing amid the hail of bullets and cannon shells. Reed was badly wounded, but when the Master asked him how he was, he said that he would carry on and refused to leave his guns. Then, seeing that the chief officer and a steward were wounded, he carried them from the bridge down two ladders to the deck below and put them in a shelter near a lifeboat. Reed then collapsed and died. It was afterwards found that his stomach had been ripped open by machine-gun fire.

Chief Officer Edward Willey, although not badly wounded, never fully recovered from the effects of the attack, and died on 28 September 1941. He is buried in the same cemetery as Henry Reed.

**Acting Lieutenant Commander WILLIAM HISCOCK**
*ST GEORGE'S BAY, Malta*
September 1941
He was 55 years old and serving in the Royal Navy when a 'torpedo machine' (a device in which the Italians specialised) was dropped in 15ft of water. Hiscock was given the task of disarming it. The salvage operation was dangerous as, quite apart from the possibility of booby traps, no information was available about the firing mechanism of the explosive head, and its behaviour when parted from the body was a matter of complete uncertainty. While working on the bomb the clock mechanism started and it was only Hiscock's cool determination and skill that brought the operation to a successful conclusion.

Hiscock had also served in the First World War. He was killed defusing a bomb on 15 February 1942.

**Temporary Lieutenant JOHN GIBBONS** (Albert Medal)
*English Channel*
22 September 1941
He was 36 years old and serving in the Royal Naval Volunteer Reserve when his motor launch hit a mine, wounding him in the head and throwing him into the sea. Despite this, when he was rescued he went at once to save others. He saw a seaman some 100yds away in the water, and swam to him through burning fuel. His gallant action saved the man's life.

Gibbons died on 12 November 1971, just twenty-three days after the announcement of the AM-GC exchange; his family declined to exchange.

**Leading Aircraftman ALBERT 'MATT' OSBORNE**
*Malta*
November 1941–1 April 1942
He was 44 years old and serving in the RAF Volunteer Reserve when, during a long period of fierce enemy air attacks, he was always first at hand to deal with emergencies. The following are examples of his bravery:
• he extinguished a burning aircraft during a heavy bombing attack;
• he attempted to save a burning aircraft and subsequently removed torpedoes from the vicinity;
• he assisted in saving the pilot of a burning aircraft and extinguishing the fire;
• he saved an aircraft from destruction by fire;
• he attempted for six hours to extricate airmen from a bombed shelter, despite continued heavy bombing and falling stonework.

On one day alone he fought fires in two aircraft, saving one of them; he freed the parachute of a burning flare that was caught on an aircraft, enabling the pilot to taxi clear, and he checked the fire in a burning aircraft, the greater part of which was undamaged.

On 1 April 1942 he was leading a party to extinguish the flames of a burning aircraft when one of the petrol tanks exploded, injuring him. On recovering, he returned to fight the fire and was killed by the explosion of an air vessel while attempting to pour water over two torpedoes that were in danger of exploding.

The Air Officer Commanding, RAF Mediterranean said Osborne was 'one of the bravest airmen it has been my privilege to meet'.

**Leading Aircraftman KARL GRAVELL**
*CALGARY, Canada*
10 November 1941
He was 18 years old and serving in the Royal Canadian Air Force when his Tiger Moth's engine cut out and the aircraft crashed into the yard of the Big Hills Springs School. The fuel tank exploded on impact. Gravell managed to get clear but lost an eye and his clothes were on fire; nevertheless, without any thought for his own safety, he rushed back to the blazing wreck and tried to pull the pilot, Flying Officer James Robinson, from the wreckage. Mrs Frances Walsh, a teacher, grabbed Gravell from behind and hauled him to the ground, rolling him over to put out the fire in his clothes. She called to her pupils to come and help. They carried the unconscious Gravell into the school, where she rendered first aid and sent for a doctor. When medical aid arrived, she would not permit anyone to treat her burns until Gravell was taken to hospital. On the way he told the medics, 'Please don't tell my Mom, she would only worry.' He subsequently died from his injuries. Frances Walsh was awarded the GM.

**Lieutenant JOHN 'MOULDY' MOULD**
*England*
14 November 1941–30 June 1942

He was 31 years old and serving in the Royal Australian Naval Reserve, attached to the Royal Navy, where he was continuously employed on most dangerous work. His outstanding work, both in dock-clearance operations and those resulting in the stripping of the early Type G German mine, had been the subject of a previous recommendation for which he was ultimately awarded the GM. Since that time he had carried out his most important recovery, rendering safe and investigating the first German magnetic-acoustic unit and a moored magnetic mine. His work included the successful handling of a wide range of disposal and clearance problems. For many of these he devised ingenious and unique solutions.

He died on 9 August 1957.

### Captain MATEEN (often incorrectly spelt MATREEN) AHMED ANSARI
*STANLEY GAOL, Hong Kong*
1942–19 or 29 October 1943

He was 27 years old and serving in the 5th Battalion, 7th Rajput Regiment, Indian Army. When the Japanese invaded Hong Kong in December 1941, he became a prisoner of war. At first he was treated reasonably well, but as he was closely related to the ruler of a great Indian state his captors tried to persuade him to renounce his allegiance to the British and help to spread subversion among the Indian ranks. He steadfastly continued both by word of mouth and example to counteract all traitorous propaganda and resolutely opposed all attempts at undermining the loyalty of his compatriots.

He was thrown into Stanley Gaol after warnings and beatings had produced no effect, where he remained until September 1942, by which time, owing to starvation and brutal treatment, which is alleged to have included mutilations, he was unable to walk. After a short time in the Matauchung Hospital Camp he was returned to the Indian Others Ranks camp, where he not only resumed his previous efforts but also organised a system for aiding escapers.

In May 1943 he was betrayed and thrown back into Stanley Gaol, where he was starved and brutally tortured for several months. Fellow prisoners, both British and Indian, have testified that during this time his outstanding courage and defiance were such as to excite the admiration of all. Finally, he was tried and beheaded on either the 19 or 29 October 1943.

### Assistant Attorney General JOHN FRASER (some times spelt FRAZER)
*STANLEY CIVIL INTERNMENT CAMP, Hong Kong*
1942–29 October 1943

He was 48 years old and serving in the Colonial Service. When the Japanese invaded Hong Kong in December 1941, he was interned. He immediately started organising escape plans and a clandestine wireless service. He was fully aware of the risk but engaged continuously in most dangerous activities and was successful not only in receiving news from outside, but also at getting important information out of the camp. Eventually he was arrested and subjected to prolonged and severe torture by the Japanese, who were determined to obtain information from him and to make him implicate those who were working with him. Despite this treatment, he steadfastly refused to utter one word that could help the Japanese investigations or bring punishment to others. His fortitude under the most severe torture was such that it was commented upon by the Japanese guards. Unable to break him, the Japanese beheaded him on 29 October 1943.

Fraser had also served in the First World War, during which he was awarded the MC and Bar.

## Flight Lieutenant HECTOR 'DOLLY' GRAY
*SHAM SHUI PO PRISON CAMP, Hong Kong*
December 1941–18 December 1943
He was 31 years old and serving in the RAF. When the Japanese invaded Hong Kong in December 1941, he became a prisoner of war. While in captivity he did all he could to sustain the morale of his fellow prisoners. He smuggled much-needed drugs into the camp and distributed them to those who were seriously ill, and he also ran a news service on information he received from people outside the camp. He was tortured repeatedly over a period of six months to make him divulge the names of his informants, but he disclosed nothing. He was executed by the Japanese on 18 December 1943.

In 1938 Gray had taken part in what was at that time the longest non-stop flight, from Egypt to Australia, a distance of 7,158 nautical miles.

## Captain MAHMOOD (or MAHMUD) KHAN DURRANI
*Malaya*
1942–1944
He was 28 years old and serving in the 1st Bahawalpur Infantry, Indian State Forces when he and a small party were cut off, but managed to remain in hiding for three mouths. He was then betrayed to the INA and was sent to a Japanese prisoner-of-war camp. He refused to become a member of the Japanese-sponsored INA and took active steps to thwart Japanese efforts to infiltrate members of that organisation into India. In fact he conceived the idea of founding a school to send Muslim agents into India to oppose the ideas the Japanese were trying to put across. To start with, his efforts were successful, but in May 1944 the Japanese arrested him and he was subjected to every form of torture in an effort to find out his accomplices. As this produced no results, he was handed over to the INA, where he was again tortured and even condemned to death, but he still refused to give away any information. He was liberated at the end of the war but his health was affected by his treatment for many years.

Durrani's autobiography is called *The Sixth Column*. He died on 20 August 1995.

## Temporary Lieutenant GEORGE 'GRANNY' GOODMAN

*Egypt/North Africa*

15 January–27 March 1942

He was 21 years old and serving in the Royal Naval Volunteer Reserve when the Egyptian Coastguard spotted a torpedo-shaped object along the coast from Alexandria. The object was covered with sand and shingle, so a working party went with him but on arrival they had to find the object by probing until they hit something. Once uncovered, it was seen to be a torpedo but it was not like any seen before. Three pistol firing mechanisms were visible.

The working party moved back to a safe distance. None of their tools fitted the screw heads, so a hammer and chisel were used to unscrew the key-rings to gain access to the pistols, primers and detonators. It was while dealing with the first of these that a loud 'phut' was heard. Instinctively the party ran from the torpedo. Having recovered their composure, they returned to the scene and completed the work of making it safe.

The device turned out to be the only Italian self-destroying surface torpedo that had been recovered. A similar weapon had killed the torpedo officer of HMS *Medway* only a few days before.

During the period 15 January–27 March 1942 Goodman's work included rendering safe fourteen parachute mines in the Suez Canal area and retrieving the first mechanism from a German C Type mine to be recovered and examined. He also made safe two torpedoes, thirty-one moored mines and the first 'Sammy' mine to be recovered in the Mediterranean.

Goodman survived the war, just; he was killed on 31 May 1945 when he entered a booby-trapped house near Rotterdam.

## Captain LIONEL 'THE DUKE' MATTHEWS

*SANDAKAN, Borneo*

August 1942–2 March 1944

He was 30 years old and serving in the 2nd Battalion, Corps of Signals, Australian Military Forces when he was taken prisoner after the fall of Singapore on 15 February 1942. From August 1942 to March 1944 he personally directed an underground intelligence organisation and arranged through native contacts for the delivery into the camp of sorely needed medical supplies, food and money, factors which not only kept up morale and the courage of the prisoners but which undoubtedly saved the lives of many. He was instrumental in arranging a radio link with the outside world and was able to send weekly news bulletins to the civil internees on Berhala Island. He was also responsible for arranging the delivery of firearms to a secret location for future use. Although a prisoner of war, Matthews was appointed to command the North British Armed Constabulary and at great danger organised that body, together with the local native population, into readiness for a rising against the Japanese. He made contact with guerrilla forces in the Philippines and successfully organised escape parties. He continued these activities at great personal risk to himself until arrested. Although subjected to brutal torture, beating and starvation, he steadfastly refused to make any admissions to implicate his associates. His conduct at all times was that of a very brave and courageous man and he upheld the highest traditions of an Australian officer. Captain Matthews was executed by the Japanese on 2 March 1944, and even at the time of his execution he defied the Japanese by saying 'Keep your chins up, boys. What the Japs do to me doesn't matter. They can't win.' He was also posthumously awarded the MC.

### Lieutenant DENNIS COPPERWHEAT
*GRAND HARBOUR, VALLETTA, Malta*
22 March 1942

He was 28 years old and serving in the Royal Navy when, during a heavy air attack, he was in charge of a party of men from HMS *Penelope* sent to scuttle a merchant ship that was laden with ammunition and burning in the harbour. Owing to the fires, it was impossible to place the scuttling charges in the hold, and they had to be slung over the side of the ship. As they worked, ammunition was exploding all around them. The ship was 40yds from shore, which was too far for the cables for firing the charges. Copperwheat sent his party to cover and stayed to fire the charges himself from an exposed position; he was lifted up bodily when the charges were fired.

Due to his actions, however, much of the ammunition was saved and some of the very heavy bombs were later dropped on targets in Italy.

He died on 8 September 1992.

### Apprentice (Merchant Navy) DONALD CLARKE
*off the coast of Trinidad*
8/9 August 1942

He was 19 years old and serving in the Merchant Navy when his ship, the tanker *San Emiliano*, was hit by two torpedoes and her cargo of petroleum burst into flames, turning the ship into an inferno. Clarke was trapped in his cabin but fought his way out on deck and boarded the only lifeboat that was still intact. It was full of burnt and wounded men, and he himself was severely burnt on the face, hands and legs. When the boat was lowered into the sea, it started to drift back towards the flaming tanker and it was evident that it would require a tremendous effort to pull it out of danger. Most of the occupants, however, were so badly injured that they were unable to help. Despite his injuries, Clarke took an oar and pulled heartily for two hours without a groan or murmur of complaint, and only when the boat was well clear did he collapse and then his hands had to be cut away from the oar as the burnt flesh had stuck to it. He had pulled as well as anyone, although he was rowing with the bones of his hands. As he lay dying in the bottom of the boat he sang cheerful songs to keep up the spirits of his injured shipmates.

The Sea Cadets of Chester-le-Street named a lunch in his honour.

## Captain DUDLEY MASON

*Mediterranean Sea*

12–15 August 1942

He was 40 years old and serving in the Merchant Navy. During Operation Pedestal, his ship, the tanker SS *Ohio*, was part of a fourteen-ship convoy taking urgently needed aviation fuel to Malta GC. On 12 August the SS *Ohio* was hit by Italian torpedoes, and for four days she was attacked by aircraft and submarines, shattering the ship. One bomb lifted her right out of the water, while another exploded in her boiler room, and a Stuka crashed and exploded on her deck. Her back was broken.

Nevertheless, although she was so badly damaged, the ship's engineers kept her going and she was steered without any compass. She was finally towed into port, the sea level almost up to her deck. Mason had sustained burns to his hands and he was flown back to Britain, together with Chief Engineer James Wyld. However, no accommodation had been arranged, there was no reception party and they were left to find their own medical treatment.

However, an invitation did come from Air Vice-Marshal Keith Park, whose fighters had given cover to the *Ohio*:

'My pilots would welcome an opportunity of seeing you and thanking you personally for bringing your ship through. Would you like to pay a visit to some of my aerodromes next Thursday 20th August departing 16.00, having tea at one of the aerodromes and having a look around, returning with me to my house for drinks? We could fix you up for dinner at our mess and return you to your ship or shore billet later.'

In addition Earl Mountbatten wrote to him, offering his 'congratulations on one of the best earned GCs of the war'. Mason, however, considered the award to be for the entire crew. He died on 26 April 1987.

## Apprentice JOHN GREGSON (Albert Medal)

*Malta*

12 August 1942

He was 18 years old and serving in the Merchant Navy when his ship SS *Deucalian* was attacked by aircraft and torpedoed, being set on fire by the explosion. The flames spread rapidly and orders were given to abandon ship. One of the ship's gunners was, however, pinned under a raft. Gregson immediately went to his assistance and, with help, freed him. The gunner had severe injuries and it was impossible to get him into a boat or onto a raft, so he was dropped overboard. Gregson dived into the sea after him and in the darkness towed his helpless shipmate to a ship 600yds away, which picked them up. But for his action, the injured man would have had little chance of survival.

Gregson declined to exchange his AM for the GC. At the time of going to publication, he is one of twenty living recipients of the GC.

**Petty Officer Cook CHARLES WALKER** (Albert Medal)

*Mediterranean Sea*

13 August 1942

He was 28 years old and serving in the Royal Navy aboard HMS *Ledbury* when the SS *Waimarama* was bombed and set on fire fore and aft. The *Ledbury* went to assist, lowering her whaler to pick up survivors. Walker then saw 16-year-old galley-boy Alan Burnett thrown into the sea with many of his fellow crew members, many of whom were dead. Seeing that he was in difficulties, and without a thought for his own safety, Walker dived over the destroyer's side and rescued him. The sea was on fire and the heat intense, and his ship was about to get under way but both men were picked up.

Sixty years later they met again to commemorate the anniversary of the battle for Malta GC, and Burnett jokingly remarked, 'I want half your medal – without me you wouldn't have got it,' and Charles retorted 'And without me you wouldn't be here to ask that!'

I had the privilege of meeting Charles in 2010, just before his 96th birthday, and I asked him if he felt he had done anything brave on that day. His reply was: 'Hell no, I was a good swimmer in those days and I would have helped anyone I saw in difficulties.' Charles died on 17 July 2011.

**Lieutenant WILLIAM FOSTER**

*ASHLEY HILL, CLARENDON PARK, WILTSHIRE, England*

13 September 1942

He was 61 years old and serving in the 7th Wiltshire (Salisbury) Battalion, Home Guard. He was instructing a group of recruits how to throw grenades when one of them threw a live grenade, which, instead of going over the top, hit the parapet and rebounded to the throwing position. Without hesitation Lieutenant Foster threw himself on the bomb one second before it exploded. It killed him instantly, but saved the lives of his men. Before the exercise he had told the men, 'If anything happens, leave it to me.'

Foster had also served in the Second Boer War and the First World War, where he fought in the same battalion as Sidney Godley VC during the battle of Mons. He was also awarded the MC and DCM.

**Chief Officer JAMES REEVES** (Albert Medal)

*Arctic Ocean*

14 September 1942

He was 30 years old and serving in the Merchant Navy when his ship SS *Atheltemplar* was torpedoed by the *U-457*. The ship was being abandoned when two men, Mr Broadbent and Mr Ridgewell, were seen floating helplessly in the oily water flooding the engine room. All the engine room ladders had been destroyed, but Reeves used a boat ladder to descend into the engine room and secure lines around them. While they were being hauled to safety, one of the men slipped back into the water. Again Reeves descended into the engine room, which was rapidly filling with surging water, and secured another rope around the injured man, who was then brought on deck. Then they were all transferred to HMS *Harrier*, which had come alongside.

Reeves died on 26 December 1984.

### Sergeant GRAHAM PARISH
*KHARTOUM AIRFIELD, Sudan*
16 September 1942

He was 30 years old and serving in the RAF Volunteer Reserve when he was navigator of a Wellington bomber being delivered to the Middle East Command. Shortly after take-off, the port engine failed and the pilot attempted to return to the airfield, but the Wellington struck a building and burst into flames. All of the crew except Sergeant Parish and a passenger named Flowers, whose legs were broken, succeeded in getting free from the burning aircraft. At the time of the crash Parish was in the astro-hatch and Flowers was by the emergency door in the floor of the bomber.

When the blaze subsided, Parish's body was found leaning against the rear gun turret; Flowers was beside him with his arms over the navigator's shoulders. It was clear that Parish had carried him from the emergency door to the rear turret, a distance of 8yds, presumably in the hope that they could both escape through the turret. Sergeant Parish could have made his escape through the astro-hatch but his unselfish desire to assist Flowers cost him his life.

Parish had also served in the First World War, and he had taken part in Operation Millennium, the first thousand-bomber raid (in fact 1,047 bombers) on Cologne on 30 May 1942. He had enlisted after receiving a white feather in the post.

### Acting Leading Seaman WILLIAM GOAD (Albert Medal)
*North Atlantic*
20/21 September 1942

He was 20 years old and serving in the Royal Navy aboard HMS *Ashanti*. When HMS *Somali* was torpedoed by *U-703*, the *Ashanti* came alongside to help rescue the crew. Goad volunteered to be lowered on a line over the side of his ship, into water that was well below freezing, to rescue an unconscious man. A full gale was blowing and there was a very great risk that he would be either washed away by the breaking waves, or swept under the bilge keel of the ship, which was rolling heavily.

Goad also served in Korea. He declined to exchange his AM for the GC, saying, 'The King put that on my chest and I'm keeping it.' He died on 25 December 1994. His brother-in-law was Driver Joseph Hughes GC.

**Assistant Works Manager Dr WILSON BALDWIN** (Edward Medal)
*GREAT OAKLEY, ESSEX, England*
20 November 1942

He was 30 years old and working at the Great Oakley Munitions Factory when a violent explosion occurred, killing two workers and completely destroying the building and causing considerable damage to adjacent buildings. In one of these, a nitrating house, a charge of 1,800lbs of nitro-glycerine was in the pre-wash tank. Although the building became filled with fumes and steam, the operator Mr Wheeler and his assistant Mr Sallows remained at their posts and took prompt steps to control the nitration and render the chemicals harmless. They were assisted by Dr Baldwin, who arrived on the scene shortly after the explosion. He noticed that the wood above the pre-wash tank was smouldering vigorously and throwing off sparks. With the operator's assistance, Dr Baldwin extinguished this very dangerous outbreak. The danger which these three men averted was a very real one, since there is little doubt that a further explosion would have killed many workers who were still in the danger zone.

Baldwin was a member of the Executive Committee of the VC&GC Association for many years. He did not exchange his EM for the GC. He died on 2 May 1994.

**Lieutenant FRANCIS 'TONY' or 'JIMMY' FASSON**
*Mediterranean Sea*
30 October 1942

He was 29 years old and serving in the Royal Navy aboard HMS *Petard*. When the *U-559* was forced to the surface by depth-charges, she was immediately fired on by destroyers, whereupon her crew abandoned ship. Allied naval commanders had been briefed about the importance of recovering documents and code-machines from enemy submarines and knew not to sink them if at all possible.

Fasson and Able Seaman Colin Grazier volunteered to swim to the sub to see what could be retrieved and dived into the water, shortly followed by Thomas Brown, who was just 16 years old. Well aware of their perilous situation, they made their way to the U-boat's control room and bundled up all the documents they could see. After finding an Enigma machine bolted to the bulkhead, Fasson managed to free it. This was all passed up to Brown and transferred to a whaler, which Sub Lieutenant Connell had brought alongside. The *U-559* then suddenly sank, taking Fasson and Grazier with it. Brown only just managed to escape.

The two most important documents taken were the Short Signal Book and the 1942 edition of the Short Weather Cipher. Within six weeks the first decrypts were made using this information and it is considered to have halved Allied losses in the Atlantic. Both men were awarded the GC. Brown was awarded the GM, but he tragically died a few years later in a house fire. It was rather odd that most of the U-boat crew survived but Fasson and Grazier died.

154

## Able Seaman COLIN GRAZIER

*Mediterranean Sea*

30 October 1942

He was 22 years old and serving in the Royal Navy aboard HMS *Petard*
When the *U-559* was forced to the surface by depth-charges, she was immediately fired on by destroyers, whereupon her crew abandoned ship. Allied naval commanders had been briefed about the importance of recovering documents and code-machines from enemy submarines and knew not to sink them if at all possible.

Fasson and Able Seaman Colin Grazier volunteered to swim to the sub to see what could be retrieved and dived into the water, shortly followed by Thomas Brown, who was just 16 years old. Well aware of their perilous situation, they made their way to the U-boat's control room and bundled up all the documents they could see. After finding an Enigma machine bolted to the bulkhead, Fasson managed to free it. This was all passed up to Brown and transferred to a whaler, which Sub Lieutenant Connell had brought alongside. The *U-559* then suddenly sank, taking Fasson and Grazier with it. Brown only just managed to escape.

The two most important documents taken were the Short Signal Book and the 1942 edition of the Short Weather Cipher. Within six weeks the first decrypts were made using this information and it is considered to have halved Allied losses in the Atlantic. Both men were awarded the GC. Brown was awarded the GM, but he tragically died a few years later in a house fire. It was rather odd that most of the U-boat crew survived but Fasson and Grazier died.

## Boatswain WILLIAM 'MAC' McCARTHY (Albert Medal)

*MOLE OF BENGHAZI, Libya*

3 January 1943

He was 31 years old and serving in the Royal Navy when some Indian seamen were thrown into the sea from a raft. McCarthy dived into a tempestuous sea and swam to them with a line which had been thrown to him. He caught hold of one of them and successfully brought him ashore. Then he returned to the rescue of another. There was grave danger that he would be dashed against the rocks by the gales and the high sea.

He died on 21 July 1978.

## Acting Able Seaman EYNON HAWKINS (Albert Medal)

*North Atlantic*

10 January 1943

He was 22 years old and serving in the Royal Navy when the SS *British Dominion* was hit by three torpedoes from *U-522* and immediately began to burn furiously. Many of the crew jumped overboard. Hawkins, with the greatest coolness and courage, organised a party of survivors in the water and kept them away from the burning oil, until they were picked up by another ship in the convoy. Twice he had to swim to the assistance of survivors who were in difficulties. This involved him swimming through the flaming water and being burned on the face as he pulled them to safety.

After the war he became a professional rugby player. Hawkins died on 17 December 2001.

## Temporary Major CYRIL MARTIN
*LONDON, England*
17/18 January 1943

He was 45 years old and serving in the Corps of Royal Engineers when a number of bombs dropped in raids failed to explode. One of these, which had landed near Lords cricket ground, had the new marking 'Y' on it. No one knew how to render the fuse safe and it was only because it was faulty that no one was killed. The fault enabled the men to uncover the secrets of the Y fuse. Later Martin worked on a large bomb that had fallen on a warehouse in Battersea, which was full of American machine tools. On instructions from the Ministry of Supply, they radiographed the bomb to see if it was the same type as the Lords bomb; after twelve hours' work they found that it was, but the means of rendering it safe were still not known.

Martin discovered that the bomb contained solid cast TNT, and so he applied high temperature steam to the explosive while at the same time keeping the fuse cold with water. It took until 8.30 the next morning to steam all the explosive out.

Martin had also served in the First World War, during which he was awarded the MC. He was the first GC to hold office in the VC&GC Association (Honorary Secretary, 1961–70). He died on 29 November 1973.

## Temporary Major HUGH SEAGRIM
*Burma*
February 1943–22 September 1944

He was 35 years old and serving in the 19th Hyderabad Regiment (now the Kumaon Regiment), Indian Army. He was the leader of a group known as Force 136, which included two other British officers and a Karen officer. They were operating in the Karen Hills. Towards the end of 1943 the presence of this group became known to the Japanese, who commenced a widespread campaign of arrests and torture in order to discover their whereabouts. In February 1944 the British officers (Nimmo and McCrindle) were ambushed and killed. The capture of their equipment furnished the enemy with the information they required about Seagrim's activities and they redoubled their efforts to capture him. The Japanese arrested at least 270 Karens, many of whom were tortured and killed.

In spite of this the Karens continued to assist and shelter Seagrim, but the enemy managed to convey a message that if he surrendered, they would cease reprisals. Major Seagrim gave himself up on 15 March 1944. He was taken to Rangoon, along with other members of his group, and on 2 September he was sentenced to death, along with eight others. On hearing the sentence, Seagrim pleaded that the others were only obeying his orders and that he alone should be executed. The degree to which he inspired his men may be realised from the fact that they all expressed their willingness to die with him. The sentence was carried out on 22 September 1944. He was also posthumously awarded the MBE and DSO.

His brother was Lieutenant Colonel Derek Seagrim VC, making them the only siblings to be awarded the VC and the GC. After the war Seagrim's mother Annabel wore her sons' medals at a parade in Eastbourne; it is believed to be the only time both these awards have been worn together in public.

## Wing Commander FOREST (known as TOMMY) 'The White Rabbit' YEO-THOMAS
*France / Germany*
February 1943–1945

He was 36 years old and serving in the RAF Volunteer Reserve when he was parachuted into France on 23 February 1943 as part of the SOE. On this mission he enabled a French officer who was being followed by the Gestapo in Paris to reach safety and resume clandestine work in another area. He also took charge of a US Army Air Corps officer who had been shot down and was in danger of capture because he spoke no French. This officer was returned to England on 15 April 1943 in the aircraft that picked up Yeo-Thomas.

Yeo-Thomas then undertook a second mission on 17 September 1943. Soon after his arrival in France many patriots were arrested. Undeterred, he continued his enquiries and obtained information that enabled the desperate situation to be rectified. On six occasions he narrowly escaped arrest. He returned to England on 15 November 1943, bringing British intelligence archives which he had secured from a house watched by the Gestapo.

He was again parachuted into France in February 1944. Despite every security precaution, he was betrayed to the Gestapo in Paris on 21 March. While being taken by car to their HQ, he was badly beaten up and then underwent four days of continuous interrogation, interspersed with beatings and torture, including being immersed head down in ice-cold water, with his legs and arms chained. Interrogations continued for two months and Yeo-Thomas was offered his freedom in exchange for information concerning the head of a Resistance Secretariat. Owing to his wrist being cut by the chains, he contracted blood poisoning and nearly lost his left arm. He made two daring but unsuccessful escape attempts. He was then confined to solitude in Fresnes prison for four months, including three weeks in a darkened cell with little food. Throughout this time of almost continuous torture, he steadfastly refused to disclose any information.

On 17 July he was sent to Compiegne prison, from which he twice attempted to escape. He and twenty-six others were then transferred to Buchenwald Concentration Camp in Germany. (It was during this train journey that Violette Szabo took water to many of the prisoners in the carriage, including

Yeo-Thomas.) On the way they stopped at Saarbrucken, where they were beaten and kept in a tiny hut. They arrived at Buchenwald on 16 August and sixteen of them were executed and cremated on 10 September. Yeo-Thomas had already started to organise resistance within the camp and remained undaunted by the prospect of a similar fate. He accepted an opportunity of changing his identity with that of a dead French prisoner, on condition that other officers would also be enabled to do so.

He was later transferred to a work kommando for Jews. In attempting to escape, he was picked up by a German patrol; claiming French nationality, he was transferred to a camp near Marienburg for French prisoners of war. On 16 April 1945 he led a party of twenty in a most gallant attempt to escape in broad daylight. Ten were killed by fire from the guards. Those who reached cover split up into small groups. After three days without food, Yeo-Thomas became separated from his group. He continued alone for a week but was recaptured only 800yds from the American lines. A few days later he escaped with a party of ten French POWs, whom he led through German patrols to the American lines.

Yeo-Thomas had also served in the US Army at the end of the First World War. As well as the GC, he was awarded the MC and Bar, the Legion d'Honneur, the Croix de Guerre and the Polish Cross of Merit. He died on 26 February 1964.

## Lieutenant Commander PATRICK O'LEARY (real name ALBERT-MARIE EDMOND GUERISSE)

*France/Germany*

March 1943–May 1945

He was 32 years old and serving in the Royal Navy when he was captured by the French police during operations off the south coast of France in April 1941. He escaped while en route to prison, and thereupon set up an organisation to help Allied prisoners and evaders. Between April and August 1941 he helped some 150 men get away.

In March 1943 he was betrayed to the Gestapo, arrested and tortured in an attempt to make him reveal the names, whereabouts and duties of other members of his organisation. He was put in a refrigerator for hours, he was beaten repeatedly, but he never disclosed any information that could be of use to the enemy. After more ferocious experiments, the Germans gave him up as a hopeless case and sent him to a concentration camp, where he was once again the victim of torture.

Throughout his time in prison his courage never faltered. Many prisoners gave evidence that his morale and support saved their lives.

On liberation, O'Leary refused to leave the camp until he had ensured that all possible steps had been taken to ease the suffering of his fellow inmates. Even then, instead of going straight to his family, he went to France to trace the surviving members of his organisation.

After the war he rejoined the Belgian Army under his real name. Guerisse also served in Korea, where he was awarded the DSC. His other awards include the

DSO, Legion D'Honneur, Croix de Guerre, the War Cross of Poland, the Medal of Freedom and the Order of Leopold. He died on 26 March 1989.

## Chief Officer GEORGE STRONACH
*TRIPOLI HARBOUR, Italy*
19 March 1943

He was 28 years old and serving in the Merchant Navy when the harbour was attacked by bombers and the SS *Ocean Voyager* caught fire. The ship had a large consignment of petrol and ammunition on board; the ammunition began exploding, and, in spite of strenuous efforts to fight the fires, she had to be abandoned. The ship's master had been killed and responsibility for further operations fell to Stronach. He had been rendered unconscious but recovered almost immediately and went forward to look for survivors. He found a number of crew sheltering in the alleyway and, braving the exploding ammunition, he led them to a boat alongside, which took them to safety. Stronach stayed on board in order to provide for the transport of any other survivors who might be found, and then lowered another boat and brought it alongside the ship. Although the ship was now burning furiously, he made his way to the officers' accommodation amidships. Finding a hose with a trickle of water coming through, he held this over his head and kept himself sufficiently wet to protect against the worst of the heat. With great difficulty he climbed into the collapsed accommodation and found one of the deck officers unconscious and badly burnt. Mr Stronach pulled him clear and dragged him along the deck to the lowered boat.

Returning amidships, he removed the debris from another officer who was trapped and by almost superhuman efforts dragged this man through the porthole and along the deck. He then tied a rope around him and lowered him down to the boat. As the situation was becoming desperate, Mr Stronach ordered a man to take the boat to safety, while once again he returned amidships, where he discovered an officer who had been severely injured. Dragging him along the deck to the side of the ship, he tied a rope around him and lowered him over the side onto a raft, which had returned in answer to his calls. Again he continued his search for survivors. Taking a look around aft, he saw a greaser lying unconscious in the scuppers. He dragged this man to the side of the ship, but, finding no boat or raft, put a lifebelt around him and threw him overboard.

When he was satisfied that there were no more survivors, he jumped overboard and swam to a raft, which, under his direction, returned to pick up the greaser. In the full knowledge that the ship could blow up at any moment, he stayed on board for an hour and twenty minutes looking for survivors, with complete disregard for his own safety.

He died on 9 December 1999.

### Second Engineer Officer GORDON BASTIAN (Albert Medal)

*Atlantic Ocean*

30 March 1943

He was 41 years old and serving in the Merchant Navy when his ship SS *Empire Bowman* was torpedoed by the *U-404* 500 miles from Brest, sustaining severe damage. He at once shut off the engines and then remembered that two men were on watch in the stoke hold. The engine room was in darkness and water was already pouring in. Although there was grave risk of disastrous flooding, Mr Bastian did not hesitate but groped his way to the door and opened it. The two men were swept into the engine room with the inrush of water; one was badly bruised and shaken, and the other had a broken arm and injuries to his feet. Mr Bastian tried to hold them both but was unable to keep hold and lost one, so he dragged the other man to the escape ladder and helped him on deck. He then returned for the other man and helped him to safety. The more seriously injured man had to be lifted up the ladder by Mr Bastian, who was choking on cordite fumes. He had taken a very great risk in opening the watertight doors, but both men undoubtedly owed their lives to his exceptional bravery.

This action took place on Mr Bastian's birthday. He died on 29 October 1987.

### Mrs ODETTE SANSOM (née BRAILLY, then CHURCHILL, later HALLOWES)

*FRESNES PRISON, France* and *RAVENSBRUCK CONCENTRATION CAMP, Germany*

April 1943–May 1945

She was 31 years old and serving in the SOE when she was infiltrated into enemy-occupied France in October 1942 with the codename Lise. She worked with great courage and distinction until April 1943, when she was arrested with Peter Churchill, her CO. While travelling between Marseilles and Paris on the way to prison at Fresnes, she was able to speak to her CO and for mutual protection they agreed to maintain the fiction that they were married. She adhered to this story and even succeeded in convincing her captors, in spite of considerable evidence to the contrary and through at least fourteen interrogations. She also drew the Gestapo's attention away from her CO and on to herself, saying he had only come to France on her insistence. She took full responsibility and agreed that it should be herself and not her CO who should be shot. By this action she caused the Gestapo to cease paying attention to her CO after only two interrogations.

In addition, the Gestapo were most determined to discover the whereabouts of a wireless operator and another British officer whose lives were of the greatest value to the Resistance. Odette was the only person who knew of their whereabouts. The Gestapo tortured her most brutally to try to make her talk. They seared her back with a red-hot iron and, when that failed, they pulled out all her toenails. Odette, however, continually refused to speak and by her bravery and determination she not only saved the lives of the two officers but also enabled them to carry on their valuable work. In June 1943 she was condemned to death and was eventually sent to Ravensbruck Concentration Camp.

During the two years in which she was in enemy hands, she displayed courage, endurance and self-sacrifice of the highest order.

After the war she was a witness at the trial in Hamburg of sixteen members of Ravensbruck Concentration Camp staff. She died on 13 March 1995.

## Boilerman FREDERICK CRADOCK (or CRADDOCK)
*GLEMSFORD, SUFFOLK, England*
4 May 1943
He was 56 years old and working as a boilerman when there was an explosion, which resulted in the boiler house being filled with scalding steam and water, trapping Albert Sterry in a well between the furnace and the boiler. Both men had been engaged in 'blowing out the boiler', something they did twice a week. Cradock, who was on top of the furnace, could have jumped to safety, but instead he called for a ladder and attempted to get to his workmate. Before he could do so, he was overcome and severely scalded. He staggered away; at this point he could still have jumped to safety, but despite his terrible injuries he made a second gallant effort to get down into the well. He died in making the attempt. Cradock showed outstanding heroism and gave his life in an endeavour to save his workmate.

He had also served in the First World War.

## Leading Aircraftman KENNETH SPOONER
*LAKE ERIE, Canada*
14 May 1943
He was 20 years old and serving in the Royal Canadian Air Force. He was on an instructional flight when, shortly after take-off, the pilot, Sergeant Dana Nelson, fainted at the controls. The other students, Sergeant William Brown, LAC J. Curtis and LAC R. Bailey were all incapable of flying the aircraft; they tried to remove the pilot, but he temporarily regained consciousness and froze at the controls, causing the aircraft to lose altitude rapidly. With extreme coolness, Spooner assumed charge, ordered the crew to bale out while he took over the controls and endeavoured to keep the aircraft at a safe height. The three crew baled out as ordered, then Spooner attempted to land, something he had never done before, but the aircraft crashed, killing him and the pilot.

With complete disregard for his personal safety, he sacrificed himself in order to save the lives of his comrades.

## Temporary Lieutenant LEON 'FICKY' GOLDSWORTHY
*Britain*
12 June 1943–10 April 1944
He was 34 years old and serving in the Royal Australian Naval Reserve and was involved in a series of underwater mine recoveries over a period of ten months.

These included four German ground mines, three magnetic mines and one acoustic mine. On one of these occasions (13 August 1943) he made safe a German ground mine off Sheerness. It was only the second time that such a weapon had been rendered safe under water, and it was regarded as a particularly hazardous assignment for the diver. On 10 April 1944 he went to Milford Haven to deal with a mine that had been there for two-and-a-half years. He remarked, 'Like an old soldier, an acoustic mine never dies; although the batteries run down, they don't run out.' He succeeded in removing the fuse and primer and, later, the intact mine. As well as the GC, he was awarded the GM and DSC.

He died on 7 August 1994.

### Private CHARLES DUNCAN
*M'SAKEN, North Africa*
10 July 1943
He was 23 years old and serving in the 4th Battalion, The Parachute Regiment when an attack on a bridge was called off due to the rapid advance of the Eighth Army. Duncan was removing primed grenades from his equipment in the company of his comrades. One grenade fell to the ground. Noticing that the pin had fallen out, Duncan threw himself onto it until it exploded, killing him. He gave his life to save his friends.

### Temporary Colonel LANCERAY (known as LANCE or LAN) NEWNHAM
*SHAM SHUI PO PRISON CAMP, Hong Kong*
10 July–18 December 1943
He was 54 years old and serving in the Middlesex Regiment (Duke of Cambridge's Own). When the Japanese invaded Hong Kong in December 1941, he became a prisoner of war. While in captivity he managed, with a numbers of others, including Captain Douglas Ford, to make contact with British agents. They were arranging a scheme for a mass break-out when on 10 July they were betrayed by Bushir Ahmed and arrested. Both men were interrogated, starved, tortured and finally sentenced to death in an endeavour to make them talk, but they refused to implicate their fellow prisoners and both were shot on 18 December 1943. Both men were awarded the GC. Newnham had played on centre court at Wimbledon in 1914 and he had served in the First World War.

### Captain DOUGLAS FORD
*SHAM SHUI PO PRISON CAMP, Hong Kong*
10 July–18 December 1943
He was 24 years old and serving in the 2nd Battalion, Royal Scots. When the Japanese invaded Hong Kong in December 1941, he became a prisoner of war. While in captivity he managed, with a numbers of others, including Temporary Colonel Lanceray Newnham, to make contact with British agents. They were arranging a scheme for a mass break-out when on 10 July they were betrayed by Bushir Ahmed and arrested. Both men were interrogated, starved, tortured and

finally sentenced to death in an endeavour to make them talk, but they refused to implicate their fellow prisoners and both were shot on 18 December 1943. Both men were awarded the GC.

### Temporary Major ANDRE KEMPSTER (formerly ANDRE GILBERTO COCCIOLETTI)
*PHILIPPEVILLE, Algeria*
21 August 1943
He was 26 years old and serving in the Royal Armoured Corps when he was conducting grenade-throwing practice. A live grenade was dropped into the pit and he at once threw himself onto it and was killed when it exploded. His action saved the lives of the two men with him.

### Temporary Lieutenant JOHN BRIDGE
*MESSINA HARBOUR, Italy*
30 August–2 September 1943
He was 27 years old and serving in the Royal Naval Volunteer Reserve when he took over the clearing of depth-charges that had already killed or wounded six members of his bomb disposal party. After a total of twenty-eight dives they were all cleared, including two that were recovered with their unknown mechanisms intact. In total, he cleared 207 depth-charges, both above and below the water.

He wrote a memoir called *Trip to Nijmegen*. As well as the GC he was also awarded the GM and Bar, both for bomb disposal. He died on 14 December 2006.

### Assistant Section Officer NOOR-UN-NISA (wrongly gazetted as NORA) INAYAT KHAN
*France / Germany*
September 1943–12 September 1944
She was 29 years old and serving in the WAAF attached to the SOE when she was infiltrated into enemy-occupied France on 16 June 1943. During the weeks following her arrival the Gestapo made mass arrests in the Paris Resistance groups to which she had been detailed. But although she was given the opportunity to return to England, she refused to abandon what had become the principal and most dangerous post in France, because she did not wish to leave her French comrades without communications, and she hoped also to rebuild her group.

By now the Gestapo had a full description of her, but knew only her codename 'Madeleine'. They deployed considerable forces in their efforts to catch her and so break the last remaining link with London. After three-and-a-half months she was betrayed and taken to the Gestapo HQ in Avenue Foch. The Gestapo had found her codes and messages and were now in a position to work back to London. They asked her to cooperate, but she refused and gave them no information of any kind. She was imprisoned in a cell on the fifth floor and remained there for several weeks, during which time she made two unsuccessful attempts at escape. She was asked to sign a declaration that she would not make any further attempts but she refused, and the Chief of the Gestapo obtained permission from Berlin to send her to Germany for 'safe custody'.

Khan was sent to Karlstuhein in November 1943. Under interrogation she refused to give any information about her work or her colleagues and was then sent to Pforzheim, where her cell was apart from the main prison. She was considered to be a particularly dangerous and uncooperative prisoner. On 12 September 1944 she and three other prisoners were taken to Dachau Concentration Camp where, on arrival, she was taken to the crematorium and shot.

Before the war she had written children's books and plays. At the time of going to publication funds are being raised for a statue of her to be erected in Gordon Square, London.

### Acting Brigadier ARTHUR NICHOLLS
*Albania*
October 1943–January 1944
He was 32 years old and serving in the Coldstream Guards, attached to the SOE, when he was parachuted into Albania as General Staff Officer to the Allied Military Mission. His task was to organise resistance against the Germans in that country. The Mission was attacked and dispersed in December and from then until the end of January Nicholls was a fugitive in the mountains in bitter weather and conditions of extreme hardship. He suffered so severely from frostbite that he ordered an inexperienced man to amputate both his legs without any anaesthetic, and he was then towed along over the mountains on his greatcoat by two men. He was determined to make contact with the nearest British Mission and eventually succeeded in making his report, upon which important questions of Allied strategy depended. However, he had taxed his body beyond its limits and he died of gangrene and heart failure on 11 February 1944.

### Warrant Electrician ERNEST WOODING (Albert Medal)
*ORILLIA, ONTARIO, Canada*
13 October 1943
He was 27 years old and serving in the Royal Canadian Naval Volunteer Reserve when there was an explosion onboard the Fairmile *ML-1116* while it was under construction. This was followed by a fire. Wooding rushed on deck immediately (not being onboard at the time of the explosion) and pulled two of the three men in the engine room to safety. He was aware that several hundred gallons of high-octane gasoline were in the tanks of the boat, and his action showed complete disregard for his own safety. He carried out much of the rescue work following the explosion and was certainly responsible for saving the lives of two men.

Although only 'discovered' to be an AM holder in 1992, Wooding declined to exchange it for the GC. At the time of going to publication, he is believed to be one of twenty living recipients of the GC but, as he is a recluse, no one really knows if he is still living.

### Acting Sergeant JOHN 'JOCK' RENNIE
*SLOUGH, England*
29 October 1943
He was 22 years old and serving in the 1st Battalion, Argyll and Sutherland Highlanders of Canada (Princess Louise's) when he was supervising live grenade-throwing by a member of his unit at a Canadian training camp. One grenade was thrown successfully, but a second grenade failed to clear the protective embankment and rolled back into the throwing area. Although Rennie had the time and opportunity to take cover, without hesitation he dashed forward, putting himself between the grenade and his men. As he attempted to pick up the grenade and throw it clear, it exploded, fatally injuring him. By his sacrifice he prevented serious and possibly fatal injuries to three other men who were within 5yds of the explosion.

### Private JOSEPH SILK (born KIBBLE)
*Burma*
4 December 1943
He was 26 years old and serving in the 1st Battalion, Somerset Light Infantry (Prince Albert's). His platoon had just driven a Japanese force from their position, and had been ordered to prepare the position for defence. Somehow, Silk accidentally removed the pin from a grenade. Shouting a warning, he clutched the grenade to his stomach and dropped onto it. The grenade exploded, killing him instantly.

There is little doubt that he appreciated at once that he could not safely throw the grenade away because of the other men nearby. Contrary to initial reports that two other men were wounded, no one else was in fact injured.

### Mr JOHN WELLER (often mistakenly called WELLER-BROWN) (Edward Medal)
*CATTERICK, YORKSHIRE, England*
4 February 1944
He was 33 years old and working at Catterick Bridge railhead, where he had just finished unloading ammunition from a lorry. He was in a traffic hut when there was an explosion some 30–40ft away; the hut collapsed and he was thrown a considerable distance from it. The explosion was followed by extensive fires in the surrounding area, caused mainly by grenades and incendiary bombs scattered from nearby trucks. Mr Weller, although badly shaken, returned to the hut, which was on fire. He was joined by another man, who, though injured himself, was able to assist him to extricate three other injured men from the ruins and carry them

to safety. They also assisted in the rescue from other burning and wrecked buildings. Mr Weller continued this work until emergency parties arrived and took over the rescue work.

He knew very well that the area still contained loads of high explosives which might well have exploded at any time.

He died on 14 December 1978.

## Deputy Party Leader LESLIE FOX
*LONDON, England*
20/21 February 1944

He was 39 years old and working for London County Council's Heavy Rescue Service when he was called to Edith Road, where some houses had been demolished by high explosive and incendiary bombs. The wreckage was alight and the walls were liable to collapse at any moment. Cries for help were heard from under the debris and Fox, without thought for himself, immediately began to tunnel his way through the burning ruins. Debris passed back by him was often too hot to handle and his men continually sprayed him with water in an attempt to keep down the intolerable heat. At great danger to himself, Fox shored up the entrance to the tunnel, adjoining which was a very dangerous party wall. After two hours of very strenuous work, and under the most difficult and dangerous conditions, Fox located the casualty, Major Guy Edney. Although in a distressed condition, he would not allow a relief to take his place and continued the rescue operation. Shortly afterwards the wall fell, blocking the entrance and causing the tunnel to collapse. Fox, however, recommenced tunnelling, straining every muscle to expedite the work. After a further two hours' work he had tunnelled 15ft and was able to clear the debris away from the head of the casualty and cover him with some sort of protection.

A medical officer was then able to enter and administer restoratives to the injured man, who was eventually brought to safety. Fox performed his duty in a most gallant and determined manner, and displayed extraordinary courage and tenacity. Sadly Major Edney died from his injuries on 26 February.

When told of the award, Fox said: 'It was just a job of work I was paid to do. If anyone ought to have a medal it's the chap we got out. He was the gamest man I've known – he apologised for causing any bother.'

Fox died on 26 December 1982.

## Factory Development Officer RICHARD (known as ARTHUR) BYWATER
*KIRKBY, LIVERPOOL, England*
22 February 1944

He was 30 years old and working for the Ministry of Supply when nineteen operatives were at work on the last stage of filling fuses; each operative had a tray of twenty-five fuses before them. The fuses were stacked on portable tables each holding forty trays. There were over 12,000 fuses in the building when one fuse detonated, immediately involving the whole tray. The girl working on that tray was killed outright and the two standing behind her were both injured, one fatally. The building was also badly damaged. Mr Bywater realised that the damaged fuses might cause an explosion of fearful magnitude. The initial blast had been caused by a defective striker and it was obvious that the same defect might be present in some of the other fuses. Mr Bywater volunteered to remove all the fuses to a place of safety and he, with three other volunteers, worked for three days removing 12,724 fuses from the wrecked building, plus a further 4,000 suspected of being defective. It was the inspiration of his leadership that enabled this dangerous work to be concluded successfully.

Bywater was the only civilian to be awarded both the GC and the GM. He died on 5 April 2005.

## Mr ANTHONY SMITH
*LONDON, England*
23 February 1944

He was 49 years old and serving in the Civil Defence Rescue Service when, during an air raid, bombs demolished a number of houses at the World's End, Chelsea. Only the party wall was still standing, but in a precarious condition. The gas and water mains were fractured and the gas ignited, turning the wreckage into a raging inferno. Smith burrowed his way through the rubble and managed to reach Sam Mitchell, who was trapped in the basement, but by the time he had freed him the front of the building was a wall of fire, the upper floors were collapsing and his escape was cut off.

Smith determinedly burrowed his way through the burning debris and brought the man out safely, just as the remaining wall fell into the basement. Smith's eyebrows and hair were burnt and he was almost overcome by smoke but, undeterred, he immediately went to the assistance of Albert Littlejohn, who was trying to rescue a woman trapped in the basement of an adjoining building, the walls of which were in a very dangerous condition. Here, Smith worked for an hour up to his waist in water, and with the walls and floors on the point of collapse, helping to release her. He then obtained a change of clothes and carried on until his squad was relieved. Albert Littlejohn was awarded the BEM.

When asked in 1957 why he never wore his GC, Smith replied, 'It was just a job, see. You get in there and do it, same as the other blokes.' Smith had also served in the First World War. He died on 20 October 1964.

## Subadar SUBRAMANIAN
*MIGNANO, Italy*
24 February 1944

He was 31 years old and serving in 11 Field Park Company, Queen Victoria's Own Madras Sappers & Miners, Indian Army when he was with a party of sappers clearing a path through a minefield. He was leading the way with a mine detector, while Lance Naik Sigamuni was using white tape to mark out the cleared path. Suddenly there was a small explosion; Sigamuni had stood on a mine, which would explode in three seconds, and he was now petrified with fear. Without hesitating, Subramanian rushed over and pushed him out of the way. Unfortunately both men were killed by the explosion, but by his unselfish act he saved the lives of the rest of his section by placing himself between them and the mine.

### Ensign VIOLETTE SZABO (née BUSHELL)
*France and Germany*
April 1944–between 25 January and 5 February 1945
She was 23 years old and serving in the SOE when she was parachuted into France. With the codename 'Corinne', she acted as a courier to a Frenchman who had survived the break-up of his resistance circuit in Rouen and was trying to re-constitute a group in this area. She had to travel from Paris to Rouen, contacting certain people believed to have remained unmolested, and report back to her chief in Paris. She was twice arrested by the Gestapo, but each time she got away. She accomplished her task successfully and after six weeks returned to England.

On D-Day +1 (7 June 1944) she dropped into France again, this time with three men. They were met by the local Maquis group. Jaques Dafour was to drive Violette by car to the next Maquis group. They set off on 10 June. Violette had with her a Sten gun concealed in the car. Shortly after leaving Sussac they picked up Jean Bariaud, a friend of Dafour. As they neared Salon-la-Tout they saw a roadblock manned by the Germans. Dafour slowed down and then stopped, allowing all three to jump out of the car. Bariaud got away while Violette and Dafour fired at the Germans and one was hit. Then they crawled into a wheat-field and, with some cover, Violette continued to fire at the Germans as the two of them retreated towards a wood. By now the Germans were approaching and Violette was hurt but she continued to fire at the advancing soldiers. She became exhausted and told Dafour to run, which he did. She was captured and taken first to Limoges and then Fresnes in Paris.

After a brutal interrogation over several weeks during which she said nothing, she was put on a train to Germany. On the journey there was an air raid and the guards ran for cover; while they were gone she managed, despite being chained to another prisoner, to carry water to badly wounded British officers in a cattle truck, including Yeo-Thomas, who would also be awarded the GC. She was imprisoned at Ravensbruck Concentration Camp, which was followed by a move to Torgau. In January 1945 she was taken back to Ravensbruck. Her physical condition had deteriorated and she was forced to make her way to the crematorium, where she was shot in the back of the neck and her body incinerated. After the war sixteen members of staff from Ravensbruck were tried in Hamburg.

Szabo's story was made into a film, *Carve her Name with Pride*. Her biography is called *Young, Brave and Beautiful*.

### Pit Deputy FRANK NIX (Edward Medal)
*PILSLEY, England*
18 April 1944

He was 29 years old and working at the Pilsley Colliery when a 'bump' occurred at the coal face on which Ernest Vickers and another man were cutting coal with a compressed-air machine. As a result the flamper over the bars from the left side of the cutter was broken for a distance of 35yds, the roof lowering about 8in. Vickers' head was pinned against the edge of the conveyor pans. His workmate was unable to get past the machine to help, so he called for assistance.

Frank Nix had three men with him behind the machine, two of whom slid down the pans and placed a prop in order to take the weight off the trapped man. Nix followed them down but, seeing that nearly all the props within 10yds of the accident were broken, he sent the others back and went himself to where Vickers was trapped. With the aid of the third man, he worked his way down the face side, resetting the broken props as he went. By this time the roof had lowered to about 15in from the floor, and this was consequently a most difficult job. After setting about twelve props Mr Nix was in a position about 3yds from Mr Vickers, but owing to the fall of earth was unable to see him. He went back to the machine to ascertain the position and then returned to begin clearing the earth, which he did with the assistance of one of the men. After reaching Mr Vickers it became obvious that the only way to free him was to lighten the bar. This could only be done by breaking the flamper with a hammer, working with care for fear of another cave-in. When the bar was sufficiently uncovered, Nix sawed off the end and pulled Vickers free; fortunately he was suffering only from shock and bruises. This whole operation took two hours, during which the work was done in a very confined space, offering little chance of escape if a further cave-in occurred.

Nix declined to exchange his EM for the GC, and became the last recipient to wear the Edward Medal. He died on 8 August 1996.

## Mr GEOFFREY RILEY (Albert Medal)
*DIGLEY VALLEY, YORKSHIRE, England*
29 May 1944
He was 14 years old and a schoolboy. After a thunderstorm, followed by a cloudburst, the river Holme became a raging torrent 50ft wide and over 15ft deep, flooding surrounding land and buildings. Riley saw 76-year-old Maude Wimpenny, who had taken refuge on a low wall. She was surrounded by floodwater that was rapidly rising. He first attempted a rescue by walking to her along the wall, but she would not leave her position. He then entered the water and rescued her from the wall, which later collapsed; he was only a moderate swimmer, and struggled to bring her to safety through the flood until he became exhausted. His father then went to his assistance, but all three were swept away into the river. Geoffrey Riley was the only survivor.

He died on 16 January 2005.

## Engine Driver BENJAMIN GIMBERT
*SOHAM STATION, CAMBRIDGESHIRE, England*
2 June 1944

He was 41 years old and working for the London & North Eastern Railway when his and James Nightall's ammunition train was just entering Soham station. As they approached the station, Gimbert noticed the wagon behind the engine was on fire. He made Nightall aware of it and stopped the train, but by the time it had come to rest the wagon was enveloped in flames. Gimbert instructed Nightall to uncouple the rest of the train. Without hesitation, he uncoupled the wagon, knowing full well that it contained explosives, and then rejoined the driver on the footplate. The blazing wagon was close to the station building and Gimbert realised that it was essential to move it into the open so set the engine in motion. As he approached the signal-box he shouted to the signalman to stop any trains that were due and indicated what he intended to do. At that moment the bombs in the burning wagon exploded and a massive crater some 20ft deep and 60ft wide was blown in the middle of the railway and all the station buildings were destroyed. As many as 600 buildings in Soham were damaged.

Nightall was killed outright and Gimbert was severely injured, later having thirty-two pieces of metal removed from his body. The signalman, Frank Bridges, died later from his injuries, but the train's guard, Herbert Clarke, survived, although he was badly shaken. The train consisted of fifty-one wagons of explosives but due to their action only one exploded.

Gimbert died on 6 May 1976.

## Fireman JAMES NIGHTALL (misspelt KNIGHTALL on his headstone)
*SOHAM STATION, CAMBRIDGESHIRE, England*
2 June 1944

He was 22 years old and working for London & North Eastern Railway when his and engine driver Benjamin Gimbert's ammunition train was just entering Soham station. As they approached the station, Gimbert noticed the wagon behind the engine was on fire. He made Nightall aware of it and stopped the train, but by the time it had come to rest the wagon was enveloped in flames. Gimbert instructed Nightall to uncouple the rest of the train. Without hesitation, he uncoupled the wagon, knowing full well that it contained explosives, and then rejoined the driver on the footplate. The blazing wagon was close to the station building and Gimbert realised that it was essential to move it into the open so set the engine in motion. As he approached the signal-box he shouted to the signalman to stop any trains that were due and indicated what he intended to do. At that moment the bombs in the burning wagon exploded and a massive crater some 20ft deep and 60ft wide was blown in the middle of the railway and all the station buildings were destroyed. As many as 600 buildings in Soham were damaged.

Nightall was killed outright and Gimbert was severely injured, later having thirty-two pieces of metal removed from his body. The signalman, Frank Bridges, died later from his injuries, but the train's guard, Herbert Clarke, survived, although he was badly shaken. The train consisted of fifty-one wagons of explosives but due to their action only one exploded.

## Mr HARWOOD FLINTOFF (Edward Medal)
*FARNDALE, YORKSHIRE, England*
23 June 1944

He was 13 years old and working at the Thunderhead Farm when farmer John Atkinson was driving a bull which turned on him, knocked him down and knelt on his chest. Flintoff immediately left his work in a nearby field and went to his aid. He could see Mr Atkinson lying on the ground covered in blood. He grabbed hold of the bull's nose ring and just hung onto it. The bull then broke loose but was caught a few minutes later and led to its shed by a farm labourer who came to assist with a pitchfork. By his courageous action this boy saved the farmer from more serious injury and possible death.

At the time of going to publication, he is one of twenty living recipients of the GC, and is the last surviving recipient of the EM.

## Air Commodore ARTHUR (known as DWIGHT) ROSS
*RAF THOLTHORPE, YORKSHIRE, England*
28 June 1944

He was 37 years old and serving in the Royal Canadian Air Force when a Halifax bomber crash-landed into another bomber that was in the dispersal area and fully loaded with bombs, bursting into flames. Ross, assisted by Corporal Maurice Marquet, extracted the pilot, who had suffered severe injuries. Then ten 500lb bombs about 30yds away exploded, throwing them to the ground. When the hail of debris had subsided, cries were heard from the rear turret of the crashed bomber. Despite the risk of further explosions, they returned to the blazing wreckage and endeavoured in vain to swing the turret to release the gunner. Ross hacked at the Perspex with an axe and then handed it through the hole to the gunner who enlarged the aperture. Taking the axe again, Ross, now assisted by Flight Sergeant Joseph St Germain and Marquet, finally broke the Perspex steel frame supports and extricated the gunner.

Another 500lb bomb then exploded, which threw the three men to the ground; St Germain quickly threw himself upon the gunner in order to shield him from flying debris. Ross's arm was practically severed between the wrist and the elbow by the blast. He calmly walked to the ambulance and an emergency amputation was performed on arrival at the station sick quarters.

Meanwhile Marquet, seeing petrol running towards two nearby aircraft, directed their removal from the vicinity. Leading Aircraftman M. McKenzie and L. Wolfe rendered valuable assistance in trying to bring the fire under control and helping to extricate the trapped gunner, both being seriously injured by flying debris. St Germain and Marquet were both awarded the GM.

Ross died on 27 September 1981.

### Lieutenant ST JOHN YOUNG
*CITTA DI CASTELLO, Italy*
23/24 July 1944

He was 23 years old and serving in the 4th Indian Division, 10 Corps, Royal Tank Regiment when he was in charge of a patrol that had been ordered to occupy Point 403, a hill feature. As the patrol neared its objective in the dark, explosions were heard and Young believed he was under mortar fire. He ordered a withdrawal but while this was happening there were three more explosions in their midst. Realising that they were in a minefield, he at once ordered every one to remain where he was until daylight.

After nearly two hours Sowar Niru, who had been wounded and was in great pain, began calling for assistance. Young began to crawl forward, probing in front with his fingers; he located and rendered harmless three mines, but then he knelt on another. The explosion blew his right leg off. He immediately called out to his men that he had been wounded but on no account was anyone to come near him. He then continued, with great determination, to crawl forward and reached Niru, whom he found to be unconscious, and in the company of Sowar Ditto Ram, who had also lost his leg on a mine. They applied a field dressing to the wounded man's thigh. It was by now 01:00 hours on the 24th. For the next four hours Lieutenant Young continually gave encouragement to his men, ordering them to remain quite still and assuring them that it would be much easier to extricate themselves as soon as it was light.

At first light Jemadar Hosenak Singh reached them. Finding both the sowars dead, he carried Lieutenant Young out of the minefield to a place of safety. Half an hour later Young was sitting up giving orders to the patrol, indicating the way and supervising the evacuation of the wounded. He died from his wounds the same day.

Initially he was considered for the VC, but this was changed to the GC.

### Sowar DITTO RAM
*CITTA DI CASTELLO, Italy*
23/24 July 1944

He was 29 years old and serving in the Central India Horse, 21st King George V's Horse when he was part of a night patrol that ran into an enemy minefield. Ditto Ram stepped on a mine, blowing his left leg off below the knee, and he applied a field dressing. On hearing calls for help from Sowar Niru, who had been wounded, he crawled forward through the minefield to assist him.

On reaching the man, whose left thigh had been shattered, he was joined by Lieutenant Young and they applied a field dressing to his comrade's wound. He was in great pain throughout, which made the operation both difficult and prolonged. Having completed his task, Ditto Ram lost consciousness and died a few minutes later, as did Sowar Niru.

## Private BENJAMIN HARDY

*COWRA, NSW, Australia*

5 August 1944

He was 45 years old and serving in the 22nd Australian Garrison Battalion, AMF when there was a mass break-out of Japanese prisoners from No. 12 POW Camp. Hardy and Private Ralph Jones were manning a machine-gun when the Japanese stormed over the perimeter armed with knives and baseball bats, and bore down on them. They stood their ground, firing the gun and cutting down hundreds before they were bashed to death by the Japanese. Both men were awarded the GC.

It should be noted that the garrison battalions were manned by men considered too old or unfit for front-line service or men with wounds too bad to be returned to front-line duty. They were often rather unfairly referred to as 'ruthless and toothless'.

## Private RALPH JONES

*COWRA, NSW, Australia*

5 August 1944

He was 43 years old and serving in the 22nd Australian Garrison Battalion, AMF when there was a mass break-out of Japanese prisoners from No. 12 POW Camp. Jones and Private Benjamin Hardy were manning a machine-gun when the Japanese stormed over the perimeter armed with knives and baseball bats, and bore down on them. They stood their ground, firing the gun and cutting down hundreds before they were bashed to death by the Japanese. Both men were awarded the GC.

It should be noted that the garrison battalions were manned by men considered too old or unfit for front-line service or men with wounds too bad to be returned to front-line duty. They were often rather unfairly referred to as 'ruthless and toothless'.

## Corporal KENNETH HORSFIELD

*BRINDISI, Italy*

18 August 1944

He was 24 years old and serving in the Manchester Regiment, attached to the SAS, when an explosion occurred in an ammunition warehouse. Horsfield, who was one of the first on the scene, looked through a window and saw a man lying inside, trapped by rubble. Although a fire was blazing, he jumped into the room to release the man, but was unable to do so because of the fire. He got a 32-gallon wheeled extinguisher and from the doorway directed it on to the fire in an attempt to keep it away from the trapped man. He knew that another explosion might occur and had in fact ordered his men away.

He continued his efforts until a second explosion fatally injured him.

### Flying Officer RODERICK 'CY' GRAY
*Atlantic Ocean*
27 August 1944

He was 26 years old and serving in 72 Squadron, RAF when his Wellington bomber attacked the *U-534* but was shot down. Despite a severe leg wound, Gray succeeded in inflating his own dinghy and then assisted the wounded captain, George Whiteley, into it. Shortly afterwards, cries were heard from Flight Sergeant John Ford, who had broken his arm. Gray helped him into the dinghy, but, knowing it could hold only two men, he refused to get into the dinghy himself, although he was suffering intense pain. He and Warrant Officer Gordon Bulley held on to the side for some hours. The pain in his leg (it is thought that the lower part of his leg had been shot off) was increasing in intensity and he was becoming exhausted. Nevertheless he steadfastly refused to endanger his comrades by entering the dinghy. He eventually lost consciousness and died in the night. When it became light, his comrades realised that he was dead and they were forced to let him go. The three remaining men were picked up after fifteen hours in the sea. Bulley wrote to his widow and said of Gray: 'Never so long as I live will I forget Cy Gray's courage. I definitely owe my life to him. In my opinion he was just about the biggest hero that ever lived.'

### Sergeant ARTHUR BANKS
*Italy*
27 August–20 December 1944

He was 21 years old and serving in 112 Squadron, RAF Volunteer Reserve. During an armed reconnaissance flight his aircraft was badly damaged by anti-aircraft fire. Banks was compelled to make a forced landing, and after destroying his aircraft he tried to reach the Allied lines. He made contact with a group of partisans and, during the following months, he became an outstanding figure among them, advising and encouraging them in action against the enemy. Early in December 1944 an attempt was made at crossing into Allied territory by boat, but the whole party was surrounded and captured. Banks was handed over to the German commander of the district, who presided at his interrogation, during which he was tortured. At one stage he succeeded in getting hold of a machine-gun, with which he could have killed most of his captors, but one of the partisans, fearing reprisals, intervened by pinning his arms to his sides.

On 8 December Banks was taken to a prison in Adria, where he remained until 19 December, when he was moved to another prison at Ariano Polesine and was again tortured to make him talk, which he never did. He was then stripped, bound and thrown into the river Po; he managed to escape, but was recaptured, taken back to the prison and shot.

### Captain SIMMON LATUTIN
*MOGADISHU, Somaliland*
29 December 1944

He was 28 years old and serving in the Somerset Light Infantry (Prince Albert's), attached to the Somalia Gendarmerie. Latutin, an officer, an NCO and a personal boy were in the training school store selecting fireworks for New Year when a fire broke out and almost simultaneously a great number of rockets began to explode and burn – there were some 170 cases of them in the store. With the force of the explosion and the fire, the store rapidly became an inferno. Latutin, regardless of the detonating rockets, the intense heat and the choking clouds of smoke, plunged into the flames and succeeded in dragging out the officer, who was almost unconscious owing to his injuries. By this time Latutin was himself alight, but without an instant's hesitation he again rushed into the flames and rescued the NCO. He was about to go back in for the boy but his men restrained him.

Latutin died of his injuries the next day.

### Signalman KENNETH SMITH
*ISLAND OF IST, Adriatic*
10 January 1945

He was 34 years old and serving in the Long Range Desert Group Signal Section, Royal Corps of Signals when he was part of a team gathering information on shipping movements in the Adriatic Sea. They were using a villager's home as a base when saboteurs laid time-bombs in vital houses on the island. After hearing firing, Smith got up and went into the main part of the house, where he saw a bomb on the table by the door. Knowing that there were partisans and children in the room, Smith immediately picked up the bomb, which was already ticking and had run only a few yards out of the house with it when it exploded, killing him. He deliberately sacrificed himself to save others.

### Constable 1st Class ERIC BAILEY
*BLAYNEY, NSW, Australia*
12 January 1945

He was 38 years old and serving in the NSW Police Force. He was on duty in Adelaide Street when he stopped a man whose movements were suspicious. While he was being questioned, the man pulled a revolver from his pocket and shot Bailey in the stomach. Bailey closed with his assailant, who fired two more shots. Although fast succumbing to shock and haemorrhaging, he continued the struggle and held the gunman on the ground until help arrived. He died shortly afterwards.

He was posthumously promoted to Sergeant 3rd Class.

### Flight Sergeant STANLEY WOODBRIDGE
*Burma*
31 January–7 February 1945

He was 23 years old and serving in 159 Squadron, RAF Volunteer Reserve when his Liberator bomber crashed in the jungle. Together with three other members of the crew he was captured by the Japanese. All four were subjected to torture in an endeavour to obtain information that would have been useful to the Japanese Intelligence Service. Eventually, Flight Sergeant Leslie Bellingham, Flight Sergeant Robert Snelling and Flight Sergeant John Woodage were separated and taken into the jungle and beheaded.

As a wireless operator, the Japanese thought Woodbridge would have information on codes and wavelengths. A Japanese technical officer was detailed to carry out the interrogation with two interpreters, but in spite of repeated torture Woodbridge steadfastly refused to give any information whatsoever. The final interrogation took place at the place of execution. Even when it was obvious to him that he was going to be put to death, he maintained his courageous attitude to the end, merely remarking that if the Japanese were going to kill him they should do it quickly. After all efforts to make him talk, including further torture, failed, he was beheaded.

Three Japanese officers and three NCOs were subsequently brought to trial by a Military Court charged with the torture and murder of the four airmen. During the trial it was revealed that the Japanese had concentrated their efforts on Woodbridge in an endeavour to obtain technical information regarding wireless equipment. They were found guilty, three being hanged and three being given long prison sentences.

### Lance Corporal DAVID RUSSELL
*PONTE DI PIAVE, Italy*
22–28 February 1945

He was 33 years old and serving in the 22nd Motorised Battalion, New Zealand Expeditionary Force when he escaped from his prisoner-of-war camp. He obtained civilian clothes and was befriended by an Italian, Giuseppe Vettorello. During this time he kept in contact with other POWs, helping them to escape. In all he is credited with the successful escapes of forty-seven men. However, he was arrested by Italian Fascist soldiers on 22 February. He knew he would be treated as a spy rather than as a soldier, because of the civilian clothes. His captors were members of a mixed German-Italian Police Regiment, and they took him and Vettorello to the HQ of Oberleutnant Haupt. Vettorello was accused of sheltering Russell but denied having ever seen him before and was released.

However, the Germans were not convinced of Russell's innocence and believed that he knew where there were other POWs. According to an Italian soldier, Russell was beaten up by Haupt but remained silent. He was chained to a wall and told he would be shot in three days if he did not talk but he refused. He was given no food or water and was repeatedly beaten. An Italian who did offer him some food tried to persuade him to save his life, but he replied, 'Let them shoot me.'

Haupt's interpreter, an Italian, said: 'The behaviour of the Englishman was splendid, and it won the admiration of Haupt himself.'

On 28 February Russell was shot and hastily buried, but was later exhumed and buried with dignity.

**Section Leader EDWARD HEMING** (misspelt **HEMMING** on his citation)
*LONDON, England*
2 March 1945
He was 34 years old and serving in the Civil Defence Rescue Service when a V2 rocket fell on the Dockhead Roman Catholic Church in Bermondsey. Heming, on hearing a faint call for help, took an axe and a saw and crawled between the joists and beams, making his way through the rubble to the trapped man. He removed the debris and broke away the furniture around the victim until it was found that he was pinned down by a main timber beam which was fixed to the floor. Any movement of the beam would have brought about a complete collapse with fatal results for both men. Gas was also leaking into the building. Despite being told the risk of continuing was too great, Heming slowly and carefully removed the debris from beneath the man until, after three hours, he was released. The rescued man, Father Arbuthnott, later presented Heming with a silver crucifix engraved 'In gratitude for 2.3.45. EA.'

Heming was assisted by George Northwood who was in the crypt below, directing light and handing tools through a hole; although he was also nominated for an award, nothing came of it. Years later Heming worked in the photographic department of the Imperial War Museum. He died on 3 January 1987.

**Lance Naik ISLAM-un-DIN**
*PYAWBWE, Burma*
12 April 1945
He was 19 or 20 years old and serving in the 6th Battalion, Jat Regiment, Indian Army when he threw himself on a live grenade to save the lives of his comrades and was killed instantly. He had previously shown high qualities of leadership and courage in action on 24 March 1945, near Khanda.

**Lieutenant GEORGE GOSSE**
*BREMEN, Germany*
8–19 May 1945
He was 33 years old and serving in the Royal Australian Naval Volunteer Reserve when a report came in that a new type of mine had been found in the Ubersee-Hafen. Gosse immediately dived and verified that it was a GD pressure type commonly known as an 'Oyster'. As it was necessary that this type of mine should be recovered intact, it was decided to attempt to render it safe underwater and on the next day Lieutenant Gosse dived on it again. Using improvised tools, he eventually succeeded in removing the primer, which was followed by a loud metallic crash. The mine was eventually lifted on to the quayside, where it was found that the detonator had fired immediately the primer had been removed. During the subsequent ten days Gosse rendered safe two similar types of mine that were lying in close proximity to shipping, and in each instance the detonator fired before the mine reached the surface.

Gosse had joined the Royal Australian Navy aged just 13 in 1925. He died on 31 December 1965.

### Mr WILLIAM WATERSON (Edward Medal)
*BIRMINGHAM, England*
18 August 1945

He was 41 years old and working at the General Electric Co. when two workmen were engaged in collecting newly manufactured lamp-black from a brick chamber. The men were unprotected and had to withstand high temperatures as well as an atmosphere made unpleasant by the presence of particles of oily lamp-black as well as carbon monoxide from burning soot. After a short time Webb collapsed and his companion, Albert Stranks, being unable to move him, sought assistance. Breathing gear was stored at the works fire station some distance away; when Stranks called for help, the alarm was sounded. To wait for the breathing gear would have led to a long delay.

Waterson, who was the first on the scene, joined Stranks and without hesitation, though fully realising the risk, entered the chamber and attempted to pull Webb out. He was covered in sweat and carbon black and the rescue work was difficult as it was not possible to get a proper grip on him. They were unsuccessful at first and when they came out Stranks collapsed; Waterson continued to try, entering the chamber four times in all. On his last attempt he was helped by John Hewitt, a member of the works fire brigade, who had arrived with some rope but no breathing gear; together they succeeded in bringing Webb out, but unfortunately he was found to be dead.

Waterson died on 24 March 1973.

### Fireman FREDERICK DAVIES
*LONDON, England*
22 August 1945

He was 32 years old and serving in the National Fire Service (London Area), now the London Fire Brigade, when his engine was called to a fire in Craven Park Road. On arrival, the officer in charge was informed that two young sisters, Avril and Jean Pike, were in the front room on the second floor. A ladder was immediately pitched to the window and before it was even in position Davies ran up it and entered the burning building. At this stage flames were pouring from the windows and licking up the front of the building. He was seen to endeavour to remove his tunic, presumably to wrap around the children, but his hands were now too badly burned for him to do so. After a short period he returned to the window with Avril in his arms; he handed her out of the window to Leading Fireman Thorn. He was next seen to fling himself out of the window on to the ladder, the whole of his clothing ablaze. Thorn held Davies under one arm and Avril under the other, then disastrously Avril slipped from his grip and fell to the ground; unbeknown to either fireman, she was already dead. Davies' uniform was still smouldering and he was taken to hospital suffering from severe burns on his face, hands, arms and back. In fact his arms were burned all the way to his elbows. He succumbed to his injuries the following day. Jean died in the fire. Leading Fireman Thorn was awarded a King's Commendation for Brave Conduct.

The fire brigade never forgot Frederick Davies' bravery; they paid for his son Raymond to go on holiday to Bournemouth every year.

# CHAPTER EIGHT

# George Crosses Awarded after the Second World War

### Naik KIRPA RAM
*THONDEBHAVI, India*
12 September 1945

He was 29 years old and serving in the 8th Battalion, 13th Frontier Force Rifles, Indian Army when he was commanding a section of men on a firing exercise. He was lying next to a sepoy who was firing rifle grenades when one fell short, landing just in front of the section. Kirpa Ram leapt up and dashed forward, shouting to his men, 'Get back and take cover.' He picked up the grenade but it exploded before he could throw it away. He died from his wounds just a few minutes later.

### Major KENNETH BIGGS
*SAVERNAKE FOREST, WILTSHIRE, England*
2 January 1946

He was 34 years old and serving in the Royal Army Ordnance Corps. A munitions train was being loaded with ammunition when there was a violent explosion and a 3-ton lorry and two railway wagons literally disappeared. Fire broke out at a dozen points around the yard. A wagon load of 5.5-inch shells, some distance off, went up and the fire spread further. Small arms ammunition started to explode in every direction and the scene became like a battlefield. Eight men died in the explosion and six more were badly injured. There were in fact few of the original working party left to do anything about the situation. However, the noise brought men hurrying from all over the area and one of the first to arrive was Staff Sergeant Sydney Rogerson.

Realising he was the senior NCO on the spot, he took charge at once. He collected together the few uninjured men and others just arriving and with great calmness he split the men up into small parties and detailed each group to one of the many fires. One party had to move an explosives truck that was close to a blaze, and then Rogerson himself climbed under a burning truck full of shells to rescue two injured men. As more men arrived on the scene, he gave them the job of carrying the wounded to safety, or sent them to join the fire parties. Some minutes later Major Biggs arrived and took over command. He remained as cool as Rogerson had been, and one of the first things he did, with the help of another officer, was to uncouple a burning wagon full of shells from the rest of the train and push it clear of the other trucks.

Then he set to work extinguishing the fires. Next he organised the removal of other wagons to create fire breaks. At this point Biggs was thrown to the ground by another heavy explosion and badly shaken. He picked himself up and went forward alone, refusing to let anyone go with him, to inspect the site of the latest detonation and to see if any further damage had been caused by it. Soon after this he decided that everything possible had been done to remove the loaded trucks from the burning ones, and that further efforts at fire-fighting could do little good and might even result in further loss of life. He therefore withdrew all his men from the siding and was the last to leave. But he did not go far, keeping an eye on the situation until the last fire had burnt itself out.

Biggs had also served in the Second World War. He died on 11 January 1998.

## Acting Staff Sergeant SYDNEY (sometimes spelt SIDNEY) ROGERSON
*SAVERNAKE FOREST, WILTSHIRE, England*
2 January 1946

He was 30 years old and serving in the Royal Army Ordnance Corps. A munitions train was being loaded with ammunition when there was a violent explosion and a 3-ton lorry and two railway wagons literally disappeared. Fire broke out at a dozen points around the yard. A wagon load of 5.5-inch shells, some distance off, went up and the fire spread further. Small arms ammunition started to explode in every direction and the scene became like a battlefield. Eight men died in the explosion and six more were badly injured. There were in fact few of the original working party left to do anything about the situation. However, the noise brought men hurrying from all over the area and one of the first to arrive was Staff Sergeant Sydney Rogerson.

Realising he was the senior NCO on the spot, he took charge at once. He collected together the few uninjured men and others just arriving and with great calmness he split the men up into small parties and detailed each group to one of the many fires. One party had to move an explosives truck that was close to a blaze, and then Rogerson himself climbed under a burning truck full of shells to rescue two injured men. As more men arrived on the scene, he gave them the job of carrying the wounded to safety, or sent them to join the fire parties. Some minutes later Major Biggs arrived and took over command. He remained as cool as Rogerson had been, and one of the first things he did, with the help of another officer, was to uncouple a burning wagon full of shells from the rest of the train and push it clear of the other trucks.

Then he set to work extinguishing the fires. Next he organised the removal of other wagons to create fire breaks. At this point Biggs was thrown to the ground by another heavy explosion and badly shaken. He picked himself up and went forward alone, refusing to let anyone go with him, to inspect the site of the latest detonation and to see if any further damage had been caused by it. Soon after this he decided that everything possible had been done to remove the loaded trucks from the burning ones, and that further efforts at fire-fighting could do little good and might even result in further loss of life. He therefore withdrew all his men from the siding and was the last to leave. But he did not go far, keeping an eye on the situation until the last fire had burnt itself out.

Rogerson also served in the Second World War. He died on 23 September 1993.

## Havildar RAHMAN (sometimes spelt REHMAN) ABDUL
*KLETEK, Java*
22 February 1946

He was 25 years old and serving in the 3rd Battalion, 9th Jat Regiment, Indian Army when his jeep hit a mine and was thrown forward into a ditch, bursting into flames. Abdul was thrown clear, but went back to try to free the other three men, who were trapped under the jeep. His task was rendered more hazardous since, owing to the fire, the ammunition began to explode. Nevertheless, he extricated one man, and, although by this time the jeep was burning fiercely, then succeeded in dragging a second man clear. He then returned to help the last man, who was lying under the jeep by the front wheel, but as Abdul took hold of him the petrol tank under the driver's seat exploded, spouting burning petrol all over him. Despite his condition, he continued his efforts until an ambulance party approached. After calling out to them to complete his work, he fell dead.

His complete disregard for his own safety and his determination to save his helpless comrades, in which he persisted even while being burned to death himself, constitute an example of courage of the highest order.

He had also served in the Second World War, being awarded the MM. NB: the year of his GC deed is often mistakenly said to have been 1945.

## Driver JOSEPH HUGHES
*LYEMUN BARRACKS, Hong Kong*
21 March 1946

He was 19 years old and serving in the Royal Army Service Corps when he was driving a 3-ton vehicle carrying ammunition and explosives into the magazine area. The truck started to smoulder and then caught fire. Knowing full well that his truck was likely to blow up at any moment, Hughes, instead of running for cover, did everything in his power to put out the fire. Notwithstanding small explosions occurring in his vehicle, he first tried to remove the burning camouflage net, and then tried a fire extinguisher, which failed to put out the fire. A few minutes later his lorry blew up, fatally wounding him. He died two days later. Hughes' courage in remaining at his task, and attempting to minimise the danger to others when he could have run to safety, was an outstanding example of devotion to duty.

His brother-in-law was Acting Leading Seaman William Goad GC.

## Squadron Leader HUBERT DINWOODIE

*LUBECK, Germany*

20–23 August 1946

He was 49 years old and serving in the RAF Volunteer Reserve. German high explosive bombs were being loaded at Lubeck for disposal at sea, and two train-loads of bomb, weighing approximately 1,100 tons, were waiting on the quayside. Loading was in progress when a 50kg bomb was accidentally dropped and exploded, killing six people and injuring twelve.

Dinwoodie was sent to Lubeck to clear the bombs; he found that they were an experimental type, fitted with a special shock-sensitive electrically operated fuse. Corporal Roland Garred was detailed to assist in dealing with these bombs and to take action to safeguard the munitions trains. Despite the considerable risk involved, Dinwoodie and Garred proceeded to defuse one of the bombs; they found that the explosion had been due to defective German workmanship or design and that in several of the bombs the fuse had already moved, rendering the bombs dangerous.

All the work on these bombs took place in an atmosphere of tension caused by lack of knowledge about the bombs and uncertainty as to whether the action of defusing them would cause another detonation. Throughout this operation both men displayed great courage and devotion to duty of the highest order.

Leading Aircraftman John Hatton was detailed to assist as motor transport driver during the four days it took to make safe the bombs, working in the full knowledge that he was working with bombs that were shock-sensitive. When it was necessary to move a damaged rail-wagon that was still loaded with bombs, he towed it very carefully along the dock side until it was in the desired position. Whenever assistance was required to move the bombs, he was always on hand. In the final operation he alone assisted in transporting the bombs to the demolition site and, although a driver, did his share of the work involved in blowing them up. Had these bombs detonated it is likely that most of Lubeck would have been destroyed. Garred was awarded the GM and Hatton the BEM.

Dinwoodie had also served in both world wars, being awarded the MC in the first. He died on 28 August 1968.

## Temporary Lieutenant ERIC WALTON (Albert Medal)

*Antarctic*

24 August 1946

He was 28 years old and serving in the Royal Navy as a member of Operation Tabarin, the forerunner of the Falklands Islands Dependencies Survey, now called the British Antarctic Survey. During a sledging journey Major John Tonkin of the survey team fell through a badly bridged crevasse and disappeared. He had fallen 40ft and was jammed in a narrow part of the crevasse. Ropes were lowered to him and he managed to get loops around his forearms, but no higher, and it was found impossible to pull him out due to his being jammed in the ice. Walton volunteered to be lowered down to help. An ice axe could not be used in the confined space; the spike was sawn off so it could be used as a hand tool. He was lowered down a wider part of the crevasse and worked his way along until he reached the major. Five times he was lowered down and it took three hours to free him.

Walton also served in the Second World War, being awarded the DSC. He and his son Jonathan are believed to be the only father and son to hold the coveted Polar Medal. He declined to exchange his AM for the GC, but was an active member of the VC&GC Association. Walton is also author of *Two Years in the Antarctic*. He died on 13 April 2009.

### Overman DAVID BROWN (Edward Medal)
*WEST CALDER, MIDLOTHIAN, Scotland*
10 January 1947
He was 46 years old and working at the Burngrange Shale Mine when firedamp ignited by an acetylene cap lamp exploded, starting fires which spread rapidly. Brown proceeded with a fireman to explore the narrow workings where men were trapped. At first they made good progress but increasingly dense smoke compelled them to withdraw. Brown then made another attempt, alone. He got as far as no. 3 Dockhead, where he shouted but got no response and could see no signs of life, smoke forcing him to withdraw again. The conditions were getting worse all the time and Overman Brown sent word explaining the position to the manager, who was dealing with the fires elsewhere, and asking for breathing apparatus.

He then set out to discover for himself where all the smoke was coming from. He was met by members of the NFS and pleaded to be permitted the use of breathing apparatus so he and a trained member of the Burngrange Mines Rescue Team could make another attempt to get into the workings beyond no. 3 Dockhead. He made two more attempts with breathing apparatus but was forced back each time by the intense heat.

It took four days to bring the fires under control and only then was it possible to send a rescue team beyond the fire area. Fourteen out of the fifteen dead were found in no. 3 Dook.

Brown died on 1 December 1977.

### Able Seaman THOMAS KELLY
*BAY OF BISCAY, North Atlantic*
18 March 1947
He was 18 years old and serving in the Merchant Navy when the SS *Famagusta* encountered very severe weather and developed a list to port. The wind was almost of gale force in squalls and the seas were high and tumbling; the list increased and the vessel pounded and shipped water.

In response to an SOS call the SS *Empire Plover* came to her assistance and stood by. The *Famagusta* launched a lifeboat, which pulled towards the *Empire Plover*, but the boat capsized and threw the ten men into the water.

The *Empire Plover* quickly manoeuvred into position and lowered ropes, ladders

185

and scrambling nets. Three of her crew entered the water; two of them remained at the nets and ladders while Kelly swam off with a line to the crew of the lifeboat, who were struggling in the raging sea. He first brought to safety an officer who had been injured. He then swam out again and returned with another man. Notwithstanding the strain through which he had already gone, he swam away from the ship a third time to the assistance of a woman who was seen struggling some 50yds away. He succeeded in reaching her but both were struck by a heavy sea and disappeared. His body was never recovered. Five of the ten in the lifeboat were drowned. The next day would have been Kelly's 19th birthday.

### Sergeant JOHN BECKETT
*LEVANT, Israel*
28 March 1947

He was 41 years old and serving in the RAF when, during a refuelling operation on a Lancaster bomber of 38 Squadron, a violent fire suddenly broke out in the pumping compartment of the refuelling vehicle of which Beckett was the driver. He was enveloped by flames, setting him alight. Another airman beat out the flames but Beckett was badly burned on the hands and face. At this time there was a grave risk that the main tank of fuel, containing over 2,000 gallons, would explode, destroying all twenty of the aircraft in the park and killing many of the aircrew. In spite of his injuries and the pain, Beckett got into the driver's seat of the burning vehicle and drove it a distance of 400yds to a point outside the aircraft park, where it could do no further damage. He was then immediately taken to the station sick quarters, but died of his injuries on 12 April.

Beckett had also served in the Second World War.

### Pit Deputy JOHN CHARLTON (Edward Medal)
*DURHAM, England*
30 March 1947

He was 52 years old and working at the Hylton Colliery when repairer John Kirkhouse was overcome by gas. Charlton was informed the man was missing and at once conducted a search, testing for gas with his flame safety lamp. He had gone only a few yards when he found gas present, at the same time noticing some 30yds ahead of him a light from an electric lamp. Accompanied by Timberman John Austin, Charlton went towards the light but had to retire owing to the presence of gas. They endeavoured to clear the air by using compressed air along the road but could still get no nearer than 12yds from Kirkhouse.

Crawling on their hands and knees, they succeeded in reaching the man, who was unconscious. While dragging him back, Charlton himself was slightly overcome and had to rest, but soon returned to help Austin, who in turn collapsed and had to be dragged clear. Other men finally helped them out, but Kirkhouse never regained consciousness. Both men were awarded the EM but only Charlton lived to exchange his for the GC.

He died on 25 February 1976.

186

**Shotfirer SYDNEY BLACKBURN** (Edward Medal)

*BARNSLEY, England*

7 May 1947

He was 48 years old and working at the Barnsley Main Colliery when an explosion killed nine men and injured twenty-three. Sydney Blackburn and Harry Crummack were at the end of the coal face away from the resulting flame. Crummack was blown over by the shock wave, but quickly recovered. Despite the fumes and dust, they assembled men who had scrambled from the face and led them to a place of safety. Then, returning, they found a number of injured men to whom they gave assistance and then proceeded through the fumes and clouds of dust in search of others. Both men, while taking every reasonable precaution, continued to disregard their own personal safety in their efforts to ensure that none of the injured was left unattended in the danger area.

Blackburn died on 15 December 1991.

**Leading Seaman PHILLIP MAY** (Albert Medal)

*Malta*

20 June 1947

He was 24 years old and serving in the Royal Navy aboard HM Cable Ship *St Margarets* when a chief petty officer entered a cable tank and was overcome by gas. The first lieutenant, the boatswain and four ratings entered the tank to rescue him and were all overcome themselves. May then entered the tank and, in a series of rescues, secured a line around each of the seven men, so enabling them to be hauled on deck. After the third rescue May was so exhausted that a ship-mate offered to relieve him, but he himself was overcome and required rescuing. May therefore continued his gallant work single-handed until the task was completed. Seven men owed their lives to his selfless bravery and determination. The chief petty officer died later.

May was the author of *Beyond the Five Points*, a book on Freemason VC&GCs, which was published posthumously. May also served in the Second World War. He died on 14 December 1994.

**Dr ARTHUR 'DICK' BUTSON** (Albert Medal)

*Antarctic*

26/27 July 1947

He was 25 years old and a member of the Falkland Islands Dependencies Survey when Mr Peterson, an American member of the Ronne Antarctic Research Expedition, fell into a crevasse. Butson was part of one rescue team, but the hazards of crossing a heavily crevassed glacier at night were much increased. On arrival, Butson immediately volunteered to be lowered into the crevasse, where he found Peterson wedged head down 106ft below the surface, and suffering from shock and exhaustion. For nearly an hour Butson chipped away at the ice in an extremely confined space in order to free the American, who was then brought to the surface and placed in a tent. The rope was again lowered and Dr Butson sent up the precious equipment before coming up himself. He then gave medical aid to Peterson and returned to base carrying the casualty on one of the sledges.

At the time of going to publication, he is one of twenty living recipients of the GC.

### Pit Deputy HARRY ROBINSON (Edward Medal)
*DURHAM, England*
22/23 August 1947

He was 30 years old and working at the Louisa Colliery when a serious explosion of firedamp and coal dust occurred. Robinson, Joseph Shanley and William Younger, who all had an intimate knowledge of the mine and could have made their way to safety, instead went to the scene of the explosion, where they were joined by John Hutchinson, who had come down from the surface on hearing the explosion. Twenty-four men, all of whom were incapacitated by injuries or carbon-monoxide, were in the district at the time. They worked for one-and-a-half hours in conditions of acute danger; the atmosphere was so thick that the beams of the cap lamps could not penetrate more than a foot. The rescuers could do nothing to stop falls of ground – a very real danger after an explosion – and the route out was almost completely blocked by tubs derailed by the blast. Nineteen of the men died and but for the prompt and continuous heroic action of Robinson, Shanley, Younger and Hutchinson there can be little doubt that not one would have survived. All four men were awarded the EM.

Robinson declined to exchange his EM for the GC. He died on 16 October 1987.

### Pit Deputy JOSEPH SHANLEY (Edward Medal)
*DURHAM, England*
22/23 August 1947

He was 40 years old and working at the Louisa Colliery when a serious explosion of firedamp and coal dust occurred. Shanley, Harry Robinson and William Younger, who all had an intimate knowledge of the mine and could have made their way to safety, instead went to the scene of the explosion, where they were joined by John Hutchinson, who had come down from the surface on hearing the explosion. Twenty-four men, all of whom were incapacitated by injuries or carbon-monoxide, were in the district at the time. They worked for one-and-a-half hours in conditions of acute danger; the atmosphere was so thick that the beams of the cap lamps could not penetrate more than a foot. The rescuers could do nothing to stop falls of ground – a very real danger after an explosion – and the route out was almost completely blocked by tubs derailed by the blast. Nineteen of the men died and but for the prompt and continuous heroic action of Robinson, Shanley, Younger and Hutchinson there can be little doubt that not one would have survived. All four men were awarded the EM.

Shanley died on 23 April 1980.

**Pit Deputy WILLIAM YOUNGER** (Edward Medal)
*DURHAM, England*
22/23 August 1947
He was 28 years old and working at the Louisa Colliery when a serious explosion of firedamp and coal dust occurred. Younger, Joseph Shanley and Harry Robinson, who all had an intimate knowledge of the mine and could have made their way to safety, instead went to the scene of the explosion, where they were joined by John Hutchinson, who had come down from the surface on hearing the explosion. Twenty-four men, all of whom were incapacitated by injuries or carbon-monoxide, were in the district at the time. They worked for one-and-a-half hours in conditions of acute danger; the atmosphere was so thick that the beams of the cap lamps could not penetrate more than a foot. The rescuers could do nothing to stop falls of ground – a very real danger after an explosion – and the route out was almost completely blocked by tubs derailed by the blast. Nineteen of the men died and but for the prompt and continuous heroic action of Robinson, Shanley, Younger and Hutchinson there can be little doubt that not one would have survived. All four men were awarded the EM.

Younger had also served in the Second World War. He died on 6 February 1993.

**Overman JOHN HUTCHINSON** (Edward Medal)
*DURHAM, England*
22/23 August 1947
He was 40 years old and working at the Louisa Colliery when a serious explosion of firedamp and coal dust occurred. Joseph Shanley, Harry Robinson and William Younger, who all had an intimate knowledge of the mine and could have made their way to safety, instead went to the scene of the explosion, where they were joined by John Hutchinson, who had come down from the surface on hearing the explosion. Twenty-four men, all of whom were incapacitated by injuries or carbon-monoxide, were in the district at the time. They worked for one-and-a-half hours in conditions of acute danger; the atmosphere was so thick that the beams of the cap lamps could not penetrate more than a foot. The rescuers could do nothing to stop falls of ground – a very real danger after an explosion – and the route out was almost completely blocked by tubs derailed by the blast. Nineteen of the men died and but for the prompt and continuous heroic action of Robinson, Shanley, Younger and Hutchinson there can be little doubt that not one would have survived. All four men were awarded the EM.

Hutchinson died on 9 June 1975.

**Pit Worker WALTER LEE** (Edward Medal)
*BARNSLEY, YORKSHIRE, England*
11 November 1947
He was 28 years old and working at Wombwell Main Colliery when a roof fall occurred at about 4pm, burying three men. The first man on the scene was

George Dorling, who had climbed over the fall in an attempt to reach the trapped men. He called for assistance and was followed by three men but the roof again began to move and a second fall occurred. The three men were able to withdraw but Dorling could not escape and was killed instantly. Shortly afterwards Lee arrived on the scene and it was clear from their shouts that two of the men trapped by the first fall were still alive. Lee then took the lead in making a way through the fall and after some two hours one of the men was extricated alive. Lee was largely instrumental in saving this man's life and exposed himself to great personal risk in doing so. Dorling was also awarded the EM.

Lee died on 24 May 1984.

### Chief Petty Officer JOSEPH LYNCH (Albert Medal)
*PORT STANLEY, Falkland Islands*
26 February 1948

He was 35 years old and serving in the Royal Navy aboard HMS *Nigeria*. Leading Seaman Hughes missed his footing on the Jacob's ladder while disembarking from the motor cutter at the port boom and fell into the sea. It was after dark, and the sea was rough and at a temperature of 42° Fahrenheit, with the wind blowing a fresh gale. Hughes managed to retain his hold on the ladder but as he was dressed in heavy oilskins he was unable to pull himself up, nor could he make for the cutter owing to the cold state of the sea and the fear of sinking in his heavy clothes.

Lynch was in the mess when he heard the pipe for the lifeboat. Dressed only in a singlet and trousers, he immediately went on deck; seeing what had happened, he made his way out along the boom, down the ladder and into the water alongside Hughes. He then persuaded Hughes to let go of the ladder and supported him to the motor cutter. Lynch then swam back to the ladder to wait until Hughes had been hauled into the boat. Only when Hughes was safe did Lynch swim back to the motor cutter, and was himself hauled to safety.

Lynch had also served in the Second World War. He died on 7 October 2006.

### Mr DAVID WESTERN (Albert Medal)
*LONDON, England*
27 February 1948

He was 10 years old and walking on a frozen lake with three other boys at Osterley Park when the ice gave way. Alan Bradley, James Sandworth (aged 9) and Leonard Edwards (aged 11) all fell through the ice. Western immediately attempted to rescue each in turn but also fell through the ice. Undaunted, he forced a channel through the ice until he linked up with Bradley, who was in difficulties, and pulled him out. He then returned with a thin rope fastened around his waist, to try to save the other boys. Though only a moderate swimmer, he swam through the channel in the ice, beating at the unbroken ice with his fists and leaning on it to make it give way. By now the boys had slipped under the ice, so he dived under the surface to look for them until he was practically exhausted and had to be pulled back to the bank. This brave work was sustained for twenty-five minutes in icy water, and in forcing his way through the ice he received multiple abrasions on his body, legs and arms. The other boys drowned.

According to his family, David Western was happy for people to know he was a holder of the GC but was always very cagey about how he'd earned it. It seems he felt some guilt because he had been unable to save the other boys, especially as at one point he had touched one's hands but could not keep hold of him. David died on 12 March 1995.

### Constable KENNETH FARROW (Albert Medal)
*CARDIFF, Wales*
21 June 1948

He was 23 years old and serving in the Cardiff City Police Force. He was on patrol when he saw a number of people running, and on making enquiry was told that a child had fallen into a feeder stream. He at once ran to the scene, divested himself of his uniform, dived into the water and swam underneath the feeder's long concrete covering for a distance of about 180yds in search of the child, despite not being a strong swimmer. The speed of the current was about 6 miles an hour, and whereas headroom at the point of entry was 2ft 2in, it decreased to only 6in. The water was murky, with considerable amounts of mud and silt at the bottom, and it was too deep to stand up in the water. Although the child's body was recovered later, Farrow greatly exhausted himself in swimming back against the current. According to witnesses, he was in the water for about fifteen minutes, in complete darkness.

Farrow had also served in the Second World War. He died on 30 March 2007.

### Boy 1st Class ALFRED LOWE (Albert Medal)
*PORTLAND HARBOUR, WEYMOUTH, England*
17 October 1948

He was 17 years old and serving in the Royal Navy when a liberty boat returning from Weymouth Pier to HMS *Illustrious* with fifty-one men on board overturned and sank 50 to 100yds from the ship's stern. Lowe was trapped under the canopy but struggled free and surfaced. He saw a lifebelt a short distance from him, which had been thrown from the *Illustrious*, and swam to it. He then removed his overcoat and shoes and swam towards the ship. When he was under the stern a line was thrown to him. At this moment he heard a faint cry of 'Help' and looking around saw that Midshipman Richard Clough, who was about 10yds away, was in great difficulty.

Lowe grabbed the line and swam to him; Clough was unconscious by the time he reached him. He tried to turn him over to keep his head above water but could not, so he pulled him to the ship's side. A fog buoy was lowered and he managed to drag Clough onto it and hold on to him until a petty officer came down the rope to assist him. Together they secured him until he was hoisted on board.

The accident took place in 8 fathoms of water, in rough seas and with a strong wind blowing. Although Richard Clough died from shock half an hour after coming on board, Lowe acted with complete disregard for his own life in leaving his place of safety in an attempt to save another. Of the fifty-one men on board the liberty boat, twenty-nine lost their lives.

Lowe also served in the Korean War. At the time of going to publication, he is one of twenty living recipients of the GC.

### Miss MARGARET VAUGHAN (later PURVES) (Albert Medal)
*SULLY ISLAND, GLAMORGAN, Wales*
28 May 1949

She was a 14-year-old schoolgirl when she saw a group of Scouts were being cut off by the rising tide. Most of the boys got safely across, but two of them were forced off the causeway by the strong tide. The Scout leader, Tony Ress, returned to help Richard Wiggins, but became exhausted in the struggle. Margaret, who was supposed to be recovering from having her appendix removed, but went to the beach instead, saw the difficulties they were in. She swam towards them over a distance of some 30yds, against strong currents, and on reaching them she towed Wiggins to shore while he supported himself by holding onto her and Ress. About 10ft from shore a lifebelt was thrown, into which Wiggins was placed, and the three reached the shore safely.

Meanwhile, 13-year-old John Davies had safely reached the mainland when he saw his friend, who was unable to swim, being forced away from the causeway into deep water. He stripped to the waist and went back along the causeway to help him. He swam out to his friend and held him up in the water. Both boys shouted for help and it was obvious that they would not get ashore unaided. By this time a rescue boat had put to sea but Davies had become exhausted by his efforts and before the boat could reach them he was forced to release his hold and the boys drifted apart. By the time the boat reached Davies' friend, there was no sign of Davies. His body was subsequently recovered. He gave his life to save his friend. Both Vaughan and Davies were awarded the AM.

At the time of going to publication, Margaret Vaughan is one of twenty living recipients of the GC.

### Miner THOMAS MANWARING (Edward Medal)
*FOREST OF DEAN, GLOUCESTERSHIRE, England*
30 June 1949

He was 32 years old and working at the Arthur & Edward Colliery when the mine was flooded by a sudden inrush of water. Evacuation was ordered as soon as the water broke in, and the escape of men underground was greatly aided by Frank Bradley, a man of 63, who took charge of the man-riding trolleys which ran up and down the long, steep main road leading to the shaft. After many men had been helped in this way, another official advised Bradley to escape at once, telling him the rising flood would soon cut off the main shaft. Bradley, however, refused to leave the pit, saying that some men were still underground. He thereupon walked back into the mine. Bradley acted deliberately and without rashness, although he knew that once he was cut off from the main shaft he would have to stay below ground for a long time and that he might never reach the surface again.

Meanwhile Oswald Simmonds was showing great calmness in the face of danger; he went around his district ordering his men out of the pit and telling them how to reach the main shaft safely through the flooding roads. When he was himself about to leave he heard that two men, Albert Sims and Ernest Barnfield, were still left in the mine. He immediately returned to help them. When he found them, they were with Thomas Manwaring, who had volunteered to stay back to help the two men. Manwaring and Simmonds, helping and sometimes carrying the men along with them, made their way towards the main shaft, meeting Bradley on the way. At the first opportunity they telephoned the surface and were told that the flood had cut them off completely from the main shaft, but they might be able to reach a second shaft through the workings of the mine.

Manwaring, Bradley and Simmonds set off, taking the other men with them, one of whom was practically exhausted. The way was very hard, and the air in parts very bad. The men had in some places to wade through torrents of water, and in others had to climb over rock falls. They never, however, abandoned their comrades. Eventually, after spending nearly seven hours underground struggling through the flooded mine, the party reached the second shaft and were hauled to safety. All three men were awarded the EM, but only Manwaring lived to exchange his for the GC.

He died on 7 March 2000.

## Mr CHARLES WILCOX (Edward Medal)
*BIRMINGHAM, England*
23 August 1949

He was 30 years old and working as a painter when he was engaged with other men on a building in the city centre. One of the painters, Alfred Burrows, mounted a ladder to begin painting an exterior window on the third floor; at the top of the ladder, about 45ft above the street, he climbed onto an arched sill about 18in wide. He then found that the window was bricked up from the inside and there was nothing for him to hold on to. He turned around to return to the ladder but could not see it and became frightened, crouching down in an attempt to retain his balance on the ledge. The foreman saw Burrows' predicament and sent another painter to his assistance but this man had to return to the ground after supporting Burrows for a few minutes. Wilcox then climbed the ladder to assist; by kneeling on a flat piece of masonry, some 18in square, at the end of the arch, he was able to support Burrows, who was now in severe shock. Mr Wilcox stayed in this position for forty-five minutes until the fire brigade arrived and Burrows, who had lapsed into unconsciousness, was brought to the ground in a safety belt which Wilcox had strapped on to him. During this time Wilcox was in considerable danger of falling had the other man kicked out or made any sudden movement.

Wilcox had also served in the Second World War. He died on 4 April 2006.

## Mr ROBERT 'TIGER' TAYLOR
*BRISTOL, England*
13 March 1950

He was 29 years old and working as a newspaper advertising representative when two armed robbers threatened a Lloyds Bank cashier and bank guard with a revolver, and stole a sum of money. When the men left the bank, followed by the bank staff shouting 'Stop them, there's been a hold-up,' Taylor, who was passing, gave chase. He caught up with the man with the gun and attempted to close with him. The robber turned and fired point-blank into his face, fatally wounding him. Taylor had intervened out of a desire to help in the preservation of law and order and gave his life in a gallant attempt to apprehend an armed and dangerous criminal. Zbigniew Gower and Roman Redel, who fired the shot, were both hanged.

Taylor had also served in the Second World War.

## Aircraftman First Class IVOR GILLETT
*SELETAR, SINGAPORE, Malaya*
26 March 1950

He was 21 years old and serving in the RAF. He was a member of the ground crew on board a Sunderland flying boat being loaded with bombs at its moorings when there was an explosion. Surface rescue craft were quickly on the scene but the aircraft and a bomb-scow alongside sank rapidly and the survivors were blown into the water. A life-belt was thrown to Gillett from a rescue launch, but he was seen to throw it to a seriously injured corporal near him who was in danger of drowning. In the confusion the rescuers had not been able to reach the corporal. Gillett was a great friend of his and knew he was not a strong swimmer. The life-belt kept him afloat until he was rescued unconscious from the water. In the meantime Gillett disappeared; his body washed ashore two days later. It was discovered that he had suffered superficial injuries and that death was due to the combined effects of the blast and drowning. By his action in deliberately saving the life of his injured friend, while in great danger himself, he displayed magnificent courage.

Gillett had also served in the Second World War.

## Vulcanologist GEORGE (aka TONY) TAYLOR
*MOUNT LAMINGTON, Papua New Guinea*
21 January–1 April 1951

He was 33 years old and working for the Commonwealth Bureau of Mineral Resources when Mount Lamington became active on 18 January. Three days later there was a violent eruption; a large part of the mountain was blown away and steam and smoke poured from the crater for a considerable time. The area of damage extended over a radius of 8 miles, while people near Higaturu, 9 miles away, were killed by the blast or burned to death. The eruptions went on until March, killing 4,000 people in total.

Mr Taylor, who arrived on 21 January, showed conspicuous courage in the face of great danger over a period of several months. He visited the crater by aircraft almost daily, and on many other occasions on foot. Sometimes he stayed at the volcano overnight. During the whole of this time the volcano was never entirely quiet, and in fact several eruptions took place without any warning. Without regard for his personal safety, Mr Taylor entered the danger area again and again, each time at great risk, both in order to ensure the safety of the rescue and working parties and to obtain scientific information relating to this type of volcano, about which little was known. His work saved many lives as he was able to warn the rescue parties of the areas to be avoided.

Taylor had also served in the Second World War. He died from a stroke on 19 August 1972 (not, as is often stated, the 20th).

## Lieutenant TERENCE WATERS
*PYONGYANG, Korea*
22 April–September/October 1951

He was 22 years old and serving in the West Yorkshire Regiment (Prince of Wales's Own) when he was wounded in the head and arm and then taken prisoner during the Battle of the Imjin River. On the way to Pyongyang with other prisoners of war, he set a magnificent example of courage and fortitude in remaining with wounded other ranks on the march, whom he felt it his duty to care for to the best of his ability. Subsequently, after a journey of immense hardship and privation, the party arrived in an area west of Pyongyang adjacent to POW Camp 12 and known generally as 'The Caves', where they were held. They found themselves imprisoned in a tunnel through which a stream of water flowed continuously, flooding a great deal of the floor in which were packed many South Korean and European prisoners in filthy rags, crawling with lice. In this cavern a number died daily from wounds, sickness or merely malnutrition: they were given two small meals of boiled maize daily and there was no medical attention.

Waters appreciated that few, if any, of his group would survive these conditions, in view of their weakness and the absolute lack of medical attention. They were visited by a North Korean political officer, who attempted to persuade them to volunteer to join a POW group known as the 'Peace Fighters' (that is, active participants in the propaganda movement against their own side) with a promise of better food, medical care and other amenities as a reward, but the offer was refused unanimously; nevertheless Waters decided to order his men to pretend to accede to the offer in an effort to save their lives. He hoped that this would save the lives of his men, but he refused to go himself, aware that the task of maintaining British prestige was vested in him as an officer.

Realising that they had failed to subvert the British officer, the North Koreans now made a series of concerted efforts to persuade him to save himself by joining the camp. This he steadfastly refused to do. He died a short while later. He was a young, inexperienced officer, yet he set an example of the highest order.

### Private HORACE MADDEN
*KAPYONG, Korea*
24 April–6 November 1951

He was 26 years old and serving in the 3rd Battalion, Royal Australian Regiment (RAR) when he was captured by Chinese communist forces. Despite repeated beatings and many forms of ill-treatment inflicted because of his defiance towards his captors, Madden remained cheerful and optimistic. Although deprived of food, resulting in severe malnutrition, he was known to share his meagre supplies, purchased from Koreans, with other prisoners who were sick. It would have been apparent to him that to pursue this course must eventually result in his death. This did not deter him, and for over six months, although he became progressively weaker, he remained undaunted in his resistance. He would in no way cooperate with the enemy. His gallant heroism was an inspiration to all of his fellow prisoners. Many officers and men made testimonials to his heroism. He died from malnutrition on or about 6 November 1951.

Madden had also served in the Second World War.

### Fusilier DEREK KINNE
*Korea*
25 April 1951–10 August 1953

He was 20 years old and serving in the 1st Battalion, Royal Northumberland Fusiliers when he was captured by the Chinese communists on the last day of the Battle of the Imjin River. From then on he had only two objectives in mind: first, to escape and second, to raise the morale of his fellow prisoners. He escaped for the first time within twenty-four hours of capture but was retaken a few days later while attempting to return to his own lines. Eventually he joined a large group of prisoners being marched north to prison camps.

In July 1952 Kinne, who was by now well known to his captors, was accused of being non cooperative and was brutally interrogated about other prisoners. As a result of his refusal to inform on his comrades, and for striking a Chinese officer who assaulted him, he was twice severely beaten and tied up for periods of twelve and twenty-four hours, being made to stand on tip-toe with a noose around his neck that would throttle him if he attempted to relax in any way.

He escaped on 27 July but was recaptured two days later. He was again beaten very severely, and put in handcuffs that were tightened so as to restrict his circulation; he was not released from them until 16 October (eighty-one days later).

He was accused of insincerity, a hostile attitude towards the Chinese, 'sabotage' of compulsory political study, attempting to escape, and of being reactionary. From 15 to 20 August he was confined in a small cell, where he was made to sit at attention all day, being beaten, prodded with bayonets, kicked and spat upon by the guards, and denied any washing facilities. On 20 August he was made to stand to attention for seven hours and when he complained he was beaten by the Chinese guard commander with the butt of his SMG, which eventually went off, killing the guard! For this Kinne was beaten senseless with belts and bayonets, stripped of his clothes and thrown into a dark rat-infested hole until 19 September.

On 16 October Kinne was tried for escape and for being a reactionary and hostile to the Chinese. He was sentenced to twelve months' solitary confinement. This was increased to eighteen months when he complained about denial of medical attention. On 5 December he was transferred to a special penal company. His last award of solitary confinement was on 2 June 1953, when he was sentenced for defying Chinese orders and wearing a rosette on Coronation Day. He was eventually exchanged at Panmunjon on 10 August 1953.

At the time of going to publication, he is one of twenty living recipients of the GC.

## Sub Officer GEORGE HENDERSON
*GIBRALTAR*
27 April 1951

He was 41 years old and serving in the Gibraltar Dockyard Fire Service when ammunition caught fire as it was being unloaded from Naval Armament Vessel *Bedenham* to a lighter. In spite of the great heat and intensity of the fire, which, Henderson must have realised, was virtually out of control and could cause a massive explosion at any time, he managed single-handedly to direct a jet of water into the lighter from a position on board the *Bedenham*, immediately alongside and above the blazing boat. The *Bedenham* had by this time been abandoned but Henderson remained at his place of duty alone, doing what he could to prevent the ammunition from exploding, although he must have known that his chance of survival was slight. It was a hopeless task and he was killed when the ammunition blew up, destroying the *Bedenham* and wrecking the quayside.

## Tracker AWANG anak RAWENG (sometimes spelt RAWANG)
*Malaya*
27 May 1951

He was 26 years old and was attached to the 1st Battalion, Worcestershire Regiment when his platoon was ambushed by about fifty bandits. The leading scout was killed instantly and the section commander fatally wounded. Awang anak Raweng was shot through the thigh, and at the same time Private Hughes was hit below the knee, shattering his leg. Although wounded and exposed to heavy automatic fire, Raweng collected his own weapon and that of the wounded Hughes and dragged the other man into the cover of the jungle.

In view of the impending attack and completely disregarding his own injury, he took up a position ready to defend the wounded man. There he remained, firing on every attempt made by the bandits to approach, successfully driving off several attacks. He was wounded again, a bullet shattering his right arm and rendering further use of his weapon impossible. Despite loss of blood, he dragged himself over to Hughes and took a grenade from him; resuming his position on guard, he pulled the pin with his teeth and, with the grenade in his left hand, defied the bandits to approach. So resolute was his demeanour that the bandits, who had maintained their attack for forty minutes, and were now being threatened by other forces, withdrew. Raweng is the only Malaysian to be awarded the GC.

At the time of going to publication, he is one of twenty living recipients of the GC.

### Flight Lieutenant JOHN (aka JACK) QUINTON
*YORKSHIRE, England*
13 August 1951

He was 30 years old and serving in the RAF when his Wellington bomber was involved in a mid-air collision. As the bomber started to break up, Quinton picked up the only parachute within reach and put it on Air Training Cadet Derek Coates. He then pointed to the ripcord and a gaping hole in the aircraft, indicating that the cadet should jump out. Quinton acted with the most commendable courage and self-sacrifice as he well knew that in giving up the only parachute he was forfeiting any chance of saving his own life.

He had also served in the Second World War, during which he was awarded the DFC.

### Mr JOHN (aka JACK) BAMFORD
*NEWTHORPE, NOTTINGHAMSHIRE, England*
19 October 1952

He was 15 years old and employed as a colliery worker when a fire started in the living room of the family home at 85 Baker Street and the stairs burst into flames. John, the eldest of six children, and his father managed to get Mrs Bamford and three of the children out of the house by climbing onto the top of a bay window that gave access to a bedroom. But two of the boys, aged 6 and 4, were trapped in their bedroom at the back of the house. John and his father climbed into the front bedroom and could hear the boys shouting in the back bedroom, which was situated immediately above the seat of the fire. John's father draped a blanket around himself and attempted to reach the children but the blanket caught fire and he was driven back. John then told his father to go out while he got on his hands and knees and crawled through the flames into the bedroom. His shirt was completely burned off him but nevertheless he snatched the two boys and managed to get them to the window. He dropped the youngest into his father's arms but the other boy struggled free and rushed back into the burning room. John could have got out himself but left the window and chased his brother through the flames, dragged him back to the window and threw him out to his father.

By this time John was fast losing consciousness. He was badly burned on his face, neck, chest, back, arms and hands but he managed to get one leg over the window sill and force himself out.

All three boys were taken to hospital, where the two youngest were soon off the danger list, but John did not go home until February 1953, after many operations and skin-grafts. At 15 years and 7 months he is the youngest direct recipient of the GC. At the time of going to publication, he is one of twenty living recipients of the GC.

## Detective Constable FREDERICK FAIRFAX
*CROYDON, SURREY, England*
2 November 1952

He was 35 years old and serving in the Metropolitan Police Force. Two men were seen to climb over the side gate of a warehouse in Tamworth Road, and reach the flat roof of a building about 22ft above. The alarm was raised and Fairfax, Constable Norman Harrison and some other officers went to the premises in a police van. At the same time Constable James McDonald and another constable arrived in a police car. Other officers took up positions around the building.

When told the suspects had climbed up a drainpipe to the roof, Fairfax immediately scaled the drainpipe, followed by McDonald, but the latter was unable to negotiate the last 6ft and returned to the ground. Fairfax reached the top and pulled himself on to the roof. In the moonlight he saw the two men about 15yds away behind a brick stack. He walked towards them and challenged them, and then, dashing behind the stack, he grabbed one of the men and pulled him into the open. The man broke away and his companion then shot Fairfax in the right shoulder. Fairfax fell to the ground but as the two criminals ran past him he got up and caught one of them, Derek Bentley, knocking him to the ground. A second shot was fired by the second man, Christopher Craig, but Fairfax held on, dragged Bentley behind a skylight and searched him. He found a knuckleduster and a dagger, which he removed from him.

McDonald had by this time climbed to the top of the drainpipe and Fairfax helped him on to the roof; he called to the gunman to drop his weapon but he refused and made further threats. During this time Harrison had climbed on to a sloping roof nearby and was edging his way towards Craig but he was seen and fired at, the shot hitting the roof close to his head. He continued his movement, however, and another shot was fired at him, which also missed. Harrison then got behind a chimney stack and went back to ground level, where he joined other officers who now entered the building, ran up to the fire escape exit door on the roof and pushed it open. Fairfax warned them that the gunman was nearby but as Constable Sidney Miles jumped from the doorway on to the roof, Bentley called out, 'Let him have it.' As he jumped, Craig shot Miles, killing him. Fairfax immediately left cover to bring in the casualty and another shot was fired at him.

McDonald also came forward and the two officers dragged Miles behind the fire escape exit. Harrison then jumped out on to the roof and, standing in the doorway, threw his truncheon at the gunman, who again fired at him. Constable Robert Jaggs then reached the roof by way of the drainpipe and was also fired upon but he joined the other officers. Fairfax, helped by Harrison, pushed Bentley through the doorway and handed him over to other officers. Fairfax was then given a police firearm and he returned to the roof. He jumped through the doorway and again called to Craig to drop his weapon. A further shot was fired at him but he advanced towards Craig firing his pistol as he went. Craig then jumped off the roof to the ground below, where he was arrested.

Much debate has raged about Bentley's phrase 'Let him have it.' It was believed at the time that he was telling Craig to shoot, but it may equally have meant hand over the gun. Craig was 16 and Bentley 19; both were tried and found guilty of murder. Bentley was hanged, but Craig was under age and was imprisoned for ten years. It was Craig who fired the fatal shot; Bentley was under Fairfax's control at the time of the murder.

As well as Fairfax's GC, Constables Norman Harrison and James McDonald were awarded the GM. Constable Robert Jaggs was awarded the BEM, and Constable Sidney Mills was posthumously awarded the Queen's Police Federation Service Medal (now called the Queen's Police Medal for Gallantry).

Fairfax had also served in the Second World War. He died on 23 February 1998.

### Radio Officer DAVID BROADFOOT
*off the coast of LARNE, Northern Ireland*
31 January 1953

He was 53 years old and serving in the Merchant Navy aboard SS *Princess Victoria* when his ferry encountered severe gales and squalls of sleet and snow. A heavy sea struck the ship and burst open the rear doors; sea water flooded in causing a list to starboard of 10 degrees. Attempts were made to secure the stern doors but without success. The captain tried to turn his ship back but the conditions were so harsh that the manoeuvre failed. Some of the ship's cargo shifted and this increased the list to starboard. From the moment the *Princess Victoria* got into difficulties, Broadfoot constantly sent out wireless messages giving the ship's position, although the listing of the ship made this task even more difficult. Despite this, he steadfastly continued his work at the radio, repeatedly sending signals to the coast radio station to enable them to ascertain the ship's exact position.

When the ship finally stopped in sight of the Irish coast her list had increased to 45 degrees. Thinking only of the crew and passengers, Broadfoot stayed at his post, receiving and sending messages, although he must have known that by doing so he had no chance of surviving. He went down with the ship, having deliberately sacrificed his own life in an attempt to save others. Of the 177 crew and passengers, 133 were lost, including all the women and children, whose lifeboat sank. Only sixty-five bodies were recovered.

### Train Driver JOHN AXON
*CHAPEL-EN-LE-FRITH, DERBYSHIRE, England*
9 February 1957

He was 56 years old and working for British Rail. He was preparing to stop his train before descending a steep gradient when suddenly the brake steam pipe fractured, destroying the braking system and filling the cab with blinding, scalding steam. Mr Axon was badly burnt. He could have abandoned his engine and saved his life, but, realising the risk of a runaway, he remained at his post and with great bravery endeavoured to get the engine under control. With the aid of his fireman, the regulator was closed and the handbrake applied but the train, which by now was descending a gradient, could not be stopped.

Axon then ordered the fireman to jump clear and apply as many wagon brakes as possible. In spite of his prompt action the train continued to gather speed. Nevertheless Axon stayed on the engine, although steam and boiling water were still pouring into the cab, making conditions almost unbearable. He waved a warning to a signalman that the train was running away and remained at his post in the hope of regaining control when a more favourable gradient should be reached. But before this the train crashed into a freight train travelling in the same direction. Mr Axon was killed in the collision. In his memory Ewan McColl and Peggy Seager recorded *The Ballad of John Axon*.

### Second Lieutenant MICHAEL BENNER
*GROSSGLOCKNER MOUNTAIN, Austria*
1 July 1957

He was 22 years old and serving in the Corps of Royal Engineers when he was in command of a party of NCOs and other ranks undergoing mountain training. They had reached the summit by 6pm but a storm caused delays and made conditions unexpectedly difficult. On the descent Sapper Phillips missed his footing and began to slide down a fairly steep snow slope. Seeing this, Benner jumped out of his own secure foothold on to the open slope and caught the falling man, holding him with one hand and trying with the other to dig his ice axe into the snow, but he could not do this. Both men slid down the slope and disappeared over the steep face of the mountain. In making his attempt to intercept Phillips, this gallant officer took, as he well knew, a desperate risk. As the two men gathered speed he must have realised that he could have saved himself by releasing Phillip's arm but he did not do so. He held on to the last, struggling to obtain a grip in the snow with his feet and axe.

### Constable HENRY STEVENS
*BROMLEY, KENT, England*
29 March 1958

He was 30 years old and serving in the Metropolitan Police Force. Stevens was on duty in plain clothes with PC Wanstall and DC Moody when they received a call to go to a house where the burglar alarm was sounding. The other officers went to the front and Stevens went around to the rear. As he reached the back of the house a man jumped from the fence only 5ft from him. Stevens said he was a police officer and called on the man to stop. The man, Ronald Easterbrook, ran off and Stevens pursued him, whereupon Easterbrook replied, 'Stop, or you'll get this,' showing him his gun. He then fired on the PC, hitting him in the mouth, shattering his teeth and part of his jaw, the bullet lodging in his tongue; despite the pain, Stevens launched himself at the gunman, who fired again but this time the gun misfired. Stevens landed on the gunman and wrenched the weapon from him and then pinned him against some railings.

Easterbrook pretended to give in, and then made a dash for it, only to find Stevens had hold of his jacket. Wriggling out of it, he escaped but in so doing left it behind, with enough evidence to identify him. He was arrested on 10 April and sentenced to ten years.

When Stevens heard of the award, he said: 'I never expected it. I was only doing my job.' I had the privilege of meeting Henry Stevens in July 2010 and he is one of the most modest men I have ever come across; he would only talk of other people's bravery and not his own. At the time of going to publication, he is one of twenty living recipients of the GC.

### Tram Conductor RAYMOND 'PUDDIN' DONOGHUE
*HOBART, Tasmania*
29 April 1960
He was 38 years old and working for the Metropolitan Transport Trust when tramcar no. 131 collided with a motor vehicle in heavy traffic. The driver's cab was wrecked and the driver injured, and the tram started to run backwards, rapidly gaining speed on the steep hill. Donoghue could have left the tramcar, or moved to the rear of the compartment with the passengers, but, realising the danger, he scorned the way to safety so that he might, by ringing the bell, warn other traffic, while also attempting to stop the tram using the handbrake. At the bottom of the hill the tram collided with a stationary tram. At the point of impact Donoghue was still trying to stop the tram but was killed. By his action he was responsible for saving the lives of a number of people. He is the only Tasmanian to be awarded the GC.

Donoghue had also served in the Second World War.

### Chief Petty Officer JONATHAN 'BUCK' ROGERS
*JERVIS BAY, off the Australian coast*
10 February 1964
He was 43 years old and serving in the Royal Australian Navy aboard MHAS *Voyager* when his ship was struck by the aircraft carrier MHAS *Melbourne*. Rogers organised the evacuation of fifty or sixty men from the ship's cafeteria, where he was organising a game of tombola. As the *Voyager* sank, Rogers realised that he was too big to fit through the escape hatch and was thus perfectly aware of the fate that awaited him, yet he remained calm and helped all he could to escape. He supported the spirits of those who could not escape and encouraged them to meet death alongside him with dignity and honour. He upheld the highest tradition of service at sea.

Rogers had also served in the Second World War, being awarded the DSM.

## Mr MICHAEL MUNNELLY
*LONDON, England*
25 December 1964

He was 23 years old and working as a journalist when fourteen youths, who had been drinking, went in a van to a flat in Regent's Park Road, to which only two of them had been invited. They were refused entry as they were extremely rowdy. Some of them then attacked the owner of the flat; others went to the dairy nearby and started bombarding the flat with milk bottles, breaking all the windows. In order to protect his property, the dairyman Mr Griffiths went into the street, where he was immediately butted, kicked and stabbed in the groin.

Munnelly, his brother and Mr Smith were in a third-floor flat; on hearing the commotion, they looked out of the window and saw the dairyman on the floor being kicked. All three men decided they must go and help him, and ran down to the street. They detained two men but Munnelly was hit on the head and let go of the man he was holding. The van, which had left the scene, then returned and was followed into the next turning by Smith, who banged on the side in an attempt to stop the van. The van stopped and he grabbed a youth in the passenger seat. The rear door of the van then opened and several of the youths jumped out and kicked him senseless. When Munnelly went to his aid, bottles were thrown at him and he was kicked and fatally stabbed by Frederick Bishop. Munnelly was also awarded the Binney Memorial Medal, as was Mr Smith, while Griffiths was awarded the BEM. Bishop was found guilty of murder and sentenced to life imprisonment.

## Mr BRIAN SPILLETT
*WALTHAM CROSS, HERTFORDSHIRE, England*
9 January 1965

He was 27 years old and working as a detail fitter when a fire broke out in a house a few doors away from his. The fire had reached an advanced stage before the family woke and it was only with difficulty that the wife, child and grand-father escaped. Mr Spillett, attracted by the shouting, came from his house, arriving only partly dressed. He asked whether everyone was out of the house and, on hearing that the father was still inside, on the first floor, he ran straight into the burning house. Attempts to hold him back were brushed aside. Mr Spillett reached the first floor but was unable to rescue the father. By now the house was a blazing inferno and he only managed to escape by jumping from a window. He was found some time later in the garden of an adjoining house, very badly burnt and with other serious injuries.

He died from his injuries a week later on 16 January 1965.

## Train Driver WALLACE OAKES
*CREWE, CHESHIRE, England*
5 June 1965

He was 33 years old and working for British Railways. He was driving a relief express passenger train when, about 7 miles from Crewe, travelling at 60 miles per hour, the engine cab suddenly filled with smoke and flames, blowing back from the firebox. The fireman at once climbed through the window and somehow managed to get on to the cab steps, where he extinguished his burning clothes. He could not get back into the cab but, realising that the brakes had been applied, remained on the steps until the train stopped.

When the flames subsided, the fireman re-entered the cab to find Oakes was missing. He saw him lying on the cutting slope just ahead of the cab; his clothes were severely burnt and it was found later that he had 80 per cent burns. Oakes was, however, still able to speak at this stage although he was dazed. Instead of leaving the cab, Oakes had remained to apply the brakes, open the blower and partly close the regulator. He had obviously not left the cab until the engine came to rest, although he must have known that to remain at the controls was to risk his own life. Mr Oakes' gallant action showed that his first thought was for the safety of his passengers. He died from his injuries a week later on 12 June.

### Constable TONY GLEDHILL
*LONDON, England*
25 August 1966
He was 27 years old and serving in the Metropolitan Police Force. He and Constable Terrance McFall were patrolling in police car 'Papa One' when they received a call that the occupants of a car had been seen acting suspiciously at Creek Side in Deptford. As the officers reached the area, the car they were looking for drove past them, containing five men. The officers immediately chased the vehicle, which was being driven recklessly through the streets, travelling on the wrong side of the road and against the one-way traffic system. Gledhill exercised considerable skill in following at high speed, and keeping up with the vehicle during a chase that covered 5 miles at speeds of up to 80 miles per hour. An attempt was made by the bandits to ambush the police car and no fewer than fifteen shots were fired at them by the bandits, using a sawn-off shotgun and revolvers, pellets from the shotgun striking the windscreen of the police car three times. Finally the escaping car crashed into a lorry at a junction.

The five men immediately left the car and a group of three, one with a pistol in his hand, ran into the yard of a transport contractor. The officers followed the three men. As the police car reached the yard gates, the men ran towards them and held the pistol to Gledhill's head, ordering the officers to get out of the car or be shot. Later Gledhill recalled: 'I just can't put into words my feelings at this point'. Both officers left the car and the man with the gun got into the driver's seat with the obvious intention of using it to make a getaway. Gledhill was then backing away across the roadway and the man reversed away from the gates towards him, pointing the pistol at him as he did so. However, when he stopped to engage first gear, he momentarily turned his head away and Gledhill immediately grabbed hold of his hand and, as the vehicle moved off, managed to grab hold of the car window with his left hand. While this was happening, McFall had run along the roadway to a group of men to get a lorry driven across the road to block it, when he heard Gledhill shout. He ran back to the police car and saw him holding on to the car window. He then saw the car gather speed, dragging Gledhill along the road. At this point the front offside tyre burst; the car veered across the road, crashed into some parked vehicles and Gledhill was thrown under one of them. McFall opened the front passenger door and, as the driver was still holding the pistol, began hitting him about the legs and body with his truncheon. Gledhill then regained his feet but as he went to the driver's door it was flung open, knocking him to the ground. The man got out of the car and backed away from the officers. He warned them not to move and at the same time fired a shot. The officers then heard the gun click and both rushed at him; McFall struck at him with his truncheon, while Gledhill grabbed the man's right hand and took the gun from him. There was a violent struggle and the gunman fell to the ground, trying desperately to reach inside his jacket. At this stage other officers arrived. The man was subdued and another gun, an automatic pistol, was found in his pocket. The officers had faced a sustained firearm attack and from the early stages knew the risks they ran of being killed. Both officers received hospital treatment. McFall was awarded the GM.

One bandit got away, but the other four – John McVicar, William Cooper, William Gentry and Frederick Davies – were all sentenced to long prison terms.

Tony Gledhill is Treasurer of the VC&GC Association. His autobiography is called *A Gun at my Head*. At the time of going to publication, he is one of twenty living recipients of the GC.

## Air Stewardess BARBARA (known as JANE) HARRISON

*HEATHROW AIRPORT, LONDON, England*
8 April 1968

She was 22 years old and working for BOAC (now British Airways) when, soon after take-off, the no. 2 engine failed on her Boeing 707 and a few seconds later caught fire. The aircraft started to turn for an emergency landing when the engine fell from the aircraft. After landing, the fuel tanks in the port wing exploded. When the aircraft landed, Harrison and the steward opened the rear galley door and inflated the emergency exit chute, which became twisted. Chief Steward Neville Davis-Gordon had to climb down the chute to straighten it before it could be used.

Once out of the aircraft, Davis-Gordon was unable to return and Harrison was left alone to the task of shepherding passengers to the rear door and helping them out of the aircraft. She encouraged some passengers to jump from the aircraft and pushed others out. With flames and explosions all around her, and escape from the rear now impossible, she directed her passengers to another exit while she remained at her post. She was finally overcome while trying to save an elderly disabled passenger, who was seated in one of the last rows, and whose body was found close to that of the stewardess. She gave her life in utter devotion to her duty. Neville Davis-Gordon was awarded the BEM.

Harrison's biography is called *Fire over Heathrow: the Tragedy of Flight 712*.

## The ROYAL ULSTER CONSTABULARY (now The POLICE SERVICE of NORTHERN IRELAND)
1969–1999

For thirty years the Royal Ulster Constabulary has been the bulwark against, and the main target of, a sustained and brutal terrorist campaign. The force has suffered heavily in protecting both sides of the community from danger – 302 officers have been killed in the line of duty and thousands more injured, many seriously. Many officers have been ostracised by their own community and others have been forced to leave their homes in the face of threats to them and their families. As Northern Ireland reached a turning point in its political development, this award was made to recognise the collective courage and dedication to duty of all those who served and accepted the danger and stress this brought to them and their families.

The award was received by Constable Paul Slane on behalf of the RUC on 12 April 2000. Paul Slane lost both legs when an IRA mortar bomb landed on his patrol car in Newry on 27 March 1992.

## District Commissioner ERROL (known as JACK) EMANUEL
*GAZELLE PENINSULA, Papua New Guinea*
July 1969–19 August 1971

He was 40 years old when he was sent to the East New Britain District of Rabaul on special duties with the objective of bringing mutual understanding and peace to the deeply hostile indigenous people. Over a period of two years Mr Emanuel visited villages at all times of the day and night, almost always alone, deliberately leaving the cover of police protection in order to talk to leaders of all factions to gain their confidence and trust. He moved among dissidents, trying to pacify them and was frequently able to avert bloodshed on both sides. He knew that he was risking his life every time he went alone into crowds such as these, but he chose to expose himself to danger rather than risk the lives of his fellow officers and the police. On 19 August 1971 he undertook the role of peaceful negotiator during a confrontation with a group of hostile people. Despite recent threats to his life and the fact that some of the Tolai people were wearing war paint, he left the protection of the police at the invitation of one group of dissidents and went alone down a bush track to try and quell the disturbance, but he was attacked and killed.

## Sergeant MICHAEL WILLETTS
*BELFAST, Northern Ireland*
25 May 1971

He was 27 years old and serving in the 3rd Battalion, The Parachute Regiment when a terrorist entered the police station in Springfield Road carrying a suitcase, from which a smoking fuse protruded. He dumped it on the floor and fled. In the room were a man and a woman, two children and several police officers. One of the officers raised the alarm and began to organise the evacuation of the hall past the reception desk, through the reception office and out via a door into the rear passage. Sergeant Willetts, who was on duty in the inner hall, heard the alarm and sent an NCO up to the first floor to warn those above. He then proceeded to the reception area and saw a police officer thrusting people through the hall and office. He held the door open while all passed safely through and then stood in the doorway, shielding them. In the next moment the bomb exploded with terrible force, mortally wounding Sergeant Willetts. He knew well the peril of going towards a terrorist bomb, having been four months in Belfast. He undoubtedly saved the lives of Elizabeth Cummings and her son Carl, aged 4, and Patrick Gray and his daughter Colette, also aged 4.

In the same incident Inspector Edward Nurse of the RUC received the GM, and Police Sergeant John Wilson and PC Hugh Shaw received the BEM.

## Superintendent GERALD 'GERRY' RICHARDSON
*BLACKPOOL, England*
23 August 1971

He was 38 years old and serving in the Lancashire Constabulary when a gang of five men robbed a jeweller's. Constable Carl Walker, having been directed to the scene by radio, arrived to see the bandits running towards a Triumph car. All the men got into the car and a shotgun was pointed at Walker; as the car drove away, Walker followed in his car. A high-speed chase then ensued; at several stages Walker briefly lost contact with the Triumph but then came upon it stationary in a blind alley. All the occupants were out of the car; Walker remained in his car, which he parked at right angles to the alley, thus blocking the exit. The men then climbed back into their car, which reversed at speed down the alley into the side of Walker's car, pushing it out of the way. As the car drove away, Constable Ian Hampson arrived at the scene in his car. He saw Walker sitting in his car, in a state of shock, and followed the Triumph. The bandits' car was driven in a fast and dangerous manner through the streets and Hampson during the whole time remained only 5–10yds behind it relaying his position.

The Triumph suddenly screeched to a halt and Hampson pulled up about 5yds behind it. One of the gunmen ran back to the police car and shot Hampson. The constable, who was badly wounded in the chest, fell from his car to the roadway but managed to reach his radio and give his position. A number of police cars were now in the area and Constable Walker, who had resumed the pursuit in his damaged car, saw the bandits, and positioned his car at a junction to block their route. As he did so Constable Patrick Jackson and Constable Andrew Hillis drove up on either side of the Triumph, trapping it. All the gunmen climbed out, and the driver threatened Jackson with a pistol and then ran towards an alley to the next street. Hillis got out of his car and followed them; the driver pointed his pistol and fired two or three shots from only 6ft away, but did not hit him. As one of the robbers broke away, Hillis ran after him and subdued him after a violent struggle.

In the meantime another police car had arrived with Inspector Edward Gray,

Inspector Stephen Radpath and Superintendent Gerard Richardson. As Radpath got out of the car, the officers saw three of the gunmen running towards an alley. Radpath ran after them, while Gray and Richardson drove into the next street in an effort to head them off. The three men were now running down the alley, followed by Walker and Jackson; when Walker was about 10yds away, the driver turned and fired a shot at him. The officer carried on towards him, and when the man reached the end of the alley he turned and fired a second time; from a distance of 6ft he fired again, hitting Walker in the groin. Then the man pointed the gun at Walker again, looked at the officer, who was holding his wounded leg, then turned away towards a Ford van which was parked outside a shop. The gunman jumped into the driver's seat and the other two got into the back; as Gray and Richardson arrived on the scene, the van moved off rapidly. Jackson got into the police car with Gray and Richardson, who then drove off in pursuit of the van, which attempted to turn into an alley but crashed into a garden wall.

While Gray went to the rear of the van to keep the doors closed and the men trapped, Richardson and Jackson ran to the front and saw that it was empty, the driver having climbed into the back of the van. The officer then went to the rear just as the doors burst open; the men jumped out and two of them ran off down the alley. Richardson and Gray tried to talk the driver into surrendering his gun, but he continued to threaten them before turning round and running off. The officers ran after him, Richardson leading, followed by Gray. A few yards into the alley Richardson caught hold of the gunman. The man thrust his gun into his stomach and fired. Before Gray could reach them, the man fired a second time and the superintendent fell to the ground. The man then escaped in a stolen van. Richardson was taken to hospital where he died later the same day.

The other bandits were seen by Sergeant Kenneth Mackay and Constable Edward Hanley, who had just arrived in the area. These officers, still in their car, joined the pursuit and caught up with the two fugitives, one of whom pointed his pistol at Mackay's head as the car drew alongside him. The sergeant swung the driver's door open and it struck the man, knocking him off balance. The police car then stalled, allowing both men to run off, with Hanley and other officers chasing them on foot. Mackay restarted the car and drove after them; he quickly overtook the men and they turned round; one, who was only 6ft away, levelled his revolver at Mackay and pulled the trigger but nothing happened. The officer drove directly at the two men, knocking them off balance; he did this several times to keep them off balance. He then got out off the car and ran towards one of them. During this chase through the alleys they ended up back at the scene where Walker had been shot. Radpath, who was still at the scene, saw them emerge from the alley running directly towards him, with Mackay behind them. Radpath stood his ground, although he could clearly see the gun in the bandit's hand. Mackay then crash-tackled the gunman and brought him down with his arms sprawled out in front of him immediately in front of Radpath, who kicked the gun from his hand. Hanley, who was chasing the other man, knocked him down and arrested him.

Richardson is the highest-ranking police officer to be killed in the line of duty. All five robbers were given long prison sentences. Joseph Sewell, who shot Richardson and Walker, said of Richardson at his trial: 'I shall see him every day of my life. He just kept coming. He was too brave.' Hampson, Hillis, Jackson and Mackay were awarded the GM. Gray and Hanley were awarded the BEM, and Radpath was awarded the Queen's Commendation for Brave Conduct.

## Constable CARL WALKER
*BLACKPOOL, England*
23 August 1971

He was 37 years old and serving in the Lancashire Constabulary when a gang of five men robbed a jeweller's. Constable Carl Walker, having been directed to the scene by radio, arrived to see the bandits running towards a Triumph car. All the men got into the car and a shotgun was pointed at Walker; as the car drove away, Walker followed in his car. A high-speed chase then ensued; at several stages Walker briefly lost contact with the Triumph but then came upon it stationary in a blind alley. All the occupants were out of the car; Walker remained in his car, which he parked at right angles to the alley, thus blocking the exit. The men then climbed back into their car, which reversed at speed down the alley into the side of Walker's car, pushing it out of the way. As the car drove away, Constable Ian Hampson arrived at the scene in his car. He saw Walker sitting in his car, in a state of shock, and followed the Triumph. The bandits' car was driven in a fast and dangerous manner through the streets and Hampson during the whole time remained only 5–10yds behind it relaying his position.

The Triumph suddenly screeched to a halt and Hampson pulled up about 5yds behind it. One of the gunmen ran back to the police car and shot Hampson. The constable, who was badly wounded in the chest, fell from his car to the roadway but managed to reach his radio and give his position. A number of police cars were now in the area and Constable Walker, who had resumed the pursuit in his damaged car, saw the bandits, and positioned his car at a junction to block their route. As he did so Constable Patrick Jackson and Constable Andrew Hillis drove up on either side of the Triumph, trapping it. All the gunmen climbed out, and the driver threatened Jackson with a pistol and then ran towards an alley to the next street. Hillis got out of his car and followed them; the driver pointed his pistol and fired two or three shots from only 6ft away, but did not hit him. As one of the robbers broke away, Hillis ran after him and subdued him after a violent struggle.

In the meantime another police car had arrived with Inspector Edward Gray, Inspector Stephen Radpath and Superintendent Gerard Richardson. As Radpath got out of the car, the officers saw three of the gunmen running towards an alley. Radpath ran after them, while Gray and Richardson drove into the next street in an effort to head them off. The three men were now running down the alley, followed by Walker and Jackson; when Walker was about 10yds away, the driver turned and fired a shot at him. The officer carried on towards him, and when the man reached the end of the alley he turned and fired a second time; from a distance of 6ft he fired again, hitting Walker in the groin. Then the man pointed the gun at Walker again, looked at the officer, who was holding his wounded leg, then turned away towards a Ford van which was parked outside a shop. The gunman jumped into the driver's seat and the other two got into the back; as Gray and Richardson arrived on the scene, the van moved off rapidly. Jackson got into the police car with Gray and Richardson, who then drove off in pursuit of the van, which attempted to turn into an alley but crashed into a garden wall.

While Gray went to the rear of the van to keep the doors closed and the men trapped, Richardson and Jackson ran to the front and saw that it was empty, the driver having climbed into the back of the van. The officer then went to the rear just as the doors burst open; the men jumped out and two of them ran off down the alley. Richardson and Gray tried to talk the driver into surrendering his gun, but he continued to threaten them before turning round and running off. The officers ran after him, Richardson leading, followed by Gray. A few yards into the alley Richardson caught hold of the gunman. The man thrust his gun into his stomach and fired. Before Gray could reach them, the man fired a second time and the superintendent fell to the ground. The man then escaped in a stolen van. Richardson was taken to hospital where he died later the same day.

The other bandits were seen by Sergeant Kenneth Mackay and Constable Edward Hanley, who had just arrived in the area. These officers, still in their car, joined the pursuit and caught up with the two fugitives, one of whom pointed his pistol at Mackay's head as the car drew alongside him. The sergeant swung the driver's door open and it struck the man, knocking him off balance. The police car then stalled, allowing both men to run off, with Hanley and other officers chasing them on foot. Mackay restarted the car and drove after them; he quickly overtook the men and they turned round; one, who was only 6ft away, levelled his revolver at Mackay and pulled the trigger but nothing happened. The officer drove directly at the two men, knocking them off balance; he did this several times to keep them off balance. He then got out off the car and ran towards one of them. During this chase through the alleys they ended up back at the scene where Walker had been shot. Radpath, who was still at the scene, saw them emerge from the alley running directly towards him, with Mackay behind them. Radpath stood his ground, although he could clearly see the gun in the bandit's hand. Mackay then crash-tackled the gunman and brought him down with his arms sprawled out in front of him immediately in front of Radpath, who kicked the gun from his hand. Hanley, who was chasing the other man, knocked him down and arrested him.

Richardson is the highest-ranking police officer to be killed in the line of duty. All five robbers were given long prison sentences. Joseph Sewell, who shot Richardson and Walker, said of Richardson at his trial: 'I shall see him every day of my life. He just kept coming. He was too brave.' Hampson, Hillis, Jackson and Mackay were awarded the GM. Gray and Hanley were awarded the BEM, and Radpath was awarded the Queen's Commendation for Brave Conduct.

Walker had also served with the RAF Police during his National Service. He is a committee member of the VC&GC Association. At the time of going to publication, he is one of twenty living recipients of the GC.

## Major STEPHEN (known as GEORGE) STYLES
*BELFAST, Northern Ireland*
20 and 22 October 1971

He was 43 years old and serving in the Royal Army Ordnance Corps as an ATO when he was called to deal with an apparently new explosive device placed in a telephone kiosk in the Hotel Europa. Styles immediately went to the scene and, having ensured that the military and police had secured the area and evacuation of personnel had been effected, took charge of the operation of neutralising the bomb. Investigation revealed that the bomb was of a new and complicated construction with anti-handling devices. Until the electrical circuit had been neutralised, the slightest movement could have set it off. The device contained between 10 and 15lbs of explosive and could have caused instant death as well as widespread damage. No one was more aware of the danger than Major Styles, yet he placed himself at great personal risk to minimise the danger to his team, to confirm the success of each stage of the operation, and to ensure the practicability of the next stage. The whole operation took seven hours to plan and execute, but was completely successful.

Two days later Major Styles was called back to the same hotel, where a second bomb had been laid by armed terrorists. This bomb was found to be an even larger device, with a charge of over 30lbs of explosive, anti-handling devices and a confusion of electrical circuits; it was clearly intended to kill the operator trying to neutralise it. Again Styles immediately took charge of the situation and successfully disarmed the device, after working on it for nine hours.

He died on 1 August 2006.

## Security Officer JAMES KENNEDY
*GLASGOW, Scotland*
21 December 1973

He was 43 years old and working for British Rail Engineering Ltd when six armed men robbed a wages train. During the attack two security guards were slightly injured by shotgun fire, and the robbers then headed towards the main exit of the works. Kennedy, who was on duty at the main gate, heard the shots; despite knowing that the criminals were armed, he stood in the gateway in an attempt to prevent their escape. He tackled the first man and prevented him leaving the yard. However, his companions then attacked Kennedy, hitting him about the head with the shotguns, inflicting two deep lacerations. At this point the raiders climbed into a van, which one of the gang had driven into position. Kennedy recovered consciousness and, undeterred, made another attempt to prevent them leaving by running towards the front passenger door of the van. He was killed by two shots fired from the front passenger seat.

The seven men involved, six raiders and the getaway driver, were all sentenced to life imprisonment.

## Sergeant MURRAY 'KINA' or 'HUDDY' HUDSON
*WAIOURU MILITARY CAMP, New Zealand*
13 February 1974

He was 35 years old and serving in the 7th Royal New Zealand Infantry Regiment. He was supervising a live grenade practice when another NCO, Sergeant Graham Fergusson, accidentally (and perhaps unknowingly) armed the grenade he was about to throw. Hudson ordered the man to throw the grenade immediately but there was no reaction. He then grasped Fergusson's throwing hand in both his hands and attempted to throw the grenade over the parapet of the throwing bay. He was within seconds of success when the grenade exploded, killing them both.

An experienced soldier, Hudson would have realised that, once the grenade was armed, there was less than four seconds to detonation. While he must have been aware of the great risk he was taking, he took no action to safeguard himself, but instead attempted to dislodge the grenade from the NCO's hand and throw it away.

He had also served in Malaya, Borneo and Vietnam.

## Inspector JAMES (known as JIM) BEATON
*LONDON, England*
20 March 1974

He was 31 years old and serving in the Metropolitan Police Force as Princess Anne's bodyguard. As the royal car approached the junction of The Mall and Marlborough Road, a white car swerved in front of it, causing the driver, Mr Callender, to stop suddenly. The driver of the white car, Ian Ball, then got out and went over to the royal car. Inspector Beaton got out to see what was wrong. As he approached, Ball shot him in the shoulder. Despite his wound, Beaton drew his pistol and fired at Ball, but missed. He was unable to fire again as his gun jammed, and as he moved to the nearside of the car and tried to clear the stoppage Ball told him to drop his weapon or he would shoot Princess Anne. As he was unable to clear the weapon, he placed it on the ground. Ball was trying to open the rear offside door of the royal car and was demanding that Princess Anne go with him, but Princess Anne and Captain Mark Phillips were struggling to keep the door closed. As soon as the lady-in-waiting left by the rear nearside door, Beaton entered the same way and leaned across to shield Princess Anne with his body. Captain Phillips managed to close the door and the inspector, seeing that Ball was about to fire into the back of the car, put his hand up to the window directly in the line of fire to absorb the impact. Ball fired, shattering the window and wounding Beaton in the hand. Despite this, he asked Captain Phillips to release his grip on the door so that he might kick it open violently and throw Ball off balance. However, before he could do so Ball opened the door and shot Beaton in the stomach. He fell from the offside door and collapsed unconscious at the gunman's feet.

Mr Callender tried to get out of the car but Ball put his pistol to his head and told him not to move. Undeterred, Callender got out at the first opportunity and grabbed Ball's arm in an attempt to disarm him. Although Ball threatened to shoot him, he clung to his arm until he was shot in the chest.

Mr McConnell was travelling in a taxi when he heard shots fired. As he could see that a royal car appeared to be involved, he stopped the taxi and ran back to the scene, where he found Ball shouting at the occupants of the car. Seeing the gun in his hand, Mr McConnell went up to him in a placatory manner and asked him to hand over the gun. Ball told him to get back, but Mr McConnell continued to approach and Ball shot him in the chest. Mr McConnell staggered away and collapsed.

Constable Hills was on duty at St James's Palace when he heard a commotion and saw the cars stationary in The Mall. Thinking there had been an accident, he reported by radio and went to the scene. He saw Ball trying to pull someone from the back of the car. He approached and touched his arm, whereupon Ball spun round and stepped back, pointing the gun at Hills. As Hills moved forward to take the gun, Ball shot him in the stomach and returned to the back of the car. Hills staggered away and, using his radio, sent a clear and concise message to Cannon Row Police Station reporting the gravity of the situation. Seeing Inspector Beaton's gun on the ground, he picked it up intending to shoot the gunman. However, he felt very faint and could not be sure of his aim.

Mr Martin was driving along The Mall. When he saw the situation, he parked his car in front of Ball's car to prevent any possible escape. He then went to the royal car to render assistance, but Ball pushed his gun into his ribs. It was at this point that Constable Hills intervened and was shot. Mr Martin assisted Hills to the side of the road.

Mr Russell was driving along The Mall when he saw Ball attempting to open the door of the royal car. He stopped, and as he ran back he heard shots. Arriving at the car, he saw Ball with the gun in his hand and Mr Martin helping Hills to the side of the road. Regardless of the obvious danger and seeing that Ball was holding Princess Anne by the forearm and trying to wrestle her from the car, he ran up and punched him on the back of the head. Ball immediately turned and fired at him, but fortunately missed. Mr Russell then tried to get Hills' truncheon, but, hearing more commotion, he returned to the royal car from which Ball was still trying to drag Princess Anne with one hand, while pointing the gun at her with the other and threatening to shoot if she refused to move. The princess is to have told Ball, 'Not bloody likely'; she managed to delay Ball and distract his attention by engaging him in conversation. Captain Phillips kept his arm firmly round her waist and was trying to pull her back into the car. Mr Russell now ran around to the other side of the car and saw that Princess Anne had broken free and was about to leave by the nearside door. She was almost out of the car when Ball came up behind Mr Russell and once again tried to reach her. Captain Phillips promptly pulled her back into the car and Mr Russell punched Ball in the face. At this point other police officers began to arrive and Ball ran off on foot.

Constable Edmonds was one of the first officers on the scene. Seeing the gunman running away he immediately gave chase, shouting to Ball to stop, but he continued to run and pointed the pistol directly at the officer. Completely undeterred, the officer charged Ball and knocked him to the ground. Other officers who also gave chase immediately threw themselves on to the man and disarmed him.

The wounded men were all taken to hospital, where bullets were removed from Inspector Beaton, Mr Callender and Mr McConnell. Constable Hill received treatment for his wounds, but no attempt has been made to remove the bullet from his liver.

As well as Inspector Beaton's GC, Constable Michael Hills and Mr Ronald Russell both received the GM. Alexander Callender, Peter Edmonds and John McConnell received the Queen's Gallantry Medal and Mr Walter Martin received the Queen's Commendation for Brave Conduct. Ball had hoped to gain a ransom of two million pounds but ended up in Rampton Hospital under the Mental Health Act. When later asked why he shot Beaton three times, Bell simply answered: 'He kept coming forward.'

At the time of going to publication, Beaton is one of twenty living recipients of the GC.

### Captain ROGER GOAD
*LONDON, England*
29 August 1975

He was 39 years old and serving as an explosives officer in the Metropolitan Police when a telephone call was made to the office of a national paper stating that a bomb had been left in a shop doorway in Kensington Street. This information was immediately passed to the police and two patrol officers were sent to the scene. They found a plastic bag in the shop doorway; one of them examined the bag and saw a pocket watch fixed to the top of the contents by adhesive tape. It was almost certainly a bomb and the officers raised the alarm. The street was taped off and cleared, along with the surrounding buildings.

Captain Goad was returning from London after having dealt with a suspect parcel and accepted the call to deal with this device. On his arrival he was briefed by a senior police officer while they walked towards the shop. Some distance from the bomb the police officer stopped and Goad walked on alone and entered the doorway. He was seen to bend over the bomb and was in the process of defusing it when it exploded, killing him instantly. He had also been awarded the BEM for bomb disposal while in the Royal Army Ordnance Corps.

### Schoolmaster JOHN CLEMENTS
*SAPPADA, Italy*
12 April 1976

He was 22 years old and a schoolteacher. On a school trip to a ski-resort in Italy he noticed smoke at about 4am. Quickly he raised the alarm and ordered the children to go downstairs. A number of children were led to safety through dense smoke by other members of the staff, who, having got out of the hotel, then helped further children to escape from a first-floor balcony. Meanwhile Mr Clements had climbed down a third-floor balcony on the west side of the building to a second-floor balcony; he then reached the first floor, where he organised a number of children into small groups and assisted them to escape by means of a rope he improvised from knotted sheets. When the room was evacuated Mr Clements refused to leave the hotel and went back into the building, which in a matter of minutes was burning fiercely. He was seen on at least two occasions going back into the hotel after carrying or dragging people out, and he ignored repeated attempts to restrain him. Mr Clements was finally overcome by fumes and died in the fire.

He displayed outstanding gallantry and devotion to duty in circumstances of extreme danger. He showed no regard for his personal safety when he remained in the fiercely burning hotel in his endeavours to save those still trapped.

One of the children Mr Clements rescued, Anita Chaytor, said of him: 'Mr Clements was in complete command of the situation and was very composed. All the time he kept lowering children one after the other, taking care to see that the youngest and those who were frightened went first.' Two schoolchildren (both boys) also died in the fire.

## Constable MICHAEL PRATT
*MELBOURNE, Australia*
4 June 1976

He was 21 years old and serving in the Victoria Police Force when three armed men entered the Clifton Hill Bank. One of the men ordered the staff to lie on the floor, another jumped over the counter and removed money from the tills, while the third remained in the public area and fired a shot in the direction of the manager and a customer when they ran towards the rear of the bank.

Constable Pratt was off duty and unarmed. He was driving past the bank and saw the men entering the bank. He could see that they were masked and carrying a firearm. He immediately turned his car, switched on the lights and, sounding the horn, mounted the kerb, blocking the entrance. He instructed a passer-by to call for police assistance.

The raiders were taken by surprise, but one of them threatened Pratt with a gun, signalling to him to move the car. He refused, removed the key from the ignition and armed himself with the handle of the car jack. The men then attempted to leave by kicking in the lower section of the glass door and climbing over the bonnet of the car. As the first man straddled the front of the car Pratt grabbed him firmly, and during the struggle the robber was knocked unconscious. By this time a second gunman had left the bank and climbed over the car; he now aimed his weapon and threatened to shoot Pratt from close range. The first man had by

215

now recovered consciousness and was getting to his feet, so the officer grabbed him again; as he did so, the man called to the gunman to shoot the officer. A shot was fired and Pratt, who was trying to protect his back and at the same time retain his hold on his captive, was seriously wounded. The three armed men received sentences of between eight and twenty-three years.

At the time of going to publication, Pratt is one of twenty living recipients of the GC.

## Captain ROBERT NAIRAC
*SOUTH ARMAGH, Northern Ireland*
14/15 May 1977

He was 28 years old and serving in 3 Infantry Brigade HQ, Grenadier Guards. He was on his fourth tour in Ireland when he was abducted while working under cover by at least seven men. Despite his fierce resistance, he was overpowered and taken to an unknown location across the border, where he was subjected to a succession of exceptionally savage assaults in an attempt to extract information that would have put other lives and operations at serious risk. These efforts to break his will failed entirely. Weakened as he was, he made repeated attempts to escape, but each time was overpowered by the weight of numbers against him. After several hours in the hands of his captors, he was callously murdered by a gunman of the Provisional IRA. His body has never been found.

Liam Townson was sentenced to life for his murder, but only served thirteen years. In 2009 another man was charged with his murder.

## Warrant Officer Class I BARRY JOHNSON (born HAMILTON WELCH)
*LONDONDERRY, Northern Ireland*
7 October 1989

He was 37 years old and serving in the Royal Army Ordnance Corps when he was called to a van containing six tube mortar bombs, near a hospital in the middle of a housing estate in the Waterside area. Due to the danger to civilian lives and to patients in the hospital, Johnson decided not to use the remote-controlled equipment to deal with the bombs, but to remove them from their tubes and dismantle them by hand. With help from Corporal W.E. Melia, he removed the tubes from the van and placed them on the ground. As the next stage was extremely hazardous, he sent Melia back into cover and then placed the tubes facing away from the hospital in case they fired. In the dark and in a bitterly cold drizzle which made handling them more hazardous, he proceeded to remove the bombs, dismantling each in turn. While he was dealing with the last bomb it exploded, causing serious injury to his face, eyes and legs. Despite being blinded by bomb fragments, being thrown across the road and in great pain, such was his courage that he refused to be evacuated until he had briefed his assistant on the precise details of the device, so that the operation could be safely completed. Melia received a Mention in Dispatches for his help that day.

When Johnson told his wife he had been awarded the GC she said, 'That's nice. Have a cup of tea.' Johnson is a committee member of the VC&GC Association. At the time of going to publication, he is one of twenty living recipients of the GC.

### Sergeant STEWART (known as STU) GUTHRIE
*ARAMOANA, New Zealand*
13 November 1990

He was 41 years old and serving in the New Zealand Police when David Gray ran amok with a firearm and massacred twelve people, including four children. Guthrie was the sole duty officer at the time the incident was reported. Realising that he knew the gunman, Guthrie went to the township alone. On arrival, he was able to call on the services of another constable. He took immediate command, armed the other officer with a privately owned rifle, and they reconnoitred the village. As they went around the houses the carnage was visible everywhere. With limited resources and with night falling, he faced the task of locating and containing the gunman, dealing with the wounded and preventing further loss of life. On approaching the gunman's house, Guthrie got the constable to cover the front while he located himself at the more dangerous position at the rear. The man, Gray, could be seen moving about the house and it can only be assumed that Guthrie chose this position based on his knowledge of the area and the gunman. All the time he gave clear and concise reports to police control and indicated his intention to contain the gunman. He saw Gray blacken his face and take up a backpack, and became concerned that he might soon try to leave. After breaking some windows and throwing what appeared to be an incendiary device, Gray left the house but was challenged by the constable and retreated in haste to the rear of the property.

Sergeant Guthrie had taken cover in some sand dunes at the rear of a crib next to the gunman's house when suddenly out of the darkness he was confronted by Gray. He challenged him, saying, 'Stop . . , stop or I shoot.' He then fired a warning shot from his police revolver. The gunman moved around and killed Guthrie with a volley of shots.

Gray himself was shot and killed the next day by police marksmen.

217

# CHAPTER NINE

# George Crosses Awarded in Iraq and Afghanistan

## Trooper CHRISTOPHER FINNEY
*SHATT-AL-ARAB WATERWAY, BASRA, Iraq*
28 March 2003

He was 19 years old and serving in the Blues & Royals, Household Cavalry Regiment when his Scimitar light tank was engaged (in friendly fire) by a pair of Coalition Forces ground-attack aircraft. Two vehicles were hit and caught fire, and ammunition began exploding inside the turrets. Finney managed to get clear of his driving position and was making his way towards cover when he noticed that his tank's gunner, Lance Corporal Alan Tudball, was trapped in the turret. He then climbed on to the burning tank, placing himself at risk from enemy fire, as well as fire from the Coalition aircraft should they return. Despite the smoke, flames and exploding ammunition, he managed to pull the wounded gunner out of the turret and get him off the vehicle, moving him to a safer position not far away, where he bandaged his wounds.

The troop officer in the other tank had been wounded and there were no senior ranks to take control. Despite his relative inexperience, the shock of the attack and the all-too-obvious risk to himself, Finney recognised the need to inform his HQ of the situation. He therefore broke cover, returned to his vehicle, which was still burning, and calmly sent a concise report by radio. He then returned to the injured gunner and began helping him towards a Royal Engineers Spartan which had come forward to help.

At this point Finney noticed that both Coalition aircraft were lining up for another attack. Notwithstanding the impending danger, he continued to help his wounded comrade towards the safety of the Royal Engineers vehicle. Both aircraft fired their cannon and Finney was wounded in the lower back and legs and the gunner in the head. Despite his wounds, he succeeded in getting Tudball to the waiting Spartan. Then, seeing that the driver of the second tank was still in the burning vehicle, he was determined to rescue him as well. Despite his wounds and the danger of exploding ammunition, he valiantly attempted to climb on to the tank but was beaten back by the heat and exploding ammunition. He collapsed exhausted a short distance from the vehicle and was recovered by the crew of the Spartan. He is the youngest serviceman to receive the award.

In 2002 he took part in 'Operation Fresco', the relief of the fire brigade during their strike. At the time of going to publication, he is one of twenty living recipients of the GC.

## Captain PETER NORTON
*BAGHDAD, Iraq*
30 April, 9 May, 23 June and 24 July 2005

He was 42 years old and serving in the Royal Logistic Corps. On 30 April Norton and his team came under fire from RPGs while they were analysing the aftermath of an Improvised Explosive Device (IED). On 9 May he was examining a supposedly neutralised suicide vest when he noticed the detonators were still connected. At great risk to himself he made the device safe by hand. On 23 June he was examining the aftermath of another IED when he identified a secondary radio-controlled Claymore IED. He cleared the area and saw to it that a US disposal team cleared the device. Then on 24 July a convoy of three vehicles was attacked by a massive IED. The ensuing explosion completely destroyed one vehicle and killed four US personnel. Parts of the vehicle, equipment and human remains were spread over a large area. On arrival, Norton was faced with a scene of carnage and the inevitable confusion which is present in the aftermath of such an incident. He quickly took charge and ensured the safety of all Coalition forces present. A short while later he was briefed that a possible command wire had been spotted in the vicinity and with a complete understanding of the potential hazard to himself and knowing that insurgents had used secondary devices before, he instructed his team and the US forces in the area to remain with their vehicles while he went alone to confirm whether another IED was present; moments later it exploded. Norton sustained a traumatic amputation of his left leg and suffered serious blast and fragmentation injuries to his right leg, both arms and his abdomen. When his team came forward to administer first aid, he was conscious, lucid and most concerned for their safety. He had deduced correctly that he had stepped on a victim-operated IED and there was a high probability that further devices were present. Before allowing them to render first aid, he instructed them on which areas were safe and where they could move. Despite having sustained serious injuries, he remained in command and coolly directed the follow-up action. It is typical of the man that he ignored his injuries and regarded the safety of his men as paramount as they administered life-saving aid to him. A further IED was discovered less than 10 metres away.

Norton had also served in Northern Ireland. He is a committee member of the VC&GC Association. At the time of going to publication, he is one of twenty living recipients of the GC.

## Corporal MARK WRIGHT
*KAJAKI RIDGE, HELMAND, Afghanistan*
6 September 2006

He was 26 years old and serving in the 3rd Battalion, The Parachute Regiment. Lance Corporal Stuart Hale was leading a sniper patrol to engage Taliban fighters when he stepped on a mine, which blew off his leg. Seeing the incident from the top of the ridge, Wright gathered a number of personnel and rushed down the slope to give assistance.

Wright made a conscious decision to enter the mined area, knowing he faced a significant risk of detonating a mine. On arriving alongside the injured Hale, he immediately took command and directed two medical orderlies to take over his treatment. Conscious of the danger of operating in a minefield, he ordered all unnecessary personnel to safety and began organising the casualty evacuation. Realising Hale was likely to bleed to death if they attempted to move him back up the steep slope, Wright called for a helicopter and ordered a route to be cleared through the minefield to a possible landing site.

Corporal Stuart Pearson undertook this task but, when moving back across the route he thought he had cleared, he stepped on another mine, blowing his left leg off. Wright at once moved to Pearson and began rendering assistance until one of the medical orderlies could take over. In doing so, he again took the risk of setting off a mine. Again Wright ordered all non-essential personnel to stay out of the minefield and sent a further situation report to his HQ. He also ensured that urgently required medical items were passed down from the ridge to treat the wounded. Shortly afterwards an RAF Chinook CH47 helicopter landed. As Wright stood up to make his way to it, he detonated a mine, sustaining serious injuries to his left shoulder, chest and face. This mine also caused chest injuries to one of the medical personnel. The remaining orderly set about treating Wright, but was himself wounded by another mine set off by a soldier treating Corporal Pearson. This blast caused further injuries to Wright and Pearson and the medical orderly. There were now seven casualties still in the minefield, three of whom had lost limbs. All were in very real danger of bleeding to death. Medical supplies were running low and initial hope of rescue disappeared as the Chinook had to abort its mission.

Despite the horrific situation, his own serious injuries and the precarious situation of the others in the minefield, Wright still strove to exercise control of the situation. He did this despite being in great pain and fully aware that he was in danger of bleeding to death. He gave his identification number and ordered the others to do the same to assist with their treatment once evacuated. Wright remained conscious and continued to give encouragement to those around him until he was finally evacuated by an American helicopter. Corporal Wright, however, died of his wounds in the helicopter during transit to the field dressing station. Corporal Paul 'Tug' Hartley, one of the medical orderlies, was awarded the GM.

Mark Wright House, an MOD centre for recovering soldiers, was named in his honour, and the Mark Wright Project, a Veterans Centre in Edinburgh, has since been opened by his parents.

### Lance Corporal MATTHEW CROUCHER
*SANGIN, HELMAND PROVINCE, Afghanistan*
9 February 2008

He was 24 years old and serving in 40 Commando, Royal Marines when he was part of a four-man team sent to check a compound suspected of being used by the Taliban. In order to determine conclusively that the compound was an IED manufacturing site, the four marines entered the site, knowing that it was believed to be occupied. Having identified numerous items that could be used to make IEDs, the team leader gave the order to leave.

Croucher was at the head of the group. As he moved he felt a wire go tight against his leg, just below knee height. This he knew to be a tripwire; he heard the fly-off lever eject and a grenade fell to the ground behind him. Instantly realising what had happened, he shouted 'grenade', then 'tripwire', in an attempt to warn his comrades but due to the low light he was unable to determine the type of grenade or how long the fuse would take to function. In an act of great courage and disregard for his own safety, he threw himself on top of the grenade, pinning it between his day sack and the ground. Quite prepared to make the ultimate sacrifice for his comrades, he lay on the grenade and braced himself for the explosion.

As it detonated, the blast was absorbed by Croucher's body. The majority of the fragmentation was contained under him but his day sack was ripped from his back and destroyed (it is now on display at the Imperial War Museum); his body armour and helmet were pitted by fragments of grenade. A large battery in the side pouch of his day sack also exploded and was burning like a flare. Astonishingly he suffered only minor injury and the only other injury was a slight wound to the team commander's face.

Immediately following the explosion they manoeuvred tactically back to their rendezvous location. Without question, Croucher's courageous and utterly selfless action had prevented the deaths of his team. He said of the incident: 'I thought, I've set this bloody thing off and I'm going to do whatever it takes to protect the others. I'm very tight with the three other guys. There have been times when they have saved my bacon. I knew a grenade like this has a killing circumference of about 5 metres. So I got down with my back to the grenade and used my body as a shield. It was a case of either having four of us as fatalities or badly wounded, or one.'

Croucher's autobiography is called *Bulletproof*. At the time of going to publication, he is one of twenty living recipients of the GC.

### Staff Sergeant KIM HUGHES
*SANGIN, HELMAND PROVINCE, Afghanistan*
16 August 2009

He was 30 years old and serving in the Royal Logistic Corps as a High Threat

Improvised Explosive Device Disposal (IEDD) operator. Along with a Royal Engineers Search Team (REST), he was providing close support to A Company, 2 Rifles Battle Group. In preparation for this, elements of A Company deployed to secure an emergency helicopter landing site and to isolate compounds along the route to the southwest of Sangin. While conducting these preliminary moves, the point section initiated a victim-operated IED (VOIED), resulting in a very serious casualty. During the casualty recovery, the stretcher-bearers initiated a second VOIED, which resulted in two more personnel being killed and four others very seriously wounded, one of whom died later from his injuries. The area was effectively an IED minefield, over-watched by the enemy, and the section was now stranded within it. Hughes and his team were called into this chaotic situation to extract the casualties and recover the bodies. Speed was essential if further loss of life was to be avoided.

Without specialist protective clothing in order to save time, Hughes set about clearing a path to the wounded men, providing constant reassurance that help was on its way. On reaching the first injured man he discovered a further VOIED within a metre of the casualty; given their proximity, it constituted a grave and immediate threat to all the casualties and himself. Without knowing the location of the power source, but acutely aware of the danger he was facing and the over-riding need to get medical aid to the casualties rapidly, Hughes calmly carried out a manual neutralisation of the device; any error would inevitably have proved fatal. This type of action is permitted only in extreme circumstances such as this. With covering fire keeping the enemy at bay, Hughes coolly turned his attention to reaching the remaining casualties and retrieving the dead. Clearing a path forward, he discovered two more VOIEDs and again carried out a manual neutralisation of both. His utterly selfless action enabled all the casualties to be extracted and the bodies recovered. Even at this stage Hughes' task was not finished. The Royal Engineers Search Team had detected a further four VOIEDs in the immediate area and stoically he set about disposing of them too.

Dealing with any form of IED is dangerous, but to deal with seven VOIEDs linked in a single circuit, in a mass casualty scenario, is the single most outstanding act of explosive ordnance disposal ever recorded in Afghanistan. In five months Staff Sergeant Hughes has dealt with over eighty other IEDs.

Hughes had also served in Northern Ireland, Bosnia and Iraq. At the time of going to publication, he is one of twenty living recipients of the GC.

### Staff Sergeant OLAF 'OZ' SCHMID
*HELMAND PROVINCE, Afghanistan*
June 2009–31 October 2009

He was 30 years old and serving in the Royal Logistic Corps as a High Threat Improvised Explosive Device Disposal (IEDD) operator. During this time he responded to forty-two IED tasks and personally dealt with seventy IEDs. A number of examples will serve to illustrate his bravery.

On 9 August an infantry company was isolated by a substantial minefield; the infamous Pharmacy Road, the only resupply route, was blocked by a medium wheeled tractor and another vehicle, both blown up by very large IEDs. Intelligence and first-hand experience indicated that the area was laced with IEDs. As the temperature soared past 45°C, Schmid started work within 100 metres of the vehicles; he initially deployed a remote-controlled vehicle (RCV), but this struck an IED and was destroyed. Schmid moved forward without hesitation and, well within the lethal arc of any device, manually placed a number of explosive charges, clearing a route to within 5 metres of the stricken vehicles. His team then moved to clear a compound adjacent to the vehicles so they could be dragged clear. When a second IED was found, Schmid made another manual approach and rapidly got rid of it. A new approach to the vehicles from the compound was created for the hulks to be dragged clear. Schmid painstakingly cleared up to both vehicles and his first trip took an hour. He was relying entirely on his eyesight and his understanding of enemy tactics. Despite the threat, Schmid again decided against explosive clearance; time was critical so he placed heavy chains on to the vehicles, a risky operation given the high likelihood of booby traps, and the vehicles were finally dragged clear. As the light started to fade, Schmid then personally led a high-risk clearance of the road, manually disposing of two further IEDs. The whole operation had lasted eleven hours.

On 8 October Schmid was tasked to deal with an artillery shell reported by the Afghan National Army (ANA). On arrival the ANA led him directly to the device. He was not only in grave personal danger but immediately realised that the many civilians around him were also in peril. Time was not on his side. Schmid quickly established that the shell was in fact part of a live radio-controlled IED intended to cause maximum casualties in a well populated area. The nature of the device also meant it was almost certainly over-watched by its operator. Without any consideration for his own safety, Schmid decided to neutralise the IED manually. To do this he knew he was employing a render-safe procedure that should only ever be carried out in the gravest of circumstances and was of the highest personal risk to himself. In an instant Schmid made the most courageous decision possible, placing his own life on the line in order to save the lives of countless Afghan civilians.

On 31 October Schmid was involved in an operation near Forward Operating Base Jackson in Battle Group North's area. Having already dealt with three IEDs that day, Schmid and his team were moving to another compound when a searcher discovered a command wire running down the alleyway they were using. Schmid and his team were trapped, with no safe route forward or back, as they did not know in which direction the IED was located. Knowing that his team was in potential danger, Schmid immediately took action to reduce the hazard. He eventually traced the wire to a complex command wire IED incorporating three linked and buried charges. While he was dealing with the device it exploded, killing him instantly. His action probably saved the lives of his team. He was due to return to the UK the next day.

These occasions are representative of the complexity and danger that Schmid faced daily throughout his tour of duty. His selfless gallantry, his devotion to duty and his indefatigable courage displayed time and again saved countless lives and is worthy of the highest recognition.

Schmid had also served in Northern Ireland, Bosnia, Sierra Leone and the Falkland Islands.

# CHAPTER TEN

# Burial Locations

H ere I have listed each country, in **bold,** followed by each cemetery, in alphabetical order; where two cemeteries have the same name I have also put the town name in *italics*; this in turn is followed by each recipient's number, in **bold**, taken from the chronological list. So anyone wishing to visit any GC holder's grave can see at a glance how many are buried in any one cemetery. Full cemetery addresses are given in the chronological list. Note that Brookwood Cemetery and Brookwood Military Cemetery are next to each other. Not all cemeteries are open to the public so check before you travel. This list does not include anyone buried at sea, those with no known grave or cremations, unless the ashes are interred in a cemetery or churchyard.

I now have over 250 cemetery plans showing the locations of both VC and GC holders, which I can email to anyone who would like them. Contact me at kib1856@yahoo.co.uk

**ALBANIA:** Tirana Park Memorial Cemetery **305.**
**ALGERIA:** Bone War Cemetery **302.**
**AUSTRALIA:** Carnelian Bay Cemetery **379;** Cheltenham Cemetery **163;** Cowra War Cemetery **323, 324;** Eastern Suburbs Memorial Park **71;** Field of Mars Cemetery **85;** Inglewood Cemetery **144;** North Road Church of England Cemetery **28;** Port Lonsdale Cemetery **7;** Rookwood Cemetery **330;** St John's Church **366;** Scone Lawn Cemetery **311.**
**BERMUDA:** Christ Church Churchyard **231.**
**BURMA:** Rangoon War Cemetery **290, 331;** Taukkyan War Cemetery **308.**
**CANADA:** Barrie Union Cemetery **294;** Bethesda United Church Cemetery **186;** Cataraqui Cemetery **320;** Featherstone Cemetery **143;** Hillcrest Cemetery **297;** Lakeview Cemetery **197;** Mountain View Cemetery **267.**
**CHINA:** Government Cemetery **342;** Stanley Military Cemetery **269, 270, 271, 300, 301.**
**CYPRUS:** English Cemetery **174.**
**ENGLAND:** All Saints Church, *Holbeton* **78;** All Saints Churchyard, *West Parley* **205;** Arksey Lane Cemetery **113;** Beighton Cemetery **6;** Bishopwearmouth Cemetery **263;** Blaydon Cemetery **184;** Bloxwich

**MALTA:** Capuccini Naval Cemetery 191, 264, 266; Ta Braxia Cemetery 35, 206.

**NEW ZEALAND:** Opotiki Cemetery 393; Purewa Cemetery 27.

**NORTHERN IRELAND:** Faughanvale Burial Ground 47; Larne Cemetery 50; Miltown Cemetery 83; St Mary's RC Cemetery 230.

**PAPUA NEW GUINEA:** Rabaul European Cemetery 387.

**SCOTLAND:** Acharacle Parish Churchyard 293; Burngrange Cemetery 345; Gifford Churchyard 254; New Cemetery 149; St Joseph's Cemetery 30; Shewlton Cemetery 200.

**SICILY:** Catania War Cemetery 213.

**SINGAPORE:** Kranji Military Cemetery 365.

**SUDAN:** Khartoum War Cemetery 55, 282.

**TUNISIA:** Enfidaville (Enfida) War Cemetery 299.

**WALES:** Llwydcoed Crematorium 51; Llysfaen Churchyard 166.

**YUGOSLAVIA:** Belgrade War Cemetery 329.

# CHAPTER ELEVEN

# Alphabetical List of George Cross Recipients

The following is a complete alphabetical list of all George Cross holders. Each entry starts with the recipient's rank or position (all ranks are at the time of GC deed). Although used extensively locally, the term Trooper did not officially come into being until 1923. This is followed by recipient's full name. Next comes the award from which they exchanged, if any. Next is their position in the chronological list (in brackets) and finally the page number in the main text.

Lieutenant Edmund Geoffrey ABBOTT (AM) **(37)**, 55
Deckhand George Fawcett Pitts ABBOTT (AM) **(19)**, 47
Inspector George John ADAMSON (EGM) **(151)**, 99
Lance Sergeant Thomas Edward ALDER (GM) **(105)**, 79
Detachment Leader Thomas Hopper ALDERSON **(224)**, 128
Qaid YOUSEF HUSSEIN ALI BEY (Arabic spelling **YOSEF BEY ALI**) (EGM) **(167)**, 106
Nurse Florence Alice ALLEN (AM) **(134)**, 92
Miner Ernest ALLPORT (EM) **(113)**, 83
Chief Engine Room Artificer Frederick Christie ANDERSON (EGM) **(168)**, 106
Flying Officer Walter ANDERSON (EGM) **(82)**, 71
Second Lieutenant Wallace Lancelot ANDREWS (EGM) **(214)**, 125
Captain MATEEN (often incorrectly spelt **MATREEN**) **AHMED ANSARI** **(269)**, 147
Acting Lieutenant Bertram Stuart Trevelyan ARCHER **(219)**, 126
Temporary Lieutenant Robert Selby ARMITAGE **(217)**, 126
Lieutenant Reginald William ARMYTAGE (AM) **(78)**, 69
Leading Aircraftman Walter ARNOLD (EGM) **(81)**, 70
Miss Doreen ASHBURNHAM (later **ASHBURNHAM-RUFFNER**) (AM) **(13)**, 45
Begum ASHRA-un-NISA (often incorrectly spelt **ASHRAF**) (EGM) **(153)**, 100

Corporal Thomas ATKINSON (EGM) **(175)**, 109
Tracker AWANG anak RAWENG (sometimes spelt RAWANG) **(371)**, 197
Train Driver John AXON **(376)**, 200

Temporary Sub Lieutenant John Herbert BABINGTON **(240)**, 135
Sub Lieutenant Arthur Gerald BAGOT (AM) **(28)**, 50
Constable 1st Class Eric George BAILEY **(330)**, 175
Lieutenant George Stewart BAIN-SMITH (AM) **(73)**, 66
Pit Lad John Thomas BAKER (EM) **(86)**, 72
Sub Inspector BALDEV SINGH (EGM) **(108)**, 81
Assistant Works Manager Dr Wilson Charles Geoffrey BALDWIN (EM)
    **(284)**, 154
Colliery Worker John BAMFORD **(373)**, 198
Sergeant Arthur BANKS **(327)**, 174
Acting Major Herbert John Leslie BAREFOOT **(216)**, 126
Naik BARKAT SINGH (EGM) **(158)**, 102
Lance Corporal William BARNETT (EGM) **(150)**, 99
Sergeant Arnold Alfred BARRACLOUGH (EGM) **(99)**, 77
Colliery Agent Norman BASTER (EM) **(143)**, 95
Second Engineer Officer Gordon Love BASTIAN (AM) **(294)**, 160
Mr William Frederick BAXTER (EM) **(261)**, 144
Trooper Clive Cyril Anthony BAYLEY (EGM) **(100)**, 78
Miner George William BEAMAN (EM) **(144)**, 96
Inspector James Wallace BEATON **(394)**, 212
Miner John Gray (spelt Grey on his headstone) BEATTIE (EGM) **(68)**, 65
Sergeant John Archibald BECKETT **(347)**, 186
Pit Manager John Frederick BELL (EGM) **(101)**, 78
Second Lieutenant Michael Paul BENNER **(377)**, 201
Sub Inspector BHIM SINGH YADAVA (EGM) **(109)**, 81
Shri BHUPENDRA NARAYAN SINGH (EGM) **(129)**, 90
Major Kenneth Alfred BIGGS **(339)**, 181
Private Richard BLACKBURN (EGM) **(142)**, 95
Shotfirer Sydney BLACKBURN (EM) **(349)**, 187
Acting Captain Michael Flood (incorrectly spelt Floud on his GC) BLANEY
    **(230)**, 131
Coxswain Henry George BLOGG (EGM) **(15)**, 45
Mulazim Theodore BOGDANOVITCH (sometimes spelt BOGDANO-
    VICH) (EGM) **(174)**, 108
Flight Sergeant Eric Watt BONAR (EGM) **(118)**, 87
Miner David Noel BOOKER (EM) **(160)**, 103
Miner Samuel BOOKER (EM) **(161)**, 103
Major Douglas Alexander BRETT (EGM) **(125)**, 89
Temporary Lieutenant John BRIDGE **(303)**, 163
Radio Officer David BROADFOOT **(375)**, 200

Sub Lieutenant Francis Haffey BROOKE-SMITH (250), 139
Private Arthur Reginald BROOKS (EGM) (139), 94
Overman David BROWN (EM) (345) , 185
Second Lieutenant Richard Leslie BROWN (AM) (18), 46
Lieutenant Oliver Campbell BRYSON (AM) (17), 46
Mate Henry BUCKLE (AM) (39), 56
Fire Officer John (incorrectly named as James on his citation) Lewis Victor
    BURKE (EGM) (40), 56
Major Herbert Edgar BURTON (EGM) (4), 40
Dr Arthur Richard Cecil BUTSON (AM) (351), 187
Lance Sergeant William John BUTTON (EGM) (212), 124
Factory Development Officer Richard Arthur Samuel BYWATER (311),
    166

Second Lieutenant Alexander Fraser CAMPBELL (242), 136
Leading Aircraftman Michael Patrick CAMPION (EGM) (196), 118
Flight Sergeant Horace James CANNON (AM) (26), 50
Mr John CHALMERS (AM) (48), 58
Petty Officer Robert Mills CHALMERS (EGM) (61), 63
Private Frederick Hector Dundonald CHANT (EGM) (44), 57
Pit Deputy John Daniel CHARLTON (EM) (348), 186
Acting Flight Lieutenant Wilson Hodgson CHARLTON (218), 126
Assistant Civil Engineer Harold Francis CHARRINGTON (EGM) (172),
    108
Mr Frederick William Henry Maurice CHILD (EGM) (177), 110
Bricklayer Joseph CLARK (EGM) (69), 65
Overman (Rescue Brigade Captain) Azariah CLARKE (EM) (162), 104
Apprentice (Merchant Navy) Donald Owen CLARKE (276), 150
Mr Walter Charles CLEALL (AM) (38), 55
Schoolmaster John CLEMENTS (396), 214
Pilot Officer Gerald Charles Neil CLOSE (EGM) (157), 102
Midshipman Anthony John COBHAM (EGM) (90), 74
Lieutenant Dennis Arthur COPPERWHEAT (275), 150
Lieutenant John Guise COWLEY (AM) (135), 93
Boilerman Frederick John CRADOCK (or CRADDOCK) (296), 161
Miner Bert (born Bertie) CRAIG (EM) (51), 60
Mr Bertram Frederick CROSBY (EM) (75), 67
Yard Foreman Edwin CROSSLEY (EGM) (146), 97
Lance Corporal Matthew Stuart CROUCHER (404), 222

Sub Lieutenant Peter Victor DANCKWERTS (247), 138
Miner Richard Edward DARKER (EM) (112), 82
Fireman Frederick DAVIES (337), 178
Temporary Lieutenant Robert John DAVIES (222), 127

Leading Seaman Thomas Neil DAVIS (AM) (22), 48
Acting Lieutenant Harry Melville Arbuthnot DAY (AM) (35), 53
Captain Richard DEEDES (EGM) (126), 89
Squadron Leader Hubert DINWOODIE (343), 184
Sowar DITTO RAM (322), 172
Mr John DIXON (EM) (173), 108
Hospital Porter Albert George DOLPHIN (220), 127
Tram Conductor Raymond Tasman DONOGHUE (379), 202
Leading Aircraftman Robert Ewing DOUGLAS (EGM) (103), 79
Fight Lieutenant John Noel DOWLAND (born DOWLAND-RYAN)
    (191), 116
Shri Joseph Baptista d'SOUZA (EGM) (102), 78
Senior Shipwright Diver Charles Godfrey DUFFIN (EGM) (155), 101
Private Charles Alfred DUNCAN (299), 162
Captain MAHMOOD (or MAHMUD) KHAN DURRANI (272), 148

Lieutenant William Marsden EASTMAN (206), 121
Temporary Sub Lieutenant Jack Maynard Cholmondeley EASTON (243),
    136
Acting Bombardier Arthur Frederick EDWARDS (EM) (11), 44
Chief Petty Officer Reginald Vincent ELLINGWORTH (227), 130
Lieutenant Bernard George ELLIS (AM) (31), 51
Private Ernest Matthew ELSTON (EGM) (140), 94
District Commissioner Errol John EMANUEL (387), 206
Auxiliary Fireman Harry ERRINGTON (228), 130
Sub Lieutenant David Hywel EVANS (AM) (32), 52

Gunner John FAIRCLOUGH (AM) (72), 66
Detective Constable Frederick William FAIRFAX (374), 199
Foundryman John Henry FARR (EGM) (209), 123
Constable Kenneth FARROW (AM) (359), 191
Lieutenant Francis Anthony Blair FASSON (285), 154
Rais RASHID ABDUL FATTAH (EGM) (165), 105
Fireman Christopher FEETHAM (AM) (36), 53
Trooper Christopher FINNEY (401), 219
Jib Crane Driver Bernard FISHER (EM) (178), 110
Coxswain William George FLEMING (EGM) (49), 58
Miner Donald FLETCHER (EM) (63), 63
Mr Harwood Henry FLINTOFF (EM) (319), 171
Sergeant Albert FORD (AM) (9), 43
Captain Douglas FORD (301), 162
Lieutenant William George FOSTER (280), 152
Deputy Party Leader Leslie Owen FOX (310), 166
Staff Nurse Harriet Elizabeth FRASER (later BARRY) (AM) (33), 52

Assistant Attorney General John Alexander FRASER (sometimes spelt FRAZER) (270), 147
Aircraftman Ernest Ralph Clyde FROST (EGM) (197), 118

Sub Inspector GHULAM MOHI-ud-DIN (EGM) (97), 77
Temporary Lieutenant John Edward GIBBONS (AM) (265), 145
Mr Stanley Frederick GIBBS (AM) (71), 61
Sergeant Michael GIBSON (244), 137
Temporary Lieutenant Ernest Oliver GIDDEN (256), 142
Aircraftman First Class Ivor John GILLETT (365), 194
Engine Driver Benjamin GIMBERT (317), 170
Constable Tony John GLEDHILL (384), 204
Captain Roger Philip GOAD (395), 214
Acting Leading Seaman William GOAD (AM) (283), 153
Mr ABDUS SAMID ABDUL WAHID GOLANDAZ (EGM) (122), 88
Temporary Lieutenant Leon Verdi GOLDSWORTHY (298), 161
Temporary Lieutenant George Herbert GOODMAN (273), 149
Lieutenant George GOSSE (335), 177
Miner John Ingram GOUGH (EM) (92), 75
Flying Officer Reginald Cubitt GRAVELEY (EGM) (180), 111
Leading Aircraftman Karl Mander GRAVELL (267), 146
Flight Lieutenant Hector Bertram GRAY (271), 148
Flying Officer Roderick Borden GRAY (326), 174
Able Seaman Colin GRAZIER (286), 155
Apprentice John Sedgwick GREGSON (AM) (278), 151
Sergeant Stewart Graeme GUTHRIE (400), 217

Pit Deputy Fred HALLER (born HAWLER) (EM) (169), 106
Sergeant William George HAND (EGM) (43), 57
Private Benjamin Gower HARDY (323), 173
Acting Sergeant Charles Thomas HARRIS (EM) (10), 43
Chief Combustion Officer Roy Thomas HARRIS (229), 131
Air Stewardess Barbara Jane HARRISON (385), 205
Able Seaman George Wilfred HARRISON (EGM) (98), 77
Civilian Armament Instructor Leonard Henry HARRISON (192), 116
Air Mechanic First Class Harrie Stephen HARWOOD (AM) (8), 42
Miner Percy Roberts HAVERCROFT (EM) (6), 41
Acting Able Seaman Eynon HAWKINS (AM) (288), 155
Cadet David George Montagu HAY (AM) (254), 141
Yuzbashi El AMIN EFFENDI HEMEIDA (sometimes spelt HUMMEIDA) (aka AGABANI) (EGM) (148), 98
Section Leader Edward Albert HEMING (spelt HEMMING on his citation) (333), 177
Sub Officer George Campbell HENDERSON (370), 197

Mr Herbert Reuben HENDERSON (EGM) **(70)**, 65
Corporal James HENDRY **(262)**, 144
Lance Corporal George HENSHAW (EGM) **(138)**, 94
Pit Manager George Christopher HESLOP (EM) **(147)**, 98
Acting Lieutenant Commander William Ewart HISCOCK **(264)**, 145
Sub Lieutenant Alexander Mitchell HODGE (EGM) **(198)**, 119
Aircraftman 1st Class Vivian HOLLOWDAY **(210)**, 123
Corporal Kenneth HORSFIELD **(325)**, 173
Research Officer Charles Rt Hon Henry George HOWARD (Earl of Suffolk
    and Berkshire) **(182)**, 112
Ordinary Seaman Albert HOWARTH (AM) **(257)**, 143
Sergeant Murray Ken HUDSON **(393)**, 212
Driver Joseph HUGHES **(342)**, 183
Staff Sergeant Kim Spencer HUGHES **(405)**, 222
Pit Manager Thomas HULME (EM) **(253)**, 141
Lieutenant Patrick Noel HUMPHREYS (EGM) **(159)**, 103
Overman John HUTCHINSON (EM) **(355)**, 189
Sergeant Albert James HUTCHISON (sometimes misspelt **HUTCHINSON**)
    (AM) **(16)**, 46

Shawish TAHA IDRIS (EGM) **(121)**, 88
Assistant Section Officer NOOR-UN-NISA (wrongly gazetted as **NORA**)
    INAYAT-KHAN **(304)**, 163
Section Commander George Walter INWOOD **(241)**, 136
Lance Naik ISLAM-un-DIN **(334)**, 177

Mine Agent Thomas JAMESON (EM) **(193)**, 117
European Shift Superintendent William JAMIESON (EGM) **(149)**, 98
Captain Robert Llewellyn JEPHSON-JONES **(205)**, 121
Warrant Officer Class I Barry JOHNSON (born Hamilton **WELCH**) **(399)**,
    216
Senior European Overseer James JOHNSTON (EM) **(60)**, 62
Commander Richard Frank JOLLY (EGM) **(181)**, 111
Quarryman Benjamin Littler JONES (EM) **(166)**, 105
Private Ralph JONES **(324)**, 173

Mr Robert Murry KAVANAUGH (AM) **(85)**, 72
Assistant River Surveyor Cecil Francis KELLY (EGM) **(152)**, 100
Able Seaman Thomas Raymond KELLY **(346)**, 185
Temporary Major Andre Gilbert KEMPSTER (formerly **Andre Gilberto**
    **COCCIOLETTI**) **(302)**, 163
Security Officer James Stirratt Topping KENNEDY **(392)**, 211
Mr Ernest William KENT (EM) **(170)**, 107

Chief Petty Officer Michael Sullivan KEOGH (born SULLIVAN) (AM) (5), 41

Acting Shawish KHALIFA MUHAMMAD (EGM) (56), 62

Miner Richard Henry KING (EM) (104), 79

Fusilier Derek Godfrey KINNE (369), 196

Naik KIRPA RAM (338), 181

Ordinary Seaman Richard John KNOWLTON (AM) (20), 47


Captain Simmon LATUTIN (328), 174

Pit Worker Walter Holroyd LEE (EM) (356), 189

Sergeant Raymond Mayhew LEWIN (248), 139

Fitter Robert Stead LITTLE (EM) (171), 107

Sub Foreman William LLOYD (EM) (76), 68

Leading Hand George LOCK (often incorrectly spelt LOCKE) (EM) (64), 64

Lieutenant John Niven Angus LOW (EGM) (201), 119

Boy 1st Class Alfred Raymond LOWE (AM) (360), 191

Lance Sergeant Alfred Herbert LUNGLEY (EGM) (141), 95

Chief Petty Officer Joseph LYNCH (AM) (357), 190


Aircraftman William Simpson McALONEY (AM) (163), 105

Private Thomas McAVOY (EGM) (176), 109

Assistant Foreman John McCABE (EGM) (200), 119

Drawer John McCABE (EM) (30), 51

Boatswain William Henry Debonnaire McCARTHY (AM) (287), 155

Corporal John Mackintosh McCLYMONT (EGM) (186), 114

Mr Thomas William McCORMACK (AM) (1), 39

Flight Cadet William Neil McKECHNIE (EGM) (88), 73

Corporal Thomas Patrick McTEAGUE (EGM) (83), 71

Private Horace William MADDEN (368), 196

Petty Officer Stoker Herbert John MAHONEY (EGM) (74), 67

The Island of MALTA (207), 121

Staff Sergeant Reginald Harry MALTBY (EGM) (65), 64

Miner Thomas George MANWARING (EM) (362), 192

Chauffeur Frederick Hamilton MARCH (EGM) (55), 61

Temporary Major Cyril Joseph Arthur MARTIN (289), 156

Captain Dudley William MASON (277), 151

Lance Naik MATA DIN (EGM) (132), 92

Captain Lionel Colin MATTHEWS (274), 149

Lieutenant Commander Alexander Henry MAXWELL-HYSLOP (AM) (89), 73

Leading Seaman Philip Stephen Robert MAY (AM) (350), 187

Assistant Store Keeper Albert John MEADOWS (EM) (110), 81

Doctor Arthur Douglas MERRIMAN (221), 127

Able Seaman Alfred MILES (AM) (251), 140

ARP Warden Leonard James (incorrectly given as **John** on his citation) **MILES** **(233)**, 133
Able Seaman Henry James MILLER (EGM) **(202)**, 120
Temporary Sub Lieutenant John Bryan Peter MILLER (later **DUPPA-MILLER**) **(234)**, 133
Private Thomas Frank MILLER (EGM) **(45)**, 57
Mr MIRGHANY AHMED MUHAMMAD (EGM) **(120)**, 87
Acting Second Hand John Henry MITCHELL (AM) **(238)**, 135
Temporary Sub Lieutenant Richard Valentine MOORE **(226)**, 129
Mill Foreman Alfred Ernest MORRIS (EM) **(52)**, 60
Constable Francis Austin MORTESHED (EGM) **(53)**, 61
Station and Rescue Officer William Radenhurst MOSEDALE **(252)**, 140
Special Constable Brandon MOSS **(246)**, 138
Private Joseph Edward MOTT (EGM) **(164)**, 105
Lieutenant John Stuart MOULD **(268)**, 146
Acting Squadron Leader Eric Laurence MOXEY **(215)**, 125
Nafar MUHAMMAD ABDULLA MUHAMMAD (EGM) **(57)**, 62
Mr Michael Joseph MUNNELLY **(381)**, 203

Captain Robert Laurence NAIRAC **(398)**, 216
Naik NANDLAL THAPA (EGM) **(137)**, 93
Private Frank NAUGHTON (EGM) **(154)**, 100
Sol IBRAHIM NEGIB (EGM) **(58)**, 62
Temporary Lieutenant Harold Reginald NEWGASS **(249)**, 139
Acting Mate Albert William NEWMAN (AM) **(21)**, 48
Temporary Colonel Lanceray Arthur NEWNHAM **(300)**, 162
Acting Brigadier Arthur Frederick Crane NICHOLLS **(305)**, 164
Fireman James William NIGHTALL (misspelt **KNIGHTALL** on his head-stone) **(318)**, 170
Able Seaman George Paterson NIVEN (EGM) **(91)**, 74
Pit Deputy Frank Emery NIX (EM) **(315)**, 168
Captain Peter Allen NORTON **(402)**, 220

Train Driver Wallace Arnold OAKES **(383)**, 203
Explosive Worker Leo Francis O'HAGEN (sometimes spelt **O'HAGAN**) (EGM) **(187)**, 114
Lieutenant Commander Patrick Albert O'LEARY (real name **Albert-Marie Edmond GUERISSE**) **(292)**, 158
Leading Seaman Dick OLIVER (AM) **(79)**, 69
Mr Edwardo OMARA (EGM) **(128)**, 90
Special Constable Samuel ORR (EGM) **(47)**, 58
Leading Aircraftman Albert Matthew OSBORNE **(266)**, 146
Reverend John Michael O'SHEA (EGM) **(3)**, 40

Sergeant Graham Leslie PARISH (282), 153
Pilot Officer Edward Donald PARKER (EGM) (208), 123
Lieutenant John Macmillan Stevenson PATTON (231), 132
Corporal Joan Daphne Mary PEARSON (EGM) (204), 121
Mr Robert PEARSON (EM) (62), 63
Jemadar Badragga (Escort) PIR KHAN (EGM) (190), 116
Under Manager James POLLITT (EM) (145), 97
Constable Michael Kenneth PRATT (397), 215
Squadron Leader the Reverend Herbert Cecil PUGH (260), 144
Pit Lad James Sidney PURVIS (EM) (87), 72

Flight Lieutenant John Alan QUINTON (372), 198

Second Lieutenant Geoffrey RACKHAM (AM) (34), 53
Havildar RAHMAN (sometimes spelt REHMAN) ABDUL (341), 183
Babu RANGIT SINGH (EGM) (124), 89
Bombardier Henry Herbert REED (263), 145
Chief Officer James Arthur REEVES (AM) (281), 152
Acting Sergeant John RENNIE (307), 165
Lieutenant Edward Womersley REYNOLDS (EGM) (211), 124
Sergeant William Ernest RHOADES (AM) (14), 45
Mr Richard Walter RICHARDS (AM) (7), 42
Superintendent Gerald Irving RICHARDSON (389), 207
Lieutenant Randolph GORDON RIDLING (AM) (29), 51
Mr Geoffrey RILEY (AM) (316), 169
Sergeant Reginald RIMMER (EGM) (84), 71
Acting Flight Commander Paul Douglas ROBERTSON (AM) (27), 50
Pit Deputy Harry ROBINSON (EM) (352), 188
Assistant Surgeon George David RODRIGUES (sometimes spelt
        RODRIQUES) (EGM) (42), 57
Chief Petty Officer Jonathan ROGERS (380), 202
Acting Staff Sergeant Sydney (sometimes spelt Sidney) George ROGERSON
        (340), 182
Air Commodore Arthur Dwight ROSS (320), 171
Acting Wing Commander John Samuel ROWLANDS (183), 112
The ROYAL ULSTER CONSTABULARY (386), 206
Lance Corporal David RUSSELL (332), 176
Lieutenant Commander Richard John Hammersley RYAN (225), 129

Mrs Odette Marie Celine SANSOM (née BRAILLY, later CHURCHILL,
        then HALLOWES) (295), 160
Dr Robert Benjamin SAUNDERS (EM) (156), 101
Staff Sergeant Olaf Sean George SCHMID (406), 223
Overman Carl Mallinson SCHOFIELD (EM) (194), 117

Corporal James Patrick SCULLY (255), 142
Temporary Major Hugh Paul SEAGRIM (290), 156
Explosive Worker Stanley William SEWELL (EM) (188), 115
Pit Deputy Joseph SHANLEY (Edward Medal) (353), 188
Mr John William Hesry (spelt Hersey on his death certificate) SHEPHERD
    (EM) (93), 75
Private Joseph Henry SILK (born KIBBLE) (308), 165
Wing Commander Laurence Frank SINCLAIR (239), 135
Chimney Sweep Anthony SMITH (312), 167
Miner Charles SMITH (EM) (184), 113
Signalman Kenneth SMITH (329), 175
Miner Oliver SOULSBY (EM) (114), 84
Ordinary Seaman Bennett SOUTHWELL (245), 137
Mr Brian Ernest SPILLETT (382), 203
Leading Aircraftman Kenneth Gerald SPOONER (297), 161
Private Robert SPOORS (AM) (133), 92
Deckhand John George STANNERS (AM) (24), 49
Constable Henry William STEVENS (378), 201
Lieutenant Colonel Jamest Ernst STEWART (EGM) (77), 68
Principal Officer John William STOVES (EGM) (80), 70
Chief Officer George Preston STRONACH (293), 159
Major Stephen George STYLES (391), 211
Subadar SUBRAMANIAN (313), 167
Miner Frank SYKES (EM) (115), 85
Explosive Worker William George SYLVESTER (EGM) (189), 115
Lieutenant Hugh Randall SYME (259), 143
Ensign Violette Reine Elizabeth SZABO (née BUSHELL) (314), 168

Shawish TAHA EL JAK EFFENDI (EGM) (59), 62
Second Lieutenant Ellis Edward Arthur Chetwynd TALBOT (EGM) (213),
    125
Mr Charles William TANDY-GREEN (EGM) (130), 91
Vulcanologist George (aka Tony) Anthony Morgan TAYLOR (366), 194
Captain Patrick Gordon TAYLOR (EGM) (131), 91
Mr Robert George TAYLOR (364), 194
Temporary Sub Lieutenant William Horace TAYLOR (237), 134
Assistant Surveyor Samuel Jarrett TEMPERLEY (EM) (111), 82
Railway Flagman Arthur Devere THOMAS (EM) (107), 80
Nursing Sister Dorothy Louise THOMAS (EGM) (127), 90
Miner Thomas Derwydd THOMAS (EM) (123), 88
Captain Jenkin Robert Oswald THOMPSON (203), 120
Miner Matthew THOMPSON (EM) (185), 114
Flying Officer Antony Henry Hamilton TOLLEMACHE (EGM) (195), 117
Miss Emma Jade (aka Jose/Jessie) TOWNSEND (EGM) (117), 86

Private Frederick Henry TROAKE (EGM) **(46)**, 58
Able Seaman Stephen John TUCKWELL **(235)**, 133
Shunter Norman TUNNA **(236)**, 134
Sub Lieutenant Geoffrey Gledhill TURNER **(232)**, 132
Radio Officer James Gordon Melville TURNER (EGM) **(179)**, 111
Prison Officer Cyril James TUTTON (EGM) **(67)**, 65
Mr Albert TYLER (EM) **(94)**, 76

Miss Margaret VAUGHAN (later PURVES) (AM) **(361)**, 192

Constable Carl WALKER **(390)**, 209
Petty Officer Cook Charles Henry WALKER (AM) **(279)**, 152
Temporary Lieutenant Eric William Kevin WALTON (AM) **(344)**, 184
Mr Granville Charles WASTIE (EM) **(96)**, 76
Park Keeper Albert WATERFIELD (EGM) **(41)**, 56
Lieutenant Terence Edward WATERS **(367)**, 195
Mr William WATERSON (EM) **(336)**, 178
Flight Lieutenant Victor Albert WATSON (AM) **(23)**, 48
Mr John WELLER (often mistakenly called **WELLER-BROWN**) (EM)
    **(309)**, 165
Mr Percy Barnard WELLER (EM) **(258)**, 143
Mr David Charles WESTERN (AM) **(358)**, 190
Mr Thomas Atkinson WHITEHEAD (EM) **(50)**, 59
Mr Charles WILCOX (EM) **(363)**, 193
Mr Robert WILD (EGM) **(66)**, 64
Sergeant Michael WILLETTS **(388)**, 206
Electrical Foreman Osmond WILLIAMS (EM) **(119)**, 87
Lance Corporal Sidney WILLIAMS (AM) **(25)**, 49
Miner Harry WILSON (EM) **(54)**, 61
Pilot Officer Sidney Noel WILTSHIRE (EGM) **(95)**, 76
Mr Gerald WINTER (EGM) **(199)**, 119
Nurse Hilda Elizabeth WOLSEY (AM) **(2)**, 39
Flight Sergeant Stanley James WOODBRIDGE **(331)**, 175
Warrant Electrician Ernest Alfred WOODING (AM) **(306)**, 164
Corporal Mark William WRIGHT **(403)**, 221
Sapper George Cameron WYLLIE (sometimes misspelt WYLIE) **(223)**, 128

Havildar AHMED YAR (EGM) **(136)**, 93
Miner Philip William YATES (EM) **(116)**, 85
Constable EL IMAM YEHIA (EGM) **(106)**, 80
Wing Commander Forest Frederic Edward YEO-THOMAS **(291)**, 157
Mr Archibald YOUNG (EM) **(12)**, 44
Lieutenant St John Graham YOUNG **(321)**, 172
Pit Deputy William YOUNGER (EM) **(354)**, 189

# BIBLIOGRAPHY

Abbott, P.E. and Tamplin, J.M.A., *British Gallantry Awards* (Guinness Superlatives & B.A. Seaby, 1981)

Ashcroft, Michael, *George Cross Heroes* (Headline Publishing, London, 2010)

Bisset, Lt Col. Ian, *The George Cross* (MacGiggon & Kee, 1961)

Gledhill GC, Tony, *A Gun at My Head* (Historic Military Press, 2006)

Hebblethwaite, Marion, *One Step Further. Those Whose Gallantry was Rewarded with the George Cross, Vols 1–9* (Chameleon H.H. Publishing, 2007)

Hissey, Terry, *GC on the Rock* (Civil Defence Association, 2001)

Hissey, Terry, *Come if ye Dare* (Civil Defence Association, 2008)

Marshall, Bruce, *The White Rabbit* (Evans Brothers Ltd, 1952)

Oliver, R.L., *Malta Besieged* (Hutchinson & Co. Ltd, 1944)

O'Shea, Philip P., *An Unknown Few* (P.D. Hasselberg, Government Printer, 1981)

Smythe VC, MC, Brig. the Rt Hon. Sir John, *The Story of the George Cross* (Arthur Barker Ltd, 1968)

Stanistreet, Allan, *'Gainst All Disaster* (Picton Publishing, 1986)

Swettenhall, J., *Valiant Men; VC and GC Winners* (Hakkert, 1973)

*The Register of the George Cross* (This England Books, 1990)

Tickell, Jerrard, *Odette* (Chapman & Hall, 1949)

Turner, John Frayn, *Awards of the George Cross 1940–2005* (Pen & Sword, Barnsley, 2006)

Wilson, Sir Arnold and McEwen, Capt. J.H.F., *Gallantry* (Oxford University Press, 1939)